NARRATING PRISON EXPERIENCE: HUMAN RIGHTS, SELF, SOCIETY, AND POLITICAL INCARCERATION IN AFRICA

KEN WALIBORA WALIAULA

NARRATING PRISON EXPERIENCE: HUMAN RIGHTS, SELF, SOCIETY, AND POLITICAL INCARCERATION IN AFRICA

KEN WALIBORA WALIAULA

First published in 2013 in Champaign, Illinois, USA
by Common Ground Publishing LLC
as part of the Interdisciplinary Social Sciences book series

Library of Congress Cataloging-in-Publication Data

Walibora, Ken, author.
Narrating prison experience : human rights, self, society, and political incarceration in Africa / Ken Walibora Waliaula.
page cm
ISBN 978-1-61229-216-8 (pbk : alk. paper) -- ISBN 978-1-61229-217-5 (pdf)
1. Political prisoners--Kenya. 2. Political prisoners' writings, Kenyan. 3. Prisoners as authors--Kenya. I. Title.

HV9846.5.W35 2013
365.4509226762--dc23

2013018625

Cover image credit: Phillip Kalantzis Cope

For my mother who never lived to see what her son would become and my father who lived to almost see, although not quite, and to my siblings who loved their brother still, and for my daughter Katila for being the one who will cry when I die.

Silence is what keeps wounds alive.
—Ngugi wa Thiong'o

Table of Contents

Acknowledgements

I am indebted to many individuals for the emergence of this book. I am grateful to Prof. Kimani wa Njogu formerly of Kenyatta University and Prof. Alamin Mazrui of State University of New Jersey, Rutgers, for helping me crystallize the idea of this book in my mind. I am immensely grateful to Prof. Nina Berman, Prof. Valerie Lee, Kwaku Korang, Prof. Rebecca Wanzo, and the late Prof. John Conteh Morgan, all of The Ohio State University, for their advice and encouragement during the earlier stages of this project. I am grateful to the University of Wisconsin-Madison Graduate School summer salary award for the year 2009 that enabled me to focus on the research of which this book is the outcome. I am grateful to Shadrack Nasong'o and Lindsay DiCuirci for meticulously reading earlier versions of this manuscript and offering candid and useful suggestions. I also benefited tremendously from my senior colleagues at the University of Wisconsin-Madison, Prof. Harold Scheub and Prof.Tejumola Olaniyan.

I should mention here that Chapter 3 of this book appeared in an earlier version as "Reading Ngugi's Detained as a manifesto" in *Du negre Bambara au Negropolitain: Littérature des mondes contemporains* (Metsz: University of Metsz Press, 2009 : 247-62). I am grateful to University of Metsz Press for permission to reuse this article. Chapter 4 is also a modified version of "Poetry, protest, and polyphony in Abdilatif Abdalla's Sauti ya Dhiki" in *Research in African Literatures*, 40.3 (2009): 129-48. I am grateful to Research in African Literatures for permission to use this material in this book.

Preface

In the mid and late 1990s I used to walk past the Central Police Station in Nairobi on my way to and from work at the government-run and government-controlled Kenya Broadcasting Corporation, (KBC). I would hear a cacophony of impassioned sermons and religious songs, uproarious laughter and piercing screams, issuing simultaneously from the police cells. Because I never entered the cells I could only, then as now, second-guess the meaning of the confused din. For one thing, I reckoned that most of the din did not come from the police officers stationed at Central Police Station. I could tell when once in a while the police yelled orders above the general din, but what struck me was how the incarcerated seemed to monopolize the noise production. I surmised that perhaps the songs and sermons and the laughter were meant to be the diversion with which to blunt the intensity of the suffering occasioned by incarceration. But as for the screams, I had strong suspicion that they were a consequence of some sort of torture or violent brutalization of the inmates, likely by overzealous police bent on squeezing out confessions.

Yet I could never muster the courage to verbalize my suspicions, much less initiate some kind of investigative journalism that would uncover the whole truth. I was then a run-of-the mill junior news editor and news anchor for the KBC, the government mouthpiece. I could only tell the government side of the story, any story. Therefore, although claims of police torture abounded then, the official position was that there was never police torture or excesses in Kenya. In fact, at KBC, we sung the song of the infallibility of the state, of flourishing democracy—we narrated only the authorized version of everything, even if privately we were keenly or vaguely aware of alternative versions. We were essentially part and parcel of the state apparatuses that perpetrated the myth that the government was right, always right. Kenya was then touted as an island of peace in a sea of turbulence in the East and Central region of Africa, a beacon of hope, and at KBC we peddled this myth with unflinching loyalty. Kenya was the only place on earth where everything went right. I knew better than to attempt raising a red flag over Kenya's human's rights record.

Official reaction to a seemingly innocuous wire story I had included in a bulletin had taught me to tread carefully so as to avoid stepping on the toes of the wrong people. In the story reporting Zambian incumbent president Fredrick

Chiluba's re-election for a second-term in office in 1996, I included some bit of background information about what I thought would be of interest to the audience. At any rate, providing background to a news story was, and I believe still is, the rule of thumb in the journalistic profession. The information I inserted was that Chiluba had been a bus conductor and driver before entering trade union politics that spurred him to prominence. Commenting on the KBC news bulletin I had edited in its November 18-22 issue, the People weekly newspaper, stated that the Chiluba story was not only interesting but quite inspiring since like, in the case of Kenya's founding father, Jomo Kenyatta, the story demonstrated the possibility for anyone to rise from humble beginnings to the highest national office in the land. The self-made Kenyatta, the newspaper added, had been a water meter reader in Nairobi before rising to become Kenya's first president.

But my immediate boss at KBC was infuriated. The Zambian Embassy had apparently called State House to complain about the story and State House had in turn called my boss to express its fury. The story was perceived as demeaning president Chiluba and capable of ruining cordial diplomatic relations between Kenya and Zambia. Because of being seen as using the official channel to disseminate an unofficial narrative about the Zambian president, I was confronted with the possibility of dismissal or incarceration. I was befuddled. Though I survived both dismissal and incarceration, it dawned on me that there was always an official narrative that was always already in existence and KBC lived by it, however fuzzy the line was between this official narrative and other versions. It also dawned on me that deviating from the official version of things was a real possibility and therefore I was a potential prisoner, if stories as innocuous as the rise of Chiluba from grass to grace would cause such trouble and trepidation. The detail on Chiluba's background had been deemed nearly sacrilegious, infuriating as it did a friendly foreign "god," but perhaps things would have turned out worse for me if the sacrilege had been directed towards a local Kenyan "god." I got away with a very stern warning.

If the fury typifying official reaction to the Chiluba story can be seen as much ado over nothing, it more importantly points to the state's anxiety to control what the public heard or read. It says something about the Kenyan nation as far as freedom of expression and access to information was concerned in the heyday of President Daniel arap Moi's regime (1978-2002). Moi was following in the footsteps of his predecessor Jomo Kenyatta (1963-1978), particularly after an attempted coup on his rule in August 22, 1982. Kenyatta on his part had embraced wholeheartedly, the despotic ethos of the British colonial administration that he had vehemently opposed in the years before independence. Indeed, the reaction is indicative of what post independence Kenya had become just few decades after the departure of the British colonial dispensation. In a sense, colonial and postcolonial Kenya remained the same site for withholding information to the unsuspecting public, a site for various forms of unfreedom.

In colonial and postcolonial Kenya as in most parts of Africa, unfreedom did not and has not always remained unchallenged, uncontested. Unlike people like me who succumbed to the culture of silence and timidity, there have been those who have dared to stick their finger in the lion's mouth. These individuals who have risen against unfreedom have often done so with astonishing boldness, alacrity, and commitment and suffered more extreme forms of unfreedom as a consequence. Historical archives abound with instances of those who were detained, imprisoned, maimed, raped, castrated, executed or who “disappeared” mysteriously because of speaking against the colonial intrusion or the postcolonial government. Some survivors of strong-handed political incarceration have documented their own individual experiences behind bars and those of silenced or silent other sufferers. In these narratives, the prison writers have almost always articulated positions that run counter to the official national narratives. The focus of *Narrating Prison Experience* is the extrapolation of these counter-narratives emerging from prison or resulting from imprisonment and detention. Like the screams from the cells of Central Police Station in Nairobi, these narratives of prisoners of conscience have always cried out to be heard and to be scrutinized. In other words, rigorous scholarly intervention into and interpretation of the meaning of these narratives for Kenya’s national myth is a venture that is long overdue.

As it should be obvious by now, these narratives of political incarceration do not sing the sort of song that we at the Kenya Broadcasting Corporation sang. They were written against the grain and as far as the official position was concerned, do not deserve to be heard or read. And yet despite official disapproval or because of it these narratives have continued to thrive ever since Josiah Mwangi Kariuki penned *Mau Mau Detainee* in 1960 in London, the belly of the British colonial beast. If accounts like that of Kariuki capturing the colonial period depict the atrocities visited on Kenyans by the colonial dispensation during the struggle for independence, the narratives of incarceration in post-independence Africa suggest that the exit of colonial rule did not translate into authentic Uhuru; post-independence Kenya had virtually become a clone of its former colonial self. Those who have written prison memoirs while incarcerated such Ngugi wa Thiong’o with his *Detained* have hence operated from the belly of the postcolonial beast.

It bears clarifying that I have a personal investment in the study of narratives of political imprisonment. Indeed *Narrating Prison Experience and Human Rights: Self, Society, and Political Incarceration in Africa* is the fruit of nearly a decade of embodied engagement with narratives of political incarceration, an engagement that blossomed particularly since my graduate school days at the Ohio State University. In a sense, therefore, this book could be seen as my atonement for the earlier sins of omission during my stint at the KBC.

Introduction

> The world may be forgiven for exuding a sense of euphoria when prison gates, which once appeared to enclose the entirety of a nation, give the appearance of being suddenly flung open, but the task remains for us to ensure that they are never again slammed shut.
>
> —Wole Soyinka, *The Burden of Memory, The Muse of Forgiveness*

Nigerian literature Nobel laureate Wole Soyinka begins his 1972 prison memoir, *The Man Died*, by suggesting that political prison literature "should become a kind of chain-letter hung permanently on the leaden conscience of the world" (11). Why should accounts by political prisoners about their prison experience, what Soyinka calls, "testimonies," become a kind of chain-letter that should be thrust upon the conscience of the world? And what is the state of the conscience of the world? Is it a seared conscience or is it sensitive enough to respond appropriately to the testimonies of human rights violations and degradation that prison literature unveils? Soyinka sees the conscience of the world as "leaden," denoting any number of things, including being dull, gloomy, spiritless, oppressive, or depressing.

The world has a leaden conscience in part because it has continually committed sins of omission and commission by winking at atrocities tyrants inflict upon their own people or supporting such tyrannical regimes, covertly or overtly. Moreover, as the epigraph above suggests, the world is all too eager to celebrate little successes over unjust incarceration without remembering to put in place solid structures and systems that could check future relapses into such tyrannical practices. The silence or inaction of the world community in the wake of genocide in Rwanda in 1994 and its protracted counterpart in Darfur, are cases in point. The world needs to be reminded of its failures, its lethargic tendencies. It would seem, in this regard, that life narratives of prisoners, particularly political prisoners, are in and of themselves emblems of gross violations of human rights. At the very least, these testimonies implicate the entire global community in the inhumanity of humans against their fellow humans.

The light prison narratives shed upon the anatomy of human rights violations may, however, easily go unnoticed and unacknowledged.[1] Prison narratives are by their very nature an outlaw genre, inhabiting a seemingly leprous and marginal space outside and beneath mainstream literature. The "criminal" tag that society engraves on the minds and bodies behind prison narratives almost always renders such narratives inadmissible to the hallowed category of respectable or highbrow works of literature deserving of critical attention. This is generally true of narratives of incarceration in Africa, as in the rest of the world. Quite unsurprisingly, even the very publication of these narratives is something that publishers undertake only at great risk, particularly in lands where autocrats reign and freedom of expression is frowned upon. Kenyan veteran publisher Henry Chakava has alluded to how publishing narratives of political prisoners often rubbed the Kenyan government the wrong way. As a consequence, the state operatives frequently harassed him and threatened him with imprisonment and closure of his audacious publishing venture. Chakava's run-ins with the Kenyan government underscore the extent to which both writing and publishing of this ostensibly outlaw narratives may be quite hazardous. When therefore Chakava claimed "African writers do not have the freedom to create freely," he was speaking from his own lived experience as a publisher, whose retinue of writers include individuals the government deemed undesirable and hence, deserving of incarceration or confinement (xxxix).

Broadly conceived, "confinement" in this book entails forceful physical detention of the body that comes in the form of capture, captivity, enslavement or imprisonment or detention without trial. For this definition of literature of confinement I draw on W. B. who Carnochan states that this kind of literature is characterized by restricting the "free movement of the body and mind" (381). Prison or imprisonment is therefore a particular kind of confinement that is the impetus and site for much of the literature constituting the focus and locus of this study. As a result, for the most part, the terms "prison," "incarceration" and "confinement" will be used interchangeably. Also, in this study the expression "political prisoner" is synonymous with "prisoner of conscience" by which, adapting a fairly broad view, I mean "anyone confined for politically motivated offences, violent or non-violent" (Nier, 351). Although the literary productions of the so-called ordinary hard criminals also merit critical consideration, these are for the moment outside the scope of this study.

Taking Kenya as its central focus *Narrating Prison Experience: Human Rights, Self, Society, and Political Prisoners in Africa* intends to bring into sharp relief instances of the prison writing of political prisoners in Africa. In order to move these narratives into the center of credible sources of human rights violations by the state, this study first and foremost decriminalizes them, stripping them of the tag of "criminality." At any rate, much of the narrative imperative of these tales of torture and trauma is informed by firsthand experience, hence they stand or fall as testimonies, to use Soyinka's term again, of individuals who at once witnessed and/or experienced. Nevertheless, it must be pointed out that rather than embark on the almost impossible task of examining all forms of prison narratives, this study concentrates only on the literature of prisoners of conscience or political prisoners. Because narratives that can be classified as narratives of confinement in these periods are also numerous, it is almost impossible to deal with all of them in one study. Hence my focus is on narratives dealing with political imprisonment, by or about political prisoners. Moreover, it is imperative to point out that the texts that I analyze are mostly those inspired by or resulting from the actual or lived prison experience of the individual authors. Yet this does not imply that fictionalized or fictional depictions of incarceration, such as Wahome Mutahi's *Three Days on the Cross*, or Aubrey Kulitera's *Prisoner's Letter*, are by any means any less important.

The works of prisoners of conscience, who for the most part were "wrongfully" detained in debasing and dehumanizing conditions and hence epitomize the anguish of victims of the state violation of individual and collective human rights, form the centerpiece of this book. By analyzing and listening to their voices of anguish and angst, as they recount their lived experiences as state captives, the study unmasks the depth of the deprivation of human dignity and human rights. That these tales of government abuses have continued in some places almost unabated is a reminder of the need for global and local mechanisms that would protect individuals and groups from tyrannical governments masquerading as champions and protectors of human rights. The world community should have its conscience pricked by these narratives and their analysis.

This book rests on a literary-critical perspective that draws upon many and varied disciplines with the objective of uncovering the interplay between self-narration and incarceration and the bigger question of human rights abuses. I therefore read these texts against the following constant variables: motivation, trauma, truth telling, and the I-pronoun. I am interested in addressing questions such as: What do prison narratives tell us about the human rights situation in colonial and postcolonial Africa? To what extent is narrating incarceration an act of self-exploration? What are the explicit and implicit motivations for narrating incarceration? What is the relationship between the conditions of confinement and the narratives of confinement or put differently, what is the link between the context of confinement and the text narrating confinement? What are the narratological tools that narratives of confinement employ? Is form/genre relevant or irrelevant in narrating and narrativizing confinement? To what extent does the collective become embedded in the individual experience of incarceration? What is the relationship between the narration of confinement and the victim's trauma? And how does narrating confinement relate to truth claims? How do aspects of truth claims, trauma, and the I-pronoun affect the prisoner's conception of self within or without society?

Debates on the genres and subgenres of literature are inevitably implicated in the larger debate as to what is literature, and what should be included in or excluded from literature. It is therefore, hardly superfluous to begin a discussion on incarceration narratives by briefly linking these narratives to this debate. The Latin term *litera*, which is the etymological basis for the English word literature at once privileges the written word and excludes oral forms of expression. The neologism "orature," preferred by many Africanist such as Ngugi wa Thiong'o, Micere Mugo, and Ochieng Anyumba is certainly an attempt to counter this exclusionary predilection of the Western idea of literature, its tendency to exclude oral forms. The primacy of the spoken word in Africa is, for the most part, the force behind the call for the celebration and inclusion of oral art forms on the high table of literature. For example, Adetayo Alabi in his book *Telling Our Stories* (2005), has advanced the argument that Africa abounds in oral autobiographies.

However, most Western critics have defined prison literature as being exclusively written. For example Carnochan observed: "Literature of the prison includes, on the one hand, fictions written about prison experience and, on the other, writings of every sort by prisoners" (384). For Carnochan, prison literature need not be about prison. But even as his notion of prison literature is quite broadly defined, it excludes oral forms. Barbara Harlow in her *Barred: Women, Writing and Political Detention*, defines prison literature as a wide range of types of writing, which is not only composed in or out of prison but is about prison (4). In other words, prison literature is inextricably tied to the "carceral," or concerned with either the fact or the fiction of the condition of incarceration.

Significantly, Harlow has drawn a distinction between what she calls "representation of prison in writing," and "the places of writing in prison" (4). Her distinction helps us to distinguish between literature about prison, which may simply be a creative or imaginative attempt to represent prison on the one hand, and the kind of literature, which has prison as the site for writing on the other. It bears adding that by "representation of prison in writing," Harlow does not necessarily mean that one must be in prison at the time of writing or must have experienced imprisonment before to write prison in this sense. In this category of prison literature therefore, we can situate both the prisoners who are experiencing or have experienced actual incarceration and the imaginative writer who is something of a potential prisoner, and is endowed with the capacity to imagine prison and to represent his idea of prison to the readers from outside the prison walls. I hasten to add that in a broader conception of prison writing or prison narratives one could be impelled to include the stories capturing the unfreedom of the prison outside, the prison that is not literal prison but that is equally suffocating and inhibiting, the figurative prison that tyrants often create for their subjects.

On the other hand, the latter kind of prison writing, "writing in prison" tends to be based on experiential reality, the reality of actual physical incarceration of the body and possibly attempts to imprison the mind as well. Regardless of whether the writer presents a real-life account or a fictionalized one and regardless of whether it is a poem, a memoir, a play, a letter or a diary; whatever the writer writes in prison constitutes prison writing, which as Harlow asserts, bears the mark of prison as the site for writing with its attendant possibilities and limitations. Moreover, the latter category of prison writing emphasizes not only the prison as the place for writing but on the *act* of writing itself as well. In a slight departure from Harlow and Carnochan, I define prison narratives as verbal compositions and expressions, written or oral, fictional or non-fictional, composed inside or outside prison and for which the carceral experience or imagination is central.

Up until the last quarter of the twentieth century, the blacklisting or ghettoizing of narratives of incarceration often rendered them unworthy or undeserving of serious critical attention. This genre of writing has a remarkably lengthy history spanning from Greek antiquity to modernity. That is to say, systematic critical evaluation and analysis of prison literature is fairly recent compared to the long literary history of works for which prison was the reason and location for writing. If classical critics and thinkers such as Aristotle, Plato, Augustine, Tertullian, paid attention to tragedies, comedies and other genres of literature, they also set the pattern that would be followed by countless generations of critics and theorists who like them would pay scanty attention the corpus of prison literature emerging in their generations and generations after them.

Yet the ancient world, ancient Greece included, evidently abounded with tales, oral and written, of incarceration, tales that narrated incarceration or had incarceration as a thematic preoccupation. The incarceration and eventual execution of Plato's mentor Socrates is a case in point. The narrative of Socrates's fate as a state captive is clearly an abiding feature of the collective memory of ancient Greeks regardless of whether one was for or against him. But more importantly, in the case of Socrates, the state's handling of its prisoner, its readiness to brand him as dissident because of his crimes of thought and its brutal execution act resonates with the trajectory of human rights violations that have become almost a permanent feature of human history.

Granted some cases have been worse than others, but the common denominator has often been the criminalization of dissent or dissidence and the state's legitimization of its inhuman and inhumane acts against its real and imagined enemies. In his capacity as prisoner of conscience in ancient Greece, Socrates had, therefore, something in common with a remarkable number of individuals who would in later centuries find themselves detained by the state for appearing to be harboring ideas considered inimical to its very existence. For instance, Paul and John, who separately wrote several portions of the Christian Bible, were detained by the Roman Empire and were perhaps executed as well; Antonio Gramsci was sentenced to a 20-year prison term by the Fascist regime of Benito Mussolini in Italy; Jacobo Timmerman was constantly persecuted and imprisoned by the Argentinean state for his ideological stance; and activist Alexander Solzhenistsyn was imprisoned by Stalin's Russia.

Africa and Political Incarceration

In the past century, Africa witnessed a tremendous increase in its incarcerated intellectuals and activists. Nelson Mandela remains perhaps the most famous of African prisoners of conscience, thanks to his 27-year jail term by the apartheid government of South Africa. But the colonial encounter in Africa had produced its long list of political prisoners from the rank and file of indigenous peoples who sought to break free from the colonial yoke. The treatment of the colonized during this turbulent period underscores the excesses and abuses of Empire as it clung to its illegitimate overseas sphere of influence. Thousands were incarcerated, persecuted, maimed, raped, castrated across Africa in some of the most appalling and atrocious instances of human rights violations in modern times.

Indeed, although the level of bloodshed and human rights violations in colonial Africa differed from country to country and from region to region, it was generally a tale of wanton and egregious violation of the human rights of indigenous populations. Incidentally, quite a number of the founding fathers of post independent African states met the full force of the colonial tyranny, becoming prisoners themselves. Ghana's Kwame Nkrumah and Kenya's Jomo Kenyatta, who soon became the first presidents of their independent nations were themselves imprisoned, hence victims of the colonial attempt to silence opposition. Could it be said that in a sense, Nkrumah and Kenyatta were "convicted criminals" who later became leaders of their respective nations? Was not the British colonial presence in Africa criminal in and of itself?

The devastating colonial encounter and its attendant violation of human rights completely sullied the pretentious and spurious "civilizing mission" in Africa that the Empire had arrogated upon itself. It is true to say that even those Africans not included in the tens and even hundreds of thousands who were literally incarcerated were virtually under the figurative colonial prison. The state of unfreedom in colonial Africa was similar to the prison life in apartheid South Africa of which Winnie Mandela would speak of as the "prison inside and the prison outside"(105). In other words, it mattered little that one was in literal prison, being outside prison was equally incarcerating, stifling, and suffocating. Not surprisingly, indigenous Africans, in the prison inside and the prison outside, began to use their inventiveness and ingenuity to come up with means to survive the hellish ambience that surrounded them. What Harold Scheub has rightly suggested in his *Uncoiling Snake*, regarding the use of narrating stories as a critical survival tool for black masses in apartheid South Africa, is also true of Africans across the continent recoiling under colonial abuses of human rights. I argue that the figures of speech and symbols that characterized these stories were coded in ways the Empire could not easily decode. Their decoding would have been hazardous both to the African story-teller and his or her audience because the stories were essentially counter-hegemonic and critical of the unwelcome presence of the Empire in the African homestead or homeland.

Moreover, the victims' penchant for narrating incarceration as a survival mechanism, as a therapeutic exercise, as well the tendency to mask meaning to the oppressor in the oral narratives of colonial Africa anticipated the written narratives of incarceration that would come in the postcolonial period. [2] It is a paradox of our times that the unfreedom that existed in colonial Africa persisted in the so-called postcolonial Africa. The conditions that necessitated the narrativation and thematization of literal and figurative prison in colonial times seem to have continued almost unabated. It is the state's determination to thwart the human spirit, to curtail freedom that in colonial and postcolonial Africa impelled victims to tell stories to capture their experiences, to survive. Additionally, fear of further reprisal and victimization motivates prison narrators to turn to fascinating inventiveness and circumlocution in colonial and postcolonial Africa. This explains for instance the absence of direct mention of Kenyatta's name in Abdilatif Abdalla's *Sauti ya Dhiki*, a collection of prison poems, in which Kenyatta constitutes the object of unflinching indictment and critique or poets' recourse to masking meaning in metaphor as a means of critiquing Kamuzu Banda in the Malawi of his reign of terror.

The list of texts that constitute the corpus of narratives of incarceration in post-independence Africa is legion. For instance, in Ethiopia the popular revolution that brought down Emperor Haile Selassie, was followed by the disenchantment and then grievous human rights violation by the military junta under Mengistu Haile Mariam that hijacked the revolution. Former political prisoners have written chilling accounts of this dark chapter in Ethiopian history, detailing the abuses and excesses visited by the state upon the populace in the prison inside and the prison outside. The Ethiopian corpus of first-hand political prison accounts include, Taffara Degueffe's *A Tripping Stone: An Ethiopian Prison Diary* (2003), Dawit Shifaw's *The Diary of Terror" Ethiopia 1974-1991*

(2006) and Nega Mezlekia in his controversial memoir *Notes from the Hyena's Belly* (2002),while Ethiopia/Eritrea has Abeba Tesfagiorgis's prison account *A Painful Season and a Stubborn Hope* (1992).

In Kamuzu Banda's Malawi jailed poet Jack Mapanje wrote And *Crocodiles are Hungry at Night* (2011) and the *The Chattering Wagtails of Mikuyu Prison* (1993), while his contemporary and senior civil servant Sam Mpasu wrote *Prison 3/75*. In Yakubu Gowon's Nigeria detained Wole Soyinka came out with his prison memoir, the *Man Died* (1972) and a prison poetry collection, *A Shuttle in the Crypt* (1987) while in Sani Abacha's Nigeria Kunle Ajibade wrote *Jailed for Life* (1981). In Zanzibar Shafi Adam Shafi fictionalized his incarceration after the 1967 Revolution in the semi-autonomous islands in his Swahili novel *Haini* (2000), while in Idi Amin's Uganda, P. M. O. Onen narrates his confinement in *Diary of an Obedient Servant During Misrule* (2000).

In apartheid South Africa, examples of political prison writings include Breyten Breytenbach's *Confessions of an Albino Terrorist* (1984), Dennis Brutus's *Letters to Martha and others poems from a South African Prison* (1968), Molefe Pheto *And Night Fell: Memoirs of a Political Prisoner in South Africa* (1983), Frances Baard's *My Spirit is Not Banned* (1986) and Tin Jenkin's *Inside Out: Escape from Pretoria Prison* (2003).

However, the production of prison narratives is not the preserve of Sub Saharan Africa. One of the better known prison writings are Nawal el Saadawi's personal prison memoir, *Memoirs from the Women's Prison* (1983) recounting her detention without trial in Anwar's Sadat's Egypt as well as her fictionalized account of a real woman's life in *Woman at Point Zero* (1975). In Morocco poet Abdellatif Laabi wrote his French prison memoir *Le Chemin des ordalies*, (1982), which has been translated in English as *Rue du Retour*, to capture his prison experience for crimes of opinion or thought.

Granted it would be naïve and myopic to gauge the level or intensity of human rights violations by looking at the number of prison tales produced. However, it certainly is germane to conclude two or three things: 1) there were real serious human rights violations in these countries of which these tales reflect or refract to a great degree 2) the publishing industry in and/or out of these countries may have made it possible for these narratives to see the light of day which may not always been the case elsewhere all the time 3) the absence or paucity of written prison narratives in certain countries is by no means a basis for concluding that those countries did not perpetuate violations of human rights of their political and non-political prisoners.

Whereas stories reveal a lot about the vicious circle of human rights violations as one independent African state after another turned its blind fury against its own peoples across the continent, these narratives also implicitly berate the world community for its silence and inaction, for turning a blind eye towards egregious violations of human rights. Moreover, these narratives pique our interest in other stories that remain untold. Indeed we should read these prison tales where they appear in plenty in places such as Kenya and South Africa, but we should also read the silences both in those stories and the loud silences from places such as Jean-Bédel Bokassa's Central Africa Republic, Chad, Zaire, and Uganda where human rights violations and incarceration and even executions went hand in hand, but from which not many such stories have been forthcoming. The stories we encounter should serve, not as substitutes or stand-ins for the untold ones, but as crystals through which we apprehend, speculate, and theorize on the conditions of political captivity in general.

All the victims involved are individuals the state detained in some way because it suspected them or their thoughts of being inimical to its survival. There were, in the view of the state a danger to society. They needed to be locked away to become object lessons or cautionary tales or simply to prevent them from contaminating obedient citizens. Yet it is important to note that the arrest, imprisonment, detention, and elimination of writers, intellectuals, and other individuals or groups perceived to be critical of the state in postcolonial Africa had its seed sown and nurtured in colonial times.

Some of these victims of colonial state terror would write their experiences in memoirs penned during or after their incarceration. These were tales of torture, trauma, deprivation and dehumanization. But even more importantly they were, as Barbara Harlow would put it, "narratives of contention" in which narrating self and reclaiming selfhood were the centerpieces (xv). Put differently, it would seem that in these narratives the incarcerated selves embarked on individual and collective voyages of self-exploration as a means of making sense of their dehumanizing and demeaning carceral experience. It is to the trajectory and context of incarceration and human rights violations in Kenya that we now turn attention.

Human Rights and Narratives of Incarceration in the Colonial Kenya

Understanding the political context of colonial Kenya and the conflict between colonial desire to dominate and demean on the one hand, and the indigenous people's desire for freedom and dignity on the other, is critical in fully grasping the nature of human rights violations that the colonist committed and how these violations are depicted in the incarceration stories capturing that period. To be sure previous studies of these memoirs and others from colonial Kenya have been conducted. Marshall S.Clough's *Mau Mau Memoirs* (1998) is arguably one of the most extensive surveys of the literature of the kind that preoccupies the current study. Other studies include, Marguerite Ylvisaker "Mau Mau" Detainee: The Account by an African of His Experiences in Detention Camps, 1953-1960 by Josiah Mwangi Kariuki" (1976). Clough investigates thirteen Mau Mau memoirs, including Kariuki's *Mau Mau Detainee* and Wanjau's *Mau Mau Author in Detention* primarily as historical sources whose validity should not be necessarily doubted or discounted. In this regard, his work establishes the "historical value" of these memoirs, validating their claims as authentic and reliable (7). While acknowledging the significance of previous studies I hasten to state that the current study is not driven by a purely historicist temperament, a desperate quest for historical facts. Neither is it averse to historical facts that help illuminate the context within which these prison texts emerged. Indeed, an historical background of the colonial encounter is quite in order at this point.

At the Berlin conference of 1884 when European powers carved up the map of Africa "like a slab of meat," to use historian David Anderson's expression, Kenya was allotted to the British (15). One of Britain's initial principal investment ventures was to build the Kenya Uganda Railway from Mombasa on the Indian Ocean coast to Kisumu on the shores of Lake Victoria in the period between 1888 and1901. The intention was to facilitate efficient and effective tapping and transportation of natural resources from inland Kenya and beyond for the European market. Desperate to find a way of paying for the massive railway project, the then governor Sir Charles Eliot encouraged Europeans to come and settle in Kenya. The first European settlers arrived in Kenya in 1902 with grandiose dreams of creating paradise for themselves in the heart of an African jungle, as it were "building a little piece of England in a foreign field"(Anderson 1). In other words as Caroline Elkins argues in her *Imperial Reckoning: The Untold Story of Britain's Gulag in Kenya* (2005), there were underpinnings of romantic and hedonistic cravings in the imperial project (11). As it turned out the actualization of such dreams was manifestly contingent upon an ethos of dispossession and denigration and abjection of Africans under the smokescreen of a largely spurious "civilizing mission." The ethos that the colonists and colonialists espoused and the actions they took were inevitably bound to raise antithetical attitudes, actions, and reactions from the indigenous population.

The raison d'être and modus operandi of the colonial administration therefore sowed the seed of rebellion that would eventuate into a bloody war in the 1950s. The famous Mau Mau struggle was largely precipitated by systematic expropriation of African lands in the fertile Central Kenya and the Rift Valley highlands. Africans soon found themselves "squatters" or tenant farmers on their own land. The vast majority of those dispossessed of land found themselves acting as sources of cheap labor on European farms or servants for European masters in the city of Nairobi. Others were dispossessed of land and forced to settle in less fertile land such as the thousands who were forcefully moved from Kiambu in Central Kenya to Olenguruone near Nakuru town in the Rift Valley. This group would soon form the nucleus of the most militant anti-colonial fighters. The land problem was compounded by the colonial legislation that barred Africans from growing cash crops and reducing their farming to subsistence only to the advantage of their white counterparts.

The draconian rules that the colonial dispensation imposed also ensured that the mobility of Kenyans was curtailed. To this end the colonial administration introduced the native reserves, which were virtual prisons or prisons outside ensuring that individuals were not permitted to go beyond the designated boundary of their community. It was a system premised on the British tactic of divide and rule or, as some have insisted, divide and ruin. Further, after World War I the administration introduced the infamous *kipande,* an identity card and a passbook without which no African could leave his home to look for work. European employers would often tear up the *kipande* of workers perceived to be errant, making it difficult or impossible for such workers to secure employment elsewhere. Hence the continual erosion of African individual rights exacerbated the antipathy between the colonized and the colonizer in a colony characterized by a politics whose complexion was essentially racial and ethnic.

After World War II Kenya entered its most turbulent moment in the colonial period, with the 5 million Africans and 97,000 Asian immigrants virtually under the economic and political domination, and hegemony of 29,000 European settlers. But even more significantly, the majority Africans were, as Anderson states, reckoned as "bottom of the pile" in the racialized hierarchy, (9). While the Legislative Council (or Legco) existed with some token Asian and African representation, it was far from democratic. Moreover, the African and Asian representatives were not only outnumbered by their white counterparts but had also been handpicked by the colonial officials. Little wonder that, like the African colonial chiefs, these African members of the council were invariably regarded as stooges and yes-men of the colonial dispensation.

Given the suffocating atmosphere of exploitation and oppression under which the majority Africans in colonial Kenya lived, it is hardly fortuitous that dissent and rebellion against British rule ensued colony-wide, culminating in what Elkins has characterized as "one of the bloodiest and most protracted wars of colonization fought in Britain's twentieth-century empire"(28). The period between 1945 and 1955 saw increased resistance, with Dini ya Maria Ragot among the Luos, Dini ya Musambwa among the Babukusu, Dini ap Mbojet among the Kipsigis being instances of insurrection mobilized on the basis of affective affiliation to some form of politicized religiosity. Other forms of resistance included those of the Masai and Pokot communities who resisted the infringement of their land rights and grazing rights and the women of Murang'a who revolted against forced labor (Atieno-Odhiambo 25).

It is against the backdrop of mounting tension between the colonized and the colonized in Kenya, which reached the pinnacle after governor Eric Barring declared a state of Emergency between 1953 and 1960 that the literature of incarceration of the colonial era emerged. Yet, it bears clarifying that whereas the bulk of the literature capturing the events precipitated by the Emergency, including the massacres, torture, rape, and castration of Africans, was written during or immediately after the events, some of the accounts were written or published years and sometimes decades after the fact. Also, it almost goes without saying that the Kikuyu of Central Kenya mounted the most enduring revolt and clearly experienced more than any other community the full force of British counter-insurgency.

Anderson makes the sobering remark that the Mau Mau war "is a story of atrocity and excess on both sides, a dirty war from which no one emerged with pride, and certainly no glory" (2). The exact toll on both sides will perhaps never be known. According to official British records the Mau Mau murdered thirty-two European settlers and 1800 African civilians while the colonial forces killed 12,000 Mau Mau combatants. In his modest estimation Anderson believes the number of Mau Mau killed exceeds 20,000. However, Elkins suggests that tens of thousands, even hundreds of thousands of Kikuyu might have died at the hands of the British colonial forces (xvi). She further claims that the entire Kikuyu population of 1.5 million during the Emergency were virtually in detention, or, one could say, swallowed up by the colonial ogre, as whole villages were surrounded by barbed wire while home-guards patrolled the land and chiefs ruled with an iron-fist. If there is cogency in insisting on the symbolic incarceration of the Kikuyu, it is certainly important to acknowledge the difference between the virtual incarceration in the villages and the actual incarceration in the detention camps to which tens of thousands languished. Chapter 2 of this book analyzes Josiah Mwangi Kariuki's *Mau Mau Detainee*, a pioneer written prison text that captured that perilous period of Kenya's history.

Political Incarceration and the Postcolonial Period in Kenya

One would have hoped that upon independence in 1963, postcolonial Kenya would cease creating an environment of repression and suppression that would produce further tales of incarceration and state terror. But what has transpired in postcolonial Kenya had striking resemblances to the scenario in Gaza during the 1990s. Norval Morris and David J. Rothman in their *The Oxford History of the Prison*, indicate that in the early 1990s, there was a record number of Palestinians held in prisons by Israel for political reasons during Israel's occupation of the disputed territory. Yet from 1994 when Gaza began to enjoy autonomy, it became increasingly a case of the Palestinian state imprisoning more and more of its own Palestinians on political grounds (Morris and Rothman 377). Similarly, in post-independence Kenya, the Kenyan state chose to silence opposition by holding other Kenyans as political prisoners, unwittingly enabling continuity in the production of narratives of incarceration for which narrating self and reclaiming selfhood were at the front and center. As a consequence, Kenya produced one of the largest corpus of the literature of political imprisonment. Kenya's share of the corpus of such narratives in Africa during the Jomo Kenyatta and Daniel arap Moi eras rivals only that of prison writers writing in apartheid South Africa.

On the whole Kenya has had a long trajectory of despotism and dictatorship during which the colonial and postcolonial potentates ruthlessly detained and silenced critics, to use Achille Mbembe's terms. These victims of state terror have consistently added to the long list of incarceration narratives that invite scholarly investigation. The corpus of the literature of political imprisonment in Kenya, particularly in the postcolonial moment, undercuts the official projection of the country as an oasis of stability, freedom, and democracy in an endless African wasteland of turbulence and tyranny. As Mbembe has argued in *On the Postcolony*, the European civilizing mission of what it then considered barbaric pre-colonial Africa amounted to little more than an imposition of colonial rule, whose despotic and dehumanizing tendencies, postcolonial African leaders notoriously and unquestioningly inherited.

Ghana's independence in 1957 had ostensibly ushered in a new dawn in Africa. The optimism and euphoria that engulfed the continent as country after country across the continent gained independence from colonial rule, has been well documented. Independence from colonial rule in Africa was largely perceived as a watershed moment in the continent's potential and possibility for confronting its own destiny without "outside" interferences. Nevertheless, as Neil Lazarus has suggested in his *Resistance in Postcolonial African Fiction* (1990) expectations exceeded reality. The optimism of independence soon turned into disillusion and dreams into nightmares. Kenya is a supreme example of how independence in Africa did not translate into total emancipation; of how there was transition from hope to despair due to tyranny and curtailment of freedom. Kenyatta had arrested under the orders colonial of Governor Evelyn Baring on October 20, 1952 and remained in prison until August 21, 1961. Three months before his release, he was elected in absentia as the president of the Kenya African National Union (KANU). As leader of KANU Kenyatta become Kenya's first Prime Minister on June 1, 1963. When Britain granted independence to Kenya in a ceremony replete with euphoria and optimism at Uhuru Park, Nairobi, with the Kenyan flag replacing the Union Jack, Kenyatta retained the position of Prime Minister. In 1964 Kenya became a republic and Kenyatta became its first president. He remained president until his death on August 22, 1978.

Nevertheless, it is the metamorphosis of Kenyatta while in power that boggles the mind. A former political prisoner and detainee himself, Kenyatta took a cue from the "colonial potentate" to detain and imprison, and even assassinate critics and dissidents. The assassinations of Pio Gama Pinto, Tom Mboya, and J.M. Kariuki are attributed to his state terror machine. Both Abdilatif Abdalla and Ngugi wa Thiong'o, whose works we analyze in chapter 5 and 6 respectively, were survivors of the Kenyatta terror machine who lived to tell the story.

Daniel Torroitich arap Moi, Kenyatta's vice president succeed his former boss, ruling Kenya for 24 years with an iron-fist until his retirement in 2001. Initially a moderate political leader, Moi seems to have been jolted into dictatorship by an abortive military coup mounted against his regime in August 1982. He espoused what he fondly called the "Nyayo philosophy," from the Swahili word "nyayo" for 'footsteps.' Upon ascending to power Moi vowed to literally walk in his predecessor's footsteps, which he claimed meant clinging tenaciously to the principles of "love, peace, and unity" in order to foster truly prosperous Kenyan nationhood. But that love, peace, and unity epitomized the Kenyatta era is a theme found only in the official authorized Kenyan national narrative.

The alternative national narrative has it that Kenyatta set the pace and precedence in silencing opposition through detention, imprisonment, and assassination. Kenyatta is therefore painted in this version of the Kenyan story as one whose example it would be a huge mistake for anyone to emulate. According to this alternative national narrative Moi became more and more inclined to emulate his predecessor's worst qualities, following Kenyatta's footsteps in turning Kenya into a virtual police state. Moi's regime saw a monumental increase in political detentions, censorship of media and books, and ruthless crackdown on opposition activism in every cranny and crook of the country. The assassination of foreign affairs minister Robert John Ouko in 1990 was the apex of political intolerance in the Moi regime. Alamin Mazrui in his *Shadows of the Moon* (1991) and *Chembe cha Moyo* (1988), Wanyiri Kihoro in his *Never Say Die* (1998), Maina wa Kinyatti in his *Kenya: A Prison Notebook* (1996) and *A Season of Blood: Poems from Kenyan prisons* (1995), Koigi wa wa Wamwere in his *I Refuse to Die* (2003) and Wahome Mutahi in his *Three Days on the Cross* (1991) and *Jail Bugs* (1992) are examples of survivors of the state terror of the Moi regime who lived to tell their experiences.

Chapter Summaries

This book is divided into five chapters.Chapter 1 revisits the debate on the oral-literate equation and makes a case for the existence of oral prison narratives. Using The Bukusu tale of Sela and Mwambu and the Swahili Liyongo epic, the chapter establishes linkages between oral and written narratives of incarceration. The chapter suggests that pre-colonial oral tales of incarceration anticipate the thematic and stylistic elements of written prison narratives of the colonial and postcolonial period. The chapter also analyzes the interplay between the human condition and human rights as depicted in these narratives. Chapter 2 examines the context and text of J.M. *Kariuki's Mau Mau Detaine*, a narrative whose appearance in print in 1963 in the London metropolis, inaugurated the publication of narratives of incarceration that capture the turbulent colonial era. The chapter analyzes the thematic and stylistic concerns in the text, which oral tales anticipated, and which are replicated in written narratives of political incarceration that emerge after Kariuki's.

Foregrounding the question of generic classification, chapter Chapter 3 revisits the debate on appropriate ways of reading *Detained*, the prison memoir of Ngugi wa Thiong'o, one of the most famous political detainees in the final phase of the Kenyatta era. In brief the chapter argues for reading Ngugi's prison narrative as a manifesto, since in its form and content, it fully conforms to a whole range of characteristics of the genre as enunciated in Janet Lyon's *Manifestoes: Provocations of the Modern* (1999). The chapter discusses the appropriateness of Ngugi's choice of genre and style in exposing state violations of inmate's human rights. Chapter 4 is an analysis of Abdilatif Abdalla's prison anthology of Swahili poems *Sauti ya Dhiki* (Voice of Agony). Following J.L. Austin's concept of "doing things with words," I examine the various voices and guises that the poet adapts and adopts to do things that help remake his world unmade by the prison experience with its concomitant deprivation and denial of human of rights.

Chapter 5 uses Alamin Mazrui's prison anthology of Swahili poems, *Chembe cha Moyo* (Arrow-Head in My Heart) to exemplify the scriptotherapeutic functions of poetry for the incarcerated. This chapter extrapolates upon the relationship between the poet's stylistic strategies and thematic concerns and how these relate to subjectivity, self-construction, and self-affirmation in the wake of gross human rights violations in a prison context. The final part of the chapter juxtaposes Mazrui's with Abdilatif Abdalla's prison poetry.

In a sense the prison narratives in this book capture and represent the carceral experience and imagination of the colonial, and postcolonial period and tend to vindicate Basil Davidson remark that postcolonial Africa is in "deep trouble" (9). Further, they tend to confirm the view propounded and advanced by any number of scholars, notably Harlow and Ioan Davies, that imprisonment hardly succeeds in its intent of silencing or much less rehabilitate political prisoners, but instead it often serves to radicalize them and harden their ideological and oppositional stances. At the very core of this often rekindled and reenergized commitment to struggle is the thirst to recapture human dignity, humane treatment in the wake of state terror and inhumane and inhuman treatment with which authoritarian regimes endeavor to legitimate their control and presence. In such beastly regimes being outside and inside prison is almost the same, hence it becomes as Winnie Mandela once indicated which prison one has in mind, the prison inside or the prison outside. It is because such despotic regimes have existed and still do exist, trampling over human rights with abandon, despite or because of the self-righteous and aloof stance of the community of nations that, as Soyinka suggests, narratives of political incarceration "should become a kind of chain-letter hung permanently on the leaden conscience of the world." In the chapters that follow, *Narrating Prison Experience* endeavors to serve as a messenger and an interpreter of this chain-letter.

Chapter 1: A Tale of Two Prison Tales

> It is a question of which prison is better, the prison outside or inside—the whole country is a prison for the black man.
>
> —Winnie Mandela, *Part of My Soul Went with Him*

> [I]n a society like ours, to be a woman or to be a prisoner is a bit the same.
>
> —Abdellatif Laabi, *Rue du Retour*

Isidore Okpewho asserts that in Africa "the moonlit square has for countless generations been the setting for songs and stories whose primary intent is more to entertain, it would seem, than to edify" (2). Okpewho's assertion is implicated in the age-old debate on the purpose of literature, not only on the question of whether literature should teach and entertain but also whether it *really* does either of these functions.[1] Okpewho's characterization of African oral literature as being fundamentally driven by the entertainment impulse should not be accepted or rejected without a more nuanced appraisal of specific conditions influencing the form and formation of the oral performances and how the performances in turn influence these conditions.

It would seem, in certain circumstances, somewhere between and betwixt the entertainment that Okpewho stresses and the edification he downplays, there is something far more profound, namely, survival of self and society. For instance, Harold Scheub has argued in the *Uncoiling Python: South African Storytellers and Resistance* (2010) that the subtle resistance of Black South African storytellers to apartheid in their narratives enabled the storytellers' survival and that of the oppressed segment of society to which they belonged. Through subterfuge and masking the message, Scheub asserts, the storytellers ingeniously assaulted the apartheid regime in South Africa in ways only the insider and downtrodden black audiences understood. There is no doubt that the social conditions and contexts within which these storytellers emerged and performed point to a more pressing survival imperative than simply seeking to satisfy the entertainment impulse or the edifying need.

This chapter presents oral texts from Kenya, not only to demonstrate that oral texts, like written ones, can and in fact *do* exhibit aspects of the carceral experience and imagination, but also to situate them in the grammar of survival in the colonial and postcolonial dispensation. Indeed, Scheub's Black South African storytellers, like their counterparts in Kenya and elsewhere across Africa particularly during colonial rule, inhabited either virtual or actual prison or both, as were their intended audiences. In her mediated memoir *Part of My Soul Went with Him* (1984), Winnie Mandela, for example, alludes to circumstances in apartheid South Africa "where it [was] a question of which prison [was] better, the prison outside or inside—the whole country [was] a prison for the black man"(105). Storytelling was therefore essentially a form of self-preservation and counter-hegemony whereby overt or tacit focus on confinement or incarceration was inescapable.

The thematization and narrativization of captivity in the oral literature of various peoples of Kenya is quite striking. The recurrence of the theme of captivity or confinement in these narratives is hardly fortuitous. The preponderance of the theme of confinement justifies moving some of these tales from the margin and placing them in the front and center of the category of literature of confinement. I am keenly aware of the real possibility of permutations in the meaning of these oral genres over time. However, what is more integral to this study is the inclusion of oral tales in the category of confinement or prison narratives.

I examine the theme of confinement in representative narratives of coastal and mainland peoples in Kenya. Going above and beyond the somewhat superficial entertainment function, I investigate the reasons why these communities tell these stories of confinement. It seems to me that any number of factors, both material and spiritual, are at plays, in the emergence and existence of these stories. But even more important is the practice of appropriating past narratives of incarceration in order to make sense of present literal or symbolic incarceration, seizing on these stories as a survival tool for the storyteller and the target audience in Scheub's sense of the term.

I have selected stories from among the Waswahili people of the Kenyan coast and the Babukusu of Western Kenya. The geographical, linguistic, and cultural divide between these two regions opens a window of opportunity for a comparative analysis of these tales. I have selected these stories because they aptly exemplify the thematization and narrativization of confinement. Also, it bears stating that the stories are case studies and that there are perhaps countless other stories or versions of the same stories that deserve attention, but that did not find space in my analysis for the moment. It also has to be borne in mind, that any attempts to strictly periodize the tales, as belonging solely to the pre-colonial era may not be exactly accurate. The tenacity, resilience, and adaptability of the oral tradition in Kenya, as is perhaps in the rest of the African world, imbue the tradition with a level of significance that is timeless.

Yet, it would be disingenuous, as Abiola Irele cautions in a different context in his "In Praise of Alienations"(1987), to undervalue the impact of the colonial encounter. To insist that African oral genres have remained unchanged or untainted by Western influences on the premise that they existed and were composed in pre-colonial times is to miss the point of the full range of the repercussions of the colonial encounter. To illustrate Peter Seitel's collections of the tales of the Haya people of Western Tanzania, *See So That We Can See* (1980), contains an oral story, "Kibwana," in which a local Haya man who lost his penis through treachery, marries the daughter of the German Kaiser, and more importantly for our purposes here, drives a motorcycle and an automobile. The motorcycle, the automobile, and formal school in the story are markers of modernity as opposed to antiquity. It is therefore a story that illustrates the adaptability and mutability of the oral tradition in the face of forces of modernity. But it also suggests the erasure of a world, as the Haya people initially knew it. Evidently, the story world of donkeys as beasts of burden, is replaced by items as alien and alienating as motorcycles. It may well be that indeed Okpewho's "moonlit square" where songs and stories entertained generations after generations, is not exempt from the forces of modernity and the oral storyteller is compelled to at once compete with and incorporate the Internet, radio television, DVDs and movies in his performance.

Who Are the Babukusu?

The Babukusu are part of the larger Luhyia ethnic group consisting of a number sub-groups that today occupy Western Kenya. The other Luhyia groups include the Abatiriki, Abalogoli, Abanyore, Abakhayo, Abanyala, Abasamia, Abesukha, Abedakho, Abakhisa, Abakhayo, Abamarachi, Abatsotso, Abakabarasi, Abatachoni, Abawanga, and Abamarama. The exact origin of the Babukusu is still shrouded in mystery. Oral tradition has it that they originated in Misri (Egypt) from where they were forced to move due to scarcity of food, water, and grazing grounds. Historians are not certain whether this "Misri" is really ancient Egypt or whether it is a fictitious creation of the myth of origin that probably refers to another place such as parts of arid Sudan or the semi-arid Lake Turkana region. Indeed, Following Makila (1978), Robert Wafula (2006) suggests that the Babukusu migrated from Northern Sudan with other Bantu groups although it was not until later that they assumed the name Babukusu from their eponymous founder Mubukusu.[3] Other historians have asserted that the Babukusu are bantuized Nilo-Hamites who preceded the Kalenjin in the Sirikwa region of the present day Rift Valley Province in Kenya. For instance, Were claims that while inhabiting the Sirikwa region before migration to the Mt. Elgon region, the Bukusu variously referred to themselves as Basilikwa basengeli and Babayi basilikwa (43). But the Masai subdued them and forced them to move westward to the land of the Pokot where again they were subdued and were forced to settle near Bukusu Hills in present-day Uganda.

At Bukusu Hill a patriarch named Mundu sired two children with different mothers, Mubukusu and Mumasaba.[2] Mundu is said to have come either "from a hole in the ground at the top of Mt. Elgon" or from the Abyssinian direction in the north" around 1517-1544 (Were, 43). When Mundu's sons grew up, a quarrel ensued between them leading to Mubukusu moving away from Bukusu Hill. Mubukusu settled at Bwayi. It is at Bwayi that the Babukusu re-instituted their elaborate circumcision rites that had fallen into limbo. According to the Babukusu oral tradition when one valiant Mubukusu man called Mango subdued and killed a fierce snake with his sword, the Barwa people rewarded him with a wife

(Wafula,1). But they insisted he must first be circumcised. Thus, Mango was circumcised and thereby inaugurated or re-inaugurated Bukusu traditional circumcision rites. These rites have continued to generate a considerable amount of interest particularly among scholars of culture. The changes brought about by modernity notwithstanding, these Bukusu rites of passage, like their oral tales, proverbs, riddles, tongue twisters, and songs, have remained resilient and tenacious even in the twenty first century. What is significant about both the Bukusu orature and culture is its hybrid nature. If the Babukusu borrowed from the Barwa their circumcision practice, it is also evident that they have over time experienced great cultural exchange between them and the entire gamut of their neighbors. Jan J. de Wolf and K.F. de Bois in their *Bukusu Stories: Sixty Chingano from Western Kenya* (2005) noted striking similarities in the oral tales of the Bukusu, the Iteso, and the Luo. Hence, whereas there is evidence that wars and skirmishes erupted from time to time between the Babukusu and their neighbors, there is no denying their remarkable cultural exchange and hydridity that marked the interaction that ensued.

If the pre-colonial skirmishes between the Babukusu and their Masai, Teso, and Kalenjin neighbors occasionally sullied their harmonious co-existence, these skirmishes pale into insignificance when compared to the almost pulverizing devastation of the colonial invasion in Bukusu land. Where they failed miserably in waging physical war against the colonial invasion, the Babukusu seemed to have turned to “doing things with words” of orality, as a survival tactic, to paraphrase J.L. Austin, as the analysis of their Sela and Mwambu story illustrates. It is to this story that we now turn.

The Sela and Mwambu Tale and Incarceration

The tale of Sela and Mwambu exists in various forms and versions among the Babukusu of Western Kenya. On the whole it is a narrative that pits human society against the tyranny of ogres. It revolves around two orphans; Mwambu, the hero of the story, and his sister Sela. Interestingly, a number of Kenyan ethnicities including the Luo, Kikuyu and Taita have their own version of the story.[3] Mwambu lived with his sister Sela and their clan at a time when man-eating ogres reigned supreme. Human life and human freedom were curtailed and threatened throughout this mythical period.

Mwambu was a fierce hunter whom the ogres would hardly vanquish. But whenever Mwambu went to the forests to hunt game the ogres would come and eat up his relatives. In the long run he was left alone with his sister Sela. He gave Sela instructions not to open the door for any stranger while he was away on his customary hunting adventures. He devised a song with a secret code signaling his arrival, with which he prompted Sela to open the door for him. She faithfully kept her brother’s instructions, declining to open the door every time the ogre knocked and pretended to be an innocuous visitor or a stranger in dire need. However, one day the ogre hid in the bush near the homestead and overheard Mwambu’s secret song. The ogre became determined to sing the song on another occasion so as to deceive Sela into opening the door. Initially the ogre’s efforts to trick Sela fell flat as he would pass by an anthill and eat termites and that changed his voice. Then when he went to the door and sung Selah would easily recognize him for the impostor that he was and would laugh her head off without opening the door.

One day the ogre held his appetite for termites in check and went to Sela's door without eating any of them. On this occasion when he sang the song, Sela thought that it was her brother Mwambu. She opened the door and was eaten alive. Later when Mwambu returned home, he sang the song but nobody opened the door. He forced his way inside and found the ogre stranded in the house, too full to walk away. Mwambu threatened to slay the ogre with his sword, but the ogre pleaded for his life to be spared. He told Mwambu to cut off his little finger. Then all Mwambu's relatives that had been swallowed up by the ogre began coming out of what remained of the finger, one after another. Mwambu was most delighted to see his beloved sister Sela come out of the ogre's finger. The last one to come out was a pipe-smoking old woman. Surprisingly, Mwambu consented to the ogre's request and allowed the ogre to swallow up the old woman again. The ogre then vanished into the woods. In brief, the rest of Mwambu's clan, including his dear sister Sela were revived and lived happily ever afterwards.

Power Dynamics and Belly Politics

It is possible to interpret this story merely as a simple human and ogre conflict story. This rather obvious and superfluous taxonomy belies the tacit thematic wave of captivity and confinement that engulfs this story. The man-eating ogre has the capacity to attack humans and confine them in its belly as it wishes, depriving them of freedom, agency and enjoyment of life. The ogre's belly is the prison to which Mwambu's entire clan including his beloved sister Sela are locked up. Their imprisonment in the belly of the mythical beast is analogous to the imprisonment of the Biblical character Jonah, who was swallowed up by the big fish for refusing to go to Nineveh as instructed by God. But compared to Jonah's experience, the victims of the ogre's imprisoning force are not only numerous, being a whole clan, but largely guiltless. In fact, Mwambu is the only human who escapes the ogre's belly prison. On the whole, he strikes the posture of a messiah, a savior who rescues other humans from the ogre's power and belly politics.

As in most narratives of confinement then, there is in this tale the playing out of power dynamics between the powerful and the powerless, between the oppressor and the oppressed, the perpetrator and the victim. The ogre arrogates powers to himself and wreaks havoc upon Mwambu's clan because he wants to satisfy an inhuman appetite. Ogre tyranny cannibalizes and effectively wipes out the entire clan. At the end of the tale, Mwambu demonstrates that his power supersedes the ogre's. It is only by virtue of being mightier than the ogre who cannot match Mwambu's skills with the sword that the reign of terror is brought to an end. The powerful ogre is hence challenged and conquered by a more powerful Mwambu. Mwambu liberates the prisoners by cutting off the ogre's little finger. The ogre concedes to suffer pain to relinquish the detainees, than to suffer complete annihilation at the hands of angry Mwambu. It is also significant that Mwambu' heroic action is prompted by love for his sister Sela. He could not bear the thought of his dear sister languishing dead in the prison of the ogre's belly.

Additionally, in enacting power dynamics the narrative can be perceived as a contest between ogre terror and the human war on that terror, or between hegemony and counter-hegemonic struggle. On both sides of the divide, violence is a necessary evil, although as Micere Mugo indicates, the extent to which the tales are sympathetic to the victims of terror and domination or the perpetrators largely depends on the milieu in which they were composed; that it is contingent upon whether the composition of the narrative serves the interests of feudal justice, capitalist justice or social justice (11).

One could argue that social justice is paramount in the tenor and thrust of the Sela and Mwambu story, meaning that the vanquishing of the ogre terror, tyranny and hegemony, translates into social justice to Mwambu and the human society he fights for. Mwambu's use of violence against the ogre is therefore as justified as the sort of violence that Frantz Fanon advocated for in the decolonization process. Suffice it to say here that if counter-hegemonic violence is rationalized and sanitized, the hegemonic violence epitomized by the ogre's human swallowing antics finds little or no sympathy or empathy in this tale.

Gender Prison and Gender Politics

Implicated in the story are gender relations. It takes the action of Sela's brother, a man, to rescue her and by extension others swallowed up by the ogre before her. Mwambu's action accords with the view that men are expected to protect women, a view to which oral tradition lends credence. According to Bukusu oral tradition, during the colonial encounter, Bukusu men at Mulukoba wa Chetambe, or Chetambe's Fort, were enticed to wage war against the colonists after the women had threatened to take action themselves. The urging by the women led the men into a battle in which they suffered devastating defeat at the hands of the British colonists who had superior weaponry. After the women incited them into fighting a battle against a formidable foe, the men either died or were imprisoned by the colonists. We will be returning to the account of the siege of British forces on Chetambe Fort shortly when we discuss songs as counter-hegemonic tools and the figurative implications of the ogre in the Sela and Mwambu story.

As for now it is necessary to stress that in the story a juxtaposition of gender roles is thrown into sharp relief. There is Sela as the servile, indefensible domestic worker on the one hand, and her brother Mwambu as the hunter, gatherer, and defender in line with the traditional role ascribed to men, on the other. Whether the story implies that the men and women were terribly enthused by their roles or not, there is an irrevocable projection of a social order whose modus operandi is gendered division of labor. In other words men and women are locked up in the prison houses of their respective rigid gender roles predetermined by cultural norms and mores. In the same vein there seems to be irrevocable evidence of patriarchy that borders on outright misogyny. When Mwambu allows the ogre to re-swallow an old woman, ageism and sexism seem to conspire against her. To a certain extent she seems to have outlived her usefulness, unlike the younger childless and unmarried Sela whose survival opens a window of opportunity for her to complete the unfinished business of, at the very least, bearing other humans. But it is significant that it is an old woman, not an old man that must suffer the fate of eternal incarceration in the belly of the beast. Clearly, ageism and/or gender discrimination are at play in this story. As far as misogyny is concerned, similar anti-women tendencies seem to have existed among other African societies such as the Kikuyu of which Mugo notes, "there was also gender discrimination. Male adults had greater freedom than their female counterparts. They were, for instance, socialized to demonstrate prowess and adventurous initiative, while females were schooled in domestication, shyness and subservience, especially towards the males, in readiness for marriage" (18).

It is also possible to interpret Sela's domesticity as virtual imprisonment. Vulnerable to danger from the ogre, Sela is compelled to remain under some kind of "house-arrest" with the door securely locked as she carries out domestic chores. This contrasts sharply with her brother's freedom from ogre danger, as he is the one endowed with the capacity and temerity to venture in and out of the house in the ogre-infested world outside. In a sense, then, Sela is already a kind of prisoner, even before the rapacious ogre swallows her up.

Songs as Subversion

It is imperative to note that recourse to an artistic composition, namely the secret song Mwambu her brother sings ensures, at least for some time, Sela's reassurance and survival. I suggest that the song anticipates the artistic works, particularly literature, that have often sustained both political and nonpolitical prisoners, works which often emanate from outside prison, and almost always arrive in the prison walls by circumventing official prison regulations. In this respect, Mwambu's song differs from artistic works produced by prisoners while in incarceration, such as Liyongo's song that we shall be analyzing shortly. Yet, it bears stressing that whether the artistic production emanates from inside or outside prison; it almost always plays a pivotal role in rescuing the prisoner's mind from breaking down. Details abound of prisoners who avidly and repeatedly read the Bible and any other form of literature for sustenance and survival. Jack Mapanje in "Of Orality and Memory in Prison and Exile" states that in Mikuyu prison in Malawi the "only book you are allowed to have is the Bible (at first only three Bibles for ninety prisoners)" (34). But one could ask, is the Bible literature? It depends. After pointing out tremendous influence on literature in general, Northrope Frye concludes, "No book could have had its influence on literature without itself having literary qualities, and the Bible is a work of literature as long as it is being examined by a literary critic" (315).

Whether we reckon the Bible as literary art, as Frye does, or as purely a book of spiritual nourishment and instruction, it is plausible to conclude that its presence in prison may serve dialectically opposed purposes for the incarcerator and incarcerated. Generally speaking, the imprisoning institution may want to use the Bible to produce repentance, obedience and subservience in the inmate, while the prisoner may want to gain solace and inner peace from the same text. Two instances of subversion of the state intentions with regard to the Bible will suffice here. One involves Alamin Mazrui, a political detainee in the Moi regime, who utilized margins and spaces between pages of the Bible to scribble his prison literary works *Chembe cha Moyo* (which we discuss in chapter 5) and *Shadows of the Moon* (Waliaula, 221). But perhaps the most extreme instance of the subversive use of the Bible is dramatized in Wahome Mutahi's *Jail Bugs* where the I-narrator witnesses a fellow inmate unashamedly transform pages torn from the holy book into toilet paper (18).

Yet the genre of songs seems to be one of the most striking resemblances between oral tales of incarceration and modern prison tales. There is no gainsaying the centrality of songs as survival and counter-hegemonic tools. In his *Detained* Ngugi tells of the songs he and other political detainees sung to find solace and form solidarity at the Kamiti Maximum Security Prison. But precedence for such counter-hegemonic songs had been set in the turbulent Mau Mau era, as previous studies of the Mau Mau memoirs would reveal.[3] In singing songs of protest and bravery the detainees in the colonial detention camps forged strong bonds of solidarity and commitment to the struggle for independence. In turn they too had borrowed a leaf from the power of counter-hegemonic songs from oral tales of incarceration of which the Sela and Mwambu tale and the Liyongo epic are instances.

The siege of Mulukoba wa Chetambe or Chetambe's Fort, inspired the Bukusu to compose and sing a song that memorializes the cataclysmic events that unfolded during the colonial invasion;

Basoreri mukhabaanga,
Amanani kali lwanyi
Basoreri mukhabaanga,
Amanani kali lwanyi

You young men always claim you are brave.
Behold, the ogres are out there right now
Young men you always claim you are brave
Behold, the ogres are out there right now

It is significant that the British soldiers are pictured in the song as *amanani*, the Tachoni equivalent of *kamanani* in Bukusu, meaning ogres. (Tachoni is one of the Luhyia dialects whose use in Bukusu folklore is emblematic of the reality of cultural exchange and hybridity among the Babukusu). The equation of the British to monsters is a fitting symbol of the oppressiveness of the British reign in the imagination of the colonized. This is nothing new in African literature. In his story "Gentlemen of the Jungle" that is fashioned after an ancient Kikuyu tale, Jomo Kenyatta narrates the account of Mr. Elephant who was hosted by a man but later usurped ownership of the hospitable man's abode and ejected him from it. The man's appeal in the court presided over by the Elephant class yields no positive results for him. He soon realizes he has to seek other means of reclaiming his property rather than depend on legal institutions skewed in his antagonist's favor. Kenyatta's short story fittingly captures the absurdity of the European dispossession of Kikuyuland, and by extension Kenyan land, a classic case of the guest responding to the host's hospitality with hostility. Regarding Kenyatta's appropriation of the story, Mugo states, "Needless to say, Kenyatta uses this story as an allegory to satirize the way settler colonialism dispossessed precolonial Kenyan people who had shown the invaders naïve hospitality on their arrival, in keeping with their customary practice" (29).

It is instructive that Mugo herself extends the frame of the story of the bully Mr. Elephant by applying it to a wider geopolitical spectrum. She writes: "This pre-colonial Orature story is the tragic tale of the workers and peasants all over Africa and in the rest of the so-called third world under imperialist domination/exploitation, facilitated by their neocolonial ruling classes" (29). Clearly, the story also showcases the capacity of orature to embrace and express new realities as a way of ensuring its own relevance and its capacity to overlap into the terrain of African written literature. At any rate the trope of tyrannical forces, both internal and external, figured as ogre, snake, or whatever monstrous beast, is commonplace in Kenyan written literature, something that attests to the tremendous influence of oral literature on written literature. Ngugi wa Thiongo's novels *A Grain of Wheat, Devil on the Cross, Matigari* and *Wizard of the Crow* as well as Margaret Ogolla's novel *The River and the Source*, are instances of this transposition of imagery from oral literature into the written text. While the analysis of what oral narratives gain or lose when they are transformed into written form is a worthwhile venture, this would perhaps be a matter for another day. Suffice it to say here that Kenyatta's conception of Europeans as the ungrateful guest Mr. Elephant and the reference to the colonists as ogres in the Chetambe song can help illuminate the meaning of ogre in the story of Sela and Mwambu.

Evidently, the image of the British as ogres reflects the oppression that they visited upon the Babukusu. It is not easy to date oral tales, particularly those "peopled" by ogres. If it is true that the ogre stories predate the colonial encounter, the transcendence of their relevance cannot be gainsaid. Given the atrocities that they suffered under colonial rule, it is not all surprising that the Babukusu would apply the metaphor of ogres to colonists. The monstrosity of the colonial machine had attributes as menacing and devastating as the ogres of the oral tales.

To the Babukusu, one could argue, the "imprisoning" forces of colonialism were ogre-like, swallowing up their freedom and existence, as they knew it. It may well be that the Selah and Mwambu tale predates the colonial encounter. Yet it is reasonable to suggest that the Bukusu, like Mugo and Kenyatta's Kikuyu, might have found the ancient tale both relevant to and expressive of their experiential reality in the colonial encounter. In a sense the narration of the famous story can be interpreted as an attempt by the Babukusu to make sense of colonial conquest whose pinnacle was the battle of Chetambe's Fort. The expression "amanani kali ilwanyi"/ [the ogres are out there right now] in the song memorializing the fall of Chetambe's Fort underscores the immediacy and proximity of the ogres' presence in the here and now of the Bukusu world.

This supports the trans-historic significance of both the Sela and Mwambu story and the ogre motif in the Bukusu thought and imagination. The urgency of the times implied by the message of the song indicated that the ogres were not merely fictive elements of tales from antiquity, but that they were real inhuman human "ogres" inhabiting the tangible Bukusu day-to-day world. Interestingly, according to oral tradition the Bukusu prophet Mutonyi wa Nabukelembe had predicted the coming of the Europeans and the impact of the devastating colonial intrusion (Wolf and Blois, 174). The centrality of Nabukelembe's accurate predictions in Bukusuphone oral literature is a measure of the importance of the European colonial experience in the collective memory of the Babukusu people. Obviously, Mwambu's messiah-like figure in the narrative is expressive of the people's desire for emancipation from the colonial yoke that held them captive for close to a century. Colonial rule for the Babukusu or other groups in Kenya meant forced labor, expropriation of land, extortion through hut tax, and restrictions on mobility within their country by being forced to carry passes.

When Kenya gained independence in 1963, it is as if the nationalist movement had severed the colonial ogre's little finger and let the Babukusu and other native Kenyans to come out of the belly of the beast that was their colonial detention camps and prisons. Ioan Davies argues in his *Writers in Prison* that prison writers "write to rescue themselves and us" (33). One could say, if the narrative was created in pre-colonial times, the Bukusu retold it over and over again amongst themselves in colonial times as a coping mechanism, as a way of rescuing themselves. There is therefore no denying the political underpinnings of the story of Sela and Mwambu and its centrality in the collective memory of the Babukusu of Western Kenya. It narrativizes the symbolic "political imprisonment" of the Babukusu under colonial rule and justifiably belongs in the class of literature of confinement. A case could also be made for likening Mwambu's failure to deal the ogre a fatal blow to the failure of post-independence African states to rid themselves of the ogre-like neocolonial influences. Colonialism, like the ogre, still looms large, albeit invisibly, in the so-called postcolonial moment.

The Waswahili People

The oral "intertextuality," which exists between the Babukusu and their neighbors is also evident between the Waswahili and their coastal neighbors. Wamitila in his *Archetypal Criticism of Kiswahili Poetry* (2001) observes that various versions of the famous Fumo Liyongo epic are found among the Gunya and Pokomo. As such, we are bound to conclude that hybridity seems to be a defining characteristic of both the Bukusu and the Swahili folklore. But just who are the Waswahili?

The exact origin of the Waswahili people is, like that of the Babukusu, shrouded in mystery. But unlike the latter, whose identity as a distinct group has never been in doubt, the Waswahili are a people whose ethnicity and existence has often been misread, misapprehended and sometimes obliterated altogether, particularly in the colonial and early postcolonial period. Three examples of explanations of Swahili identity will suffice to illustrate the related mystification. First, The ministry of tourism in Kenya, for instance, boldly proclaimed as recently as 1974 that there was no group of people called the Waswahili.[4] The implication of the ministry's assertion was that the Swahili language did not depend on the existence of a community of indigenous speakers. Second, University of Dar es Salaam scholar M. Madoshi listed ten different things that being a Mswahili connotes including trickster, European who masters the language, poor person, rich person, upcountry person who assimilates into the East African cultural culture, etc.[5] Lastly, some scholars have advanced the view that to be Swahili was synonymous with being Tanzanian or East African.[6] The multiple and conflicting explanations epitomize the extent to which the existence and identity of the Waswahili has been locked up in the prison-house of confusion, doubt, and even outright deletion. Liberating Swahili identity out of this figurative incarceration has been a task accomplished admirably through blending astute scholarship with Swahili cultural nationalism.

Shihabudin Chiraghdin, Alamin Mazrui, and Ibrahim Noor Sharif are some of the most principal players in the demystification of Swahili identity. In 1974, the same year in which the Kenyan ministry of tourism negated or discounted the existence of the Waswahili, Chiraghdin wrote "Kiswahili na Wenyewe," in which he forcefully and compellingly argued for the existence of the Swahili as a *kabila*, a distinct ethnic group. He listed five attributes of a *kabila*, all of which he indicated the Waswahili fulfilled totally. In brief he argued that the Waswahili people: (1) claim the same origin on the Kenyan coast; (2) are bound by the same traditions and customs; (3) inhabit the same geographical location; (4) have a unique language; (5) and are known or recognized by other *Makabila* (ethnic groups).

Mazrui and Shariff would later expound on the same premise in their work. For example, *Swahili Idiom and Identity of an African People* (1994), they strongly discount the notion of Swahili language as "a bastard, hybrid child of an unholy African-Arab union" (Mazrui & Shariff 59). They maintain, like Chiraghdin that Swahili is a language with its own African native speakers, who existed before the Arabic encounter. However, they concede that these people did not always call themselves the Waswahili, but preferred their own clan names such as Wabajuni, Wamalindi, Wajomvu, Wakilindi, etc. Mazrui and Shariff acknowledge the divergent explanations of the term Waswahili (the people) and Kiswahili (the language). One etymological explanation is that these terms came from the Arabic expression *Suahel*, meaning people of the coast. The other one is that the term had indigenous roots, coming as it did from the Swahili expression, *Siwa hili* "this island" and *Wa siwa hili*, "people of this island."

The existence of the Waswahili is no longer a debate that generates too much heat, not least the question of whether their nomenclature is perceived as too Arabized or too de-Arabized. As Mazrui points out in *Swahili Beyond Boundaries* (2007) despite the transethnic and transnational pretensions of the Swahili language, it has increasingly become pertinent to acknowledge the existence of the ethnicity of the native speakers. The paradox of Swahili language enjoying pride of place as the bona fide *lingua franca* of the East and Central African region, whereas doubts are cast upon the existence of native Swahili speakers has gradually waned.

The Liyongo Epic as a Prison Narrative

Understanding the story of Fumo Liyongo as an epic is an important point of departure for its analysis, because like the oral autobiography, the recognition of the African epic has been long delayed and denied. Isidore Okpewho has shown how Western scholars of African orature such as Ruth Finnigan dismissed the possibility of the existence of epics in Africa. And yet as Okpewho cogently demonstrated Africa abounds in epics including the epics of Shaka of the Zulu, Sundiata of Mali, and the Mwindo epic from the Congo. In his definition of epic Okpewho states: "An epic is fundamentally a tale about the fantastic deeds of a man or men endowed with something more than the normal human might and operating in something larger than the normal human context and it is significant in portraying some stage of the cultural or political developments of a people" (34).

Liyongo's story fits Okpewho's apposite definition. The Fumo Liyongo epic is a narrative about the eponymous poet-hero at the heart of the collective memory of the coastal peoples of East Africa. The epic enjoys pride of place as one of the most outstanding literary productions and cultural artifacts of classical

Swahili literature. The other literary productions that share similar prominence include Sayyid Nassir's *Al Inkshafi,* Abu Bakr bin Mwengo's *Utendi wa Tambuka,* Mwana Kupona's *Utendi wa Mwana Kupona* and numerous quatrains of Muyaka bin Hajji. As already noted, the influence of the Liyongo epic spans across ethnic frontiers, with for instance, the Pokomo and the Swahili each staking claim on it as a defining feature of their cultural heritage and the epitome of their system of oral expression. Initially a product of the oral tradition, the Liyongo epic has been appropriated, narrated and interpreted in many and varied ways by the communities that lay claim to it. But the potency of the oral narrative is demonstrated by the extent to which it is transformed into the written form in various genres and subgenres, for examples, as a poem in Muhamed Kijumwa's and Sayyid Nassir's renditions and as a play in Bitugi Matundura's *Shujaa Liyongo.* The epic has generated tremendous scholarly attention with many theses and dissertations being devoted to its elucidation and interpretation. These include I.N. Shariff in "The Liyongo Conundrum: Re-Examining the Historicity of Swahili's National Poet-Hero" (1991); Fussi Nagy in "The Ethnic Situation in East Africa and the Folklore figure of Liongo Fumo" (1984); and K.W. *Wamitila's Archetypal Criticism of Kiswahili Poetry* (2001).

Wamitila's study is important in a number of ways 1) he conceives of the epic as at once an oral and written text; 2) he examines various versions of the epic; and 3) he undertakes a painstaking close reading of the epic with particular attention to stylistic and linguistic features. Following Wamitila, I intend to approach the Liyongo epic as an oral text, which has been preserved in a written form. But I intend to go beyond Wamitila and other critics' focus upon what is lost or gained by the metamorphosis of the text from its oral to the written form, and to read the Liyongo epic as a quintessential narrative of confinement. In this regard I premise my analysis on the assumption that there is a close connection between Liyongo's prison narrative and the political or prison context contemporaneous with the experience or the creation of the narrative. I examine how individual experience is an embodiment of collective experience. Equally interesting to me is the centrality of the female relative in the fate and life of the male victim of incarceration. Lastly, I examine what it means for a prisoner to be an artist as Liyongo was.

I will assume my readers' ignorance of the epic, as in the case of the story of Sela and Mwambu, and provide a summary of the epic before turning to its analysis. The account takes place in the ancient city-state of Shanga along the Kenyan coast. The story's hero Liyongo lives outside the city, and is extremely famous for his outstanding musical and supernatural physical prowess. He is the archrival of King Mringwari, who feels threatened by Liyongo's superhuman strength and mounting popularity. Quite early on the narrative suggests the existence of a political problem. But at first things are not as bad. In fact when some of the neighboring Galla people visit Shanga, the King is the first to extol Liyongo's extraordinary physical strength. He tells them that Liyongo was so gigantic if they saw him they would flee or urinate on themselves in fear. He then proceeds to summon Liyongo from the outskirts of Shanga. When the Galla see for themselves the stature and strength of the man, they are absolutely terrified. They are afraid of the Waswahili for having such an extraordinarily mighty man on their side. They therefore propose a marriage alliance by providing Liyongo with a Galla wife as a means of forestalling future conflicts with the Waswahili.

With the Galla wife Liyongo sires a son, who in some versions of the story committed what Wamitila , following Freud, has called "oedipal murder."

If in the beginning King Mringwari appears to use Liyongo's strength and fame to ward off enemy attack, it was only a matter of time before there would be absolute fallout between the Swahili archrivals. The king attempts to use the Sanye or Dahalo neighboring community to kill Liyongo. They trick Liyongo into a *kikoa* feast. Participants are required to gather palm fruits in turns in the feast. When it is Liyongo's turn to gather the fruits he is given an unusually tall palm tree. The objective was to shoot him with arrows when he was on the tree. To the chagrin of the would-be killers, Liyongo decides against climbing the tree and instead fells the fruits using arrows as some versions of the tale indicate.[4] Other versions such as the Pokomo one indicate that he shook the trunk of palm tree until the fruits fell.

The King plots to have Liyongo arrested and detained. The immediate impetus of the King's drastic step is not immediately clear in extant versions of the narrative. The Zanzibar version collected by Edward Steere, however, casts Liyongo in negative light as someone who constantly harassed people: "Naye ana nguvu sana, mtu mkubwa katika mji. Akaud]hi mno watu, hatta siku hiyo, wakafanya shauri kumwendea nyumbani kwake kumfunga. Wakaenda watu wengi sana wakamingilia nyumbani ghafula, wakamkamata wakamfunga, wakaenda naye hata gerezani, wakamtia" (438-439). He had great strength and was a great man in the city. And he oppressed the people exceedingly, till one day they made a plan to go to him in his house and bind him. And a great number of people went and came upon him suddenly into his house, and seized him and bound him, and put him into prison).

In the tale Steere collected there is no mention of the king and the apparent power struggle that existed between him and Liyongo. It is the people's thoughts and actions that are placed front and center in this version, and yet we can implicitly discern the King's influence in the whole scenario as the people use "state apparatus" namely the prison, to contain and to tame Liyongo, something that would otherwise be impossible without the King's consent and coercion.

The next crucial stage in the narrative is the King's attempt to have Liyongo executed. After learning that he is to be executed in three days' time, Liyongo makes a request that a *gungu* and *mwao* dance tourney be organized outside his prison so he could bid farewell to the people. His request is accepted. Meantime he sends a message in a cryptic poem to his mother through their slave girl, requesting her to bake a loaf of bran and to hide iron files in it. Only his mother and the slave girl could tell the meaning of the poem that appeared superficially to be at once innocuous and silly.

At the farewell dance, he requests for cymbals and *upato*. On this occasion soldiers do not rob the slave girl of the bread she brings for Liyongo, as was their custom. They regard bran as inferior food befitting only slaves and hence hand it over to the prisoner for whom it was intended. Liyongo sung with his melodious voice and played the musical instruments to the delight of all those gathered outside. But he uses the music and the sound of the instruments to muffle the sound of his filing away the chains with which he was bound. Before they knew it, he had broken out of his prison cell and confronted the people assembled outside. He kills several of them by smashing their heads together.

Liyongo retreats to the countryside after breaking out of prison. Having failed to eliminate him through frontal attacks, the King decides to use Liyongo's own son. After some nagging and probing, Liyongo somewhat reluctantly and unwittingly reveals to his son the secret of his invincibility. He reveals to him that the only way to kill him is to insert a copper needle in the navel. After reporting to the king the outcome of his "espionage" the son returns to his father Liyongo with the copper needle. While the father is fast asleep the son pierces his navel with the copper needle.

Liyongo then picks up his bow and arrows and goes to the village well where he kneels down ready to shoot someone or something. One of the oddities of this tale lies in the fact that as he kneels there at the well, Liyongo dies. Yet, when the villagers came to draw water from the well in the morning they were too scared, thinking he was aiming at them in fierce fury with his bow and arrow. They approach his mother and request her to plead with to him to move away so they can draw water from the well. The mother touches him and tries to soothe him with songs, only for him to drop down. So she wept, knowing that indeed her son was dead.[7]

The thematization and narrativization of incarceration is self-evident in the Liyongo epic. There are obvious attempts to arrest Liyongo that ultimately succeed. Norval Morris and David J. Rothman in their *Oxford History of the Prison* opine that the conventional answer to the question "why prison?" often encompasses one or more of the following reasons; 1) deterrence; 2) retribution/expiation; 3) reform; and 4) incapacitation (xi). Of all these motives for incarceration it would seem reform was the furthest in the mind of King Mringwari when he decreed the imprisonment of his nemesis Liyongo. Liyongo is eventually incarcerated pending execution, a move that virtually curtails his freedom or as some versions suggest checks his harassment of the populace with his superhuman abilities. If there is validity in the claim that Liyongo harassed the people, he was not only imprisoned as a form of retribution for his actions but so that he is incapacitated, essentially becoming an object lesson for others likely to choose the same path of harassment.

There is clearly power dynamics at work in the incarceration of Liyongo as was with the case of the victims of the ogre's tyranny in the Sela and Mwambu story. Liyongo's bloody escape from prison resonates with and supersedes the counter-hegemonic violence that obtains in the case of Mwambu's violent response to ogre hegemony. However, the contending forces in the Liyongo epic are both human, even though one is bound to qualify this reality by noting that Liyongo was a human but imbued with abilities of a superhuman being. And unlike the Bukusu tale that is set in a mythical past, the Liyongo epic is set in a historical past. Beyond the mystery surrounding the life and death of Liyongo, his historicity is not really a matter of doubt in both the oral and written history of the Swahiliphone East African coast. Also, the Kenyan coast has been the terrain of countless power struggles of which, the one enacted in the Fumo Liyongo epic is exemplary[8] (see Mulokozi (1995) and Abdulaziz (1979)). King Mringwari imprisons Liyongo because he views him as a threat to his kingship, in the same way that King Saul of the Jewish nation was irked by the popularity of David, and according to Jewish tradition, on several occasions, attempts to assassinate him. The similarity between David and Liyongo is accentuated by the fact that both are not only skilled fighters but exceptional musicians, notwithstanding the fact that unlike David, Liyongo was a giant.

In the Zanzibar version of the Liyongo epic the hero is depicted as anti-social and anti-heroic for his harassment of the people. In contrast in the Bukusu story Sela and other members of Mwambu's clan are imprisoned in the belly of the ogre for no offence at all, unless their being born human was in itself a crime. According to the Zanzibar version, Liyongo is reprehensible and culpable and deserving of the incarceration. Yet, this version tends to downplay the significance of what Joseph Roach would term the "raging paranoia" of the King that might have evidently influenced negation of Liyongo's positive attributes in the public imagination (2). Feeling his power threatened by Liyongo's mounting popularity, the King might have poisoned the people's minds and decidedly perpetrated the image of Liyongo as a pariah and a danger to society.

How though is incarceration linked to Liyongo's heroism? It could be said that even before his incarceration Liyongo was already performing extraordinary feats befitting of heroism. He had exaggerated physical masculinity, exceptional musical talent as well as unprecedented ingenuity and intelligence. And according to the Zanzibar version of the story, he had also earned himself the dubious reputation of a bully largely because of the gift of physical strength. King Mringwari's raging panaroia ensures that Liyongo is incarcerated despite or because of his extraordinary attributes. In a way, one could argue, Liyongo did not need incarceration to make him stand apart from his contemporaries. Yet it would be incorrect to claim that incarceration does not augment his heroism. Incarceration makes him a victim of state terror in the form of captivity that attempts to dissolve his world and uncreate his sense of self as Elaine Scarry would put it. The sense of victimhood that arises from the incarceration enhances audience identification with Liyongo's fate. The audience is bound to sympathize or even empathize with him albeit with the awareness that the hero presumably vacillates or oscillates between victimhood and villainy. When he stages a successful escape bid from prison toward the end of the epic with the help of his mother and the slave girl, he reaches the apex of his heroism. Prison with its apparent deprivation of agency and freedom therefore becomes the location of Liyongo's most heroic act. Even though he is assisted in his escape, the bid is essentially his brainchild and signifies the highest watermark of his heroic acts, outwitting and outsmarting King Mringwari and his state apparatus. Thus, Liyongo's incarceration is inextricably tied up with counter-hegemonic heroism.

What is also remarkable is the striking similarity between Liyongo's situation and that of prisoners of conscience of the colonial and postcolonial periods in Kenya. For one thing, it would seem, oftentimes whenever the government detained or imprisoned dissenters and dissidents, it made them essentially both victims and heroes in the public imagination. Jomo Kenyatta, JM Kariuki, Raila Odinga, Koigi wa Wamwere, Martin Shikuku, Kenneth Matiba, George Moseti Anyona, and Gitobu Imanyara are cases of politicians whose incarceration tended to endear them to rather than alienate them from the electorate, enabling them to gain significant capital in certain stages of their political careers. Also, the way Liyongo earns himself a bad name in the purview of the state, leading to being branded an anti-social bully, resonates with the demonization of dissent that has been replicated over and over again in Kenya's more recent political history. For instance, as both JM Kariuki and Wambui Otieno state in their memoirs, the Mau

Mau freedom fighters were painted in colonial propaganda as cannibals and killers of children and women (see the analysis of *Mau Detainee* in the next chapter of this book). In her *Imperial Reckoning: The Untold Story of Britain's Gulag in Kenya*, historian Carolyne Elkins also alludes to the British official projection of the colonists as civilized and humane and the Mau Mau fighters as barbaric and savage. The result was the emergence in colonial Kenya of what Benedict Anderson would call "the quandary of definition" as both the terms "freedom fighters" and "terrorists" applied to the same people at the same time, depending on which side of the divide one was. Similar scenarios have often been replayed in postcolonial Kenya with, for instance, the Kenyatta regime branding Ngugi wa Thiong'o's involvement with community theatre at Kamiriithu as subversive and detaining him without trial for almost two years.

Almost always the ruling regime felt threatened by the art and activism of the victims of political imprisonment. Individuals on the long list of political prisoners in the colonial period was perceived as enemies because of the at once real and imagined fear that they wanted to topple the colonial dispensation. Similarly, the detention and imprisonment of political opponents of the Kenyatta and the Moi administration were predicated on the belief that those individuals and groups were, at the very least, like Liyongo, undermining and undercutting the authority of the regime, and at the very worst, plotting to overthrow it.

The Question of Gender

Gender issues also emerge in the Liyongo epic. But the women of the Liyongo epic do not have the passivity that we find in the Bukusu story of Sela and Mwambu. To be sure the phallocentric structures that demean women in society are reflected in the narrative as when the Wagalla in one version want to appease the Waswahili by giving Liyongo a wife. This angle of the story resembles the legend of Mango among the Bukusu who was rewarded with a wife by the Barwa for his heroic feat of killing the feared mythical snake. But the passivity of women of Liyongo epic is illusory. Both Liyongo's mother and the slave girl play a central role in the hero's successful escape from custody. Liyongo sends his mother a cryptic message through his slave girl. He states:

> Ewe kijakazi nakutuma uwatumika,
> Kamwambia mama, ni mwinga siyalimka
> Afanye mkate, pale kati tupa kuweka,
> Nikeze pingu na minyoo ikinyoka,
> Ningie ondoni ninyinyirike ja mana nyoka,
> Tatange madari na makutano kuno kimeta,
>
> You slave girl, let me send you to my mother,
> Tell my mother, she is a simpleton, unaware of the ways of the world
> Let her bake bread, and put files in the middle,
> So that I may cut my fetters, and unchain myself,
> That I may go to the road, and glide like a snake,
> That I may mount the roofs and walls, and look this way and that way.
> (Steere, 442)

The slave girl faithfully delivers the message. Liyongo's mother does as instructed by the son and hides metal files in the prisoner's bread. It is with these files that he saws away the prison chains and breaks free. The actions and reactions of these two women make them central in the drama. Their complicity in the prison escape is a mark of their valor and loyalty to Liyongo, qualities that embolden them to participate in an enterprise fraught with danger and risk. In both the Sela and Mwambu tale and the Liyongo epic, coded messages are passed between the male protagonist and key female characters. But in the former the coded message is decoded by the enemy with disastrous results, while in the latter, the foe remains oblivious and clueless. Another point of contrast is that, rather than being victims of trickery as Sela was, Liyongo's mother and the slave girl are tricksters themselves, not simpletons, as the song seems to suggest.

In the Liyongo epic, hence, there is a reversal of roles, with women paving the way for the end of captivity for Liyongo, a male character. Yet, most analyses of the story gloss over the heroic acts of these women that enhance and enable Liyongo's heroism. As Joseph Mbele stipulated in his essay "Women in the African Epic" (2006), the trajectory of folktale scholarship has a predilection toward downplaying or ignoring the heroic deeds of female characters. Mbele elegantly incriminates students of the African folktales when he states; "We have eyes and ears but we are conditioned neither to fully see nor fully hear the female characters" (62). The women are viewed as mere props in the drama with Liyongo, the man, as the center of focus, recalling Achebe's acerbic critique of the use of Africans as props and a backdrop to the European imagination in Joseph Conrad's *Heart of Darkness.*[9] It is to be noted that at the end of the narrative it is only to Liyongo's mother that the entire village turns because it believes only she would have the audacity and temerity to confront her son and persuade him to move away from the well so people can draw water. She succeeds where all men have failed by approaching him valiantly in an attempt to persuade him, only to discover he was long dead. She is the first to discover and announce the reality of the demise of this great man. But I suppose, not enough of the femininity of Liyongo's heroism has been acknowledged.

Without any doubt Liyongo shares some characteristics with mystical Lwanda Magere of the Luo people of Western Kenya and Samson of the Jewish tradition in possessing uncanny power that is inextricably tied to what we may call a certain "somatic mystery." For Lwanda Magere, his power was in the shadow of his body hence the futile and ineffectual impact of enemy spears and arrows on the body itself. For Samson, the secret of his power was in the long unshaved hair. For Liyongo the only way of conquering him was to insert a cooper needle in his navel as the son discovered and consequently executed the action that brings down the otherwise invincible fighter. Hence, on the whole, when the secret is revealed in an act of betrayal each of these heroes is dealt a fatal blow.

Liyongo's epic is also an example of a prisoner whose artistic impulse defies the reality of the prison experience. As a prisoner, Liyongo not only can but does indeed compose poetry and perform music. Unlike Sela of the Bukusu tale, Liyongo is a producer of art not merely a consumer. The resilience of his artistic ability while incarcerated anticipates the artistic productions of jailed writers such as Ngugi wa Thiong'o's *Devil on the Cross*, Alamin Mazrui's *Chembe cha Moyo* and *Shadows of the Moon*, and Abdilatif Abdalla's *Sauti ya Dhiki*, and others discussed in subsequent chapters of this study.

In composing a somewhat silly song carrying a secret message to his mother, it may seem as if Liyongo uses prison as an allegoresis or excuse for writing nonsense. But it is within this putatively "artless art" coupled with a display of his musical talent, that he schemes his escape bid. It is a classic example of art as functional rather than "art for art's sake" since it enables or attempts to enable escape from prison. Secondly, the silly poem is an artistic venture that links the prisoner with the community outside the prison walls, opening dialogue that would otherwise be missing were the prisoner to choose resigning to fate. These two aspects are inextricably intertwined in the sense that they both impinge on the place and space of aesthetics in the literary production emanating from prison. When Barbara Harlow stated that for most prison writers, questions of style are best left in the schoolbag, she was hinting at the primacy of function over aesthetics in the genre of prison writing (73). Put differently, the form tends to be less important for the prison artist than the content.

The tenacity and versatility of the Liyongo epic makes it adaptable and applicable not only to the socio-political context within which it was first conceived, but also to the colonial and postcolonial moments. This perhaps explains its widespread popularity and continued relevance to the Swahiliphone East African coast and beyond. Liyongo can thus be easily substituted for any number of political prisoners and revolutionaries of any period while King Mringwari could, like the ogre in the Bukusu tale, symbolize the reactionary despots, dictators, and tyrants who brutalize and demonize political opposition at all times, and immensely contribute to making life or existence prison-like.

The I-pronoun, Truth, and Trauma

In sum, the Sela and Mwambu story and the epic of Liyongo demonstrate how oral expression carries the weight of the experience of incarceration; the capacity of orality to exhibit the carceral experience and imagination. Bound up with these oral incarceration narratives is meditation on issues such as power dynamics, gender, violence and counter-hegemonic violence, and the use of artistic productions from within and without the prison walls. Although these issues are not by any means exclusive to prison narratives, they are pervasive enough to be considered salient features of this genre of literature. It is important to note that these issues also figure prominently in the written prison narratives that we will consider in the subsequent chapters of this study. I would suggest, in addition, that the oral tales that constitute the focus of our analysis in this chapter also implicitly point to an engagement with the ideas of the I-pronoun, truth, and trauma, ideas that find more explicit dramatization in the written texts. In what follows I briefly expound on how each of these variables is implied in both the tale of Sela and Mwambu and the Liyongo epic.

The centrality of truth–telling cannot be overemphasized in these tales of imprisonment. Generally speaking the stories are implicated in what Achebe in his collection of essays *Hopes and Impediments* has called "the truth of fiction," whose governing principle is "let us pretend," the mutual acceptance between audience and narrator that in the story world both the improbable and the impossible can and will occur (40). In respect of the Sela and Mwambu story, both audience and narrator pretend that it is true that ogres exist, that a whole population can be swallowed up into the belly of the ogre and remain alive, and be rescued by cutting off the ogre's finger. That almost goes without saying. Perhaps what does not go without saying is Liyongo's narrative because it is based on a real historical personality who lived and died on the Kenyan coast. How true is the Liyongo epic in recording and representing the incarceration and exploits of this historical figure? While a similar question may not arise with regard to the Sela and Mwambu story, it bears stating that in both narratives emphasis is laid on the fictive element and therefore it would be safer to underscore the "let us pretend" of the truth of fiction, than to insist upon historical veracity or literary verisimilitude. But it seems as if this question does not easily go away since the thin line between fiction and fact inevitably impinges on truth claims.

Further, in both the Sela and Mwambu story and the Liyongo epic, the characters' truth-claims propel the plots. The ogre's inversion and subversion of truth when he imitates Mwambu's voice leads to Sela's misrecognition and ultimately to her being swallowed up. Liyongo's truth claim in his poem that either his mother or he himself is a simpleton, belie the ingenuity with which the two, assisted by the slave girl, execute the escape plan. Both the ogre in the Sela and Mwambu story and Liyongo in the epic subvert the truth, make false truth claims or simply lie. They seem to vindicate Stephen Spenders's intriguing statement on self-narrating: "Everyone is a liar about certain things" (121). Do the so-called real-life accounts of incarceration also bear lies? What does it mean that former Mau Mau detainees would write that their so-called confessions were lies to avoid torture or further torture? Are there situations where lying is justified and justifiable? Is lying sometimes a form of truth telling? These are some of the questions that this study will attempt to address in subsequent chapters.

Also implicated in these stories is trauma. Freud is one of the earliest scholars credited with establishing connections between traumatic experience and literature. Acknowledging Freud's seminal attempt to marry literature with trauma Cathy Caruth writes: "If Freud turns to literature to describe traumatic experience, it is because literature, like psychoanalysis, is interested in the complex relation between knowing and not knowing" (3). One of the literary compositions to which Freud "turns" to describe trauma is Tasso's *Gerusalemme Liberata.* Freud turns to this romantic epic in an attempt to extrapolate upon "traumatic neurosis" (Caruth 2). In brief Tancred kills his lover Clorinda unknowingly in a duel while she is disguised as an enemy knight. Later blood comes out of a tall tree he slashes with his sword in the magic forest. He hears Clorinda's voice, whose soul is imprisoned in the tree complaining that he has wounded her again. Tancrid "hears" Clorinda's voice, long after he has inflicted the fatal wound on her body. As Caruth remarks, Freud uses the story to underscore the inassimilable nature of trauma, how it is not fully grasped initially or ever but returns to haunt the survivor later on. What is also significant about trauma personified in Clorinda is that it becomes a belated voice, barely heard in the beginning and almost incomprehensible or unrecognizible in its subsequent occurrences. Following Freud, Caruth argues that trauma "is always the story of a wound that cries out, that addresses us in the attempt to tell us of a reality or truth that is not otherwise available" (5).

Whether we reckon trauma to be a wound to the body, as the Greeks originally conceived of it, or as a wound to the psyche, as trauma scholars have come to embrace it lately, there are elements of trauma in the Sela and Mwambu story and the Liyongo epic that are implicit, although perhaps not articulated enough. Some contend that to ascribe trauma to fictional characters like Sela and Mwambu or Liyongo (as we encounter him in the epic) is to wrongly assume that these are "real living people" (Roland, 92). Yet, it is apparent that the imaginative world of both oral and written literature is almost always fashioned after real living people, a *mimesis*—to borrow Aristotle's term—of both how they live and how they die. Hence, beneath and beyond the impulse to pretend that fiction is truth is the awareness that there is close affinity between story characters and real living people. Thus we perceive the fictive world as peopled by people like us or who could be like us, people whose experiences, actions and attitudes are either reflections or refractions of our own. That is why we care about them in the first place. As Elizabeth Wright has cogently argued, although characters are not real living people, they must bear sufficient resemblance to real humans like us to attract our attention and interest or sympathy and empathy (16).

In a nutshell, the dramatization of issues of the I-pronoun, truth telling and trauma in the two stories composed and set in pre-colonial times, anticipates the issues that would preoccupy incarceration narratives in both colonial and postcolonial times in Kenya. The analysis of these tales illustrates that oral tales too carry the weight of the carceral experience and imagination as to deserve inclusion in the category of prison or incarceration narratives. The Bukusu story of Sela and Mwambu and the Swahili epic of Liyongo continue to manifest their relevance and usefulness, not only because they have the propensity to entertain but they also can interrogate and extrapolate on the meaning of being, by narrativizing and thematizing confinement.

Therefore, to overestimate the entertainment value of African oral tales is to overlook the deep moral, gender and metaphysical questions that these tales evoke and invoke. Particularly, significant is the way these narratives capture the literal and figurative imprisonment of the peoples from whom they emerge, a means of meaning making and breaking any number of prison chains. It could therefore be said, that to insist as Okpewho's claims that African tales are there merely or mostly for entertainment, is to miss the point. This chapter has demonstrated the centrality of incarceration in oral narratives. Chapter 2 illustrates how orality manifests itself in J.M. Kariuki's memoir *Mau Mau Detainee*, the first ever written and published prison narrative in Kenya's literary history.

Chapter 2: Articulating Human Rights Violations in the Pioneer Prison Memoir

> Memory is an action: essentially it is the act of telling a story.
>
> — Pierre Janet, *Trauma: Exploration in Memory*

> Every text is an intertext form that borrows, knowingly or unknowingly, from the immense archive of the previous culture.
>
> — Vincent B. Leitch, *The Nortorn Anthology of Theory and Criticism*

This chapter examines the context and text of Josiah Mwangi Kariuki's, *Mau Mau Detainee*, a narrative whose appearance in print in 1963 in the London metropolis, inaugurated the publication of narratives of incarceration that capture the turbulent colonial era.[1] Chapter one illustrated how the Kenyan peoples sustained themselves under colonial tyranny and incarceration through oral narratives that for the most part thematized and narrativized incarceration or captivity. This chapter analyzes the thematic and stylistic concerns in Kariuki's pioneering written prison text. The analysis of Kariuki's account of his experience in colonial detention camps, sheds light on how oral tales anticipated, and are replicated in, written narratives of political incarceration that emerge in the colonial and the postcolonial eras. Kariuki's written text therefore is a milestone in the literary history of Kenya's prison narratives. If oral tales such as the Fumo Liyongo epic would later find expression in the written form, there is no doubting that they were originally composed and existed as oral texts of incarceration. Conversely, the emergence of *Mau Mau Detainee* has to be appraised and appreciated from the premise that it was originally conceived as a written text. That implies that questions regarding the interplay between the individual and the collective whole take on particular significance when analyzing his account. This is so because some of his early critics lamented about the memoirist's failure to include enough of the Mau Mau movement collectively as will soon be evident in this chapter. Also, more recent theorization on the impact of the print culture on the African oral tradition tends to suggest the privileging of the self and diminution of the collective, the society. Kwame Anthony Appiah's assertion in his *In My Father's House*, that in the print culture the "we" of society is replaced by the "I" of the individual, is an instance of this kind of theoretical stance. This chapter therefore engages the individual--communal nexus, as well as truth-telling, torture, and trauma as determined by the context and text of Kariuki's *Mau Mau Detainee*.

But that these issues and Kariuki's account of his odious prison ordeal constitute matters of human rights concern is beyond any shadow of doubt. It could well be said that Kariuki's account merits attention, not simply because of its special status as the first Kenyan written prison memoir, but also because it sets the pattern of courageous exposure of egregious violation of human rights by the colonial and postcolonial governments in Kenya which subsequent prison tales would follow. This means that even though questions of style and whether or not it coheres with themes may be tantalizingly riveting in the analysis of this prison tale, one should not lose sight of the human rights dimension, or afford to be oblivious to the human cost inextricably tied up to political incarceration and its attendant torture and trauma. It indeed could well be said that *Mau Mau Detainee* is first and foremost an account of human rights violation by the state presented by an individual who witnessed and experienced it and who eventually became a political martyr.

That the colonial government's treatment of the Mau Mau insurgency entailed wanton violation of human rights is attested to by the fact that the issue resolutely refuses to go away. It has virtually become a perennial thorn in the flesh of the British government almost over half a century after it granted Kenyan political independence. As recently as 2010, a Kenyan newspaper reported how the debate was still raging in Britain about the colonial government's culpability. As the report indicates the current British government, despite offering an official apology to its victims, it was still trying to shift blame and to shirk away from responsibility for the atrocities visited on Kenyans in the heyday of colonial control: "Despite a plea from an all-party group of MPs in the House of Commons and questions raised in the House of Lords, the British government appears determined to resist any attempts at financial compensation to elderly Mau Mau victims in Kenya. Recently, a cross-party group of UK MPs published an open letter demanding an apology and the creation of a welfare fund to help the alleged victims through old age."[2]

Kariuki did not live long enough to be among the former Mau Mau victims treated to the intriguing legal gymnastics over compensation by the British Government, which claims it bears no ethical or criminal responsibility for crimes committed during colonial times in Kenya. But his memoir aptly encapsulates the essence of the horrid detention conditions during colonial rule in Africa in general and in Kenya in particular. The memoir is a record of human rights abuses of unimaginable proportions. Kariuki's memoir therefore enjoys pride of place not only as the first ever published prison memoir in Kenya, but also one that recounts the horrors of detention in a manner that runs counter to the official British narrative.

A Martyr in the Making

Josiah Mwangi Kariuki disappeared from the Hilton Hotel, Nairobi, on March 2, 1975.[3] Several days later, a Masai herdsman, Musaita ole Tunda, found his mutilated body in a thicket at Ngong Hills on the outskirts of Nairobi. Kariuki's fingers were missing. A firebrand leftist backbench Member of Parliament, JM, as he was popularly known in Kenya, had been assassinated to stem the tide of opposition to Kenyatta's despotic rule. Like the assassination of Tom Mboya six-years earlier and Robert Ouko fifteen years later, Kariuki's assassination raised political temperatures to an all-time high and nearly brought the country to the brink of civil war.[4] Kariuki paid the ultimate price for opposing Kenyatta and what Ngugi in his prison memoir *Detained* terms the "comprador class" around Kenyatta that continually amassed wealth by impoverishing the masses of Kenyans. The tragic irony of Kariuki's demise lies in the fact that he had been inspired by Kenyatta's own activism and charisma to join the struggle for freedom from the tyranny of British colonial rule and had been a close ally of Kenyatta upon independence in 1963. Kenyatta's political speech in 1946 at Njoro, near Nakuru town, had had a telling effect on young Kariuki. Kariuki writes in his memoir: "I myself was fundamentally changed by his statemanshiplike words and his burning personality. I vowed there and then that I would struggle with him for justice and freedom for our country and I dedicated myself to follow him in his crusade to remove sufferings and humiliations of our people" (38).

Kariuki had heard what he describes as the "great man from London" whose oratorical skills as he mixed Kikuyu and Kiswahili, were peerless, and whose words forever changed Kariuki's life (37). Like Karari Njama who wrote *Mau Mau from Within*, Kariuki was among countless Kikuyu who were awakened by Kenyatta's oratory (Clough 70). Kariuki was determined to acquire some education that would facilitate his role in the struggle. Commenting on his connection to the illiterate detainees, he wrote: "I personally never considered escaping since I felt my place was with the illiterates in the camps, who were fighting for freedom as strongly as many of those outside" (146). Throughout the memoir he stresses the importance of education and how it behooved the few educated people to assist the illiterate masses. Between his initiation into politics at Njoro in 1946 during Kenyatta's speech and 1952, Kariuki went to Uganda to seek further education at the King's College Budo then run by the Church Missionary Society (CMS). The education he acquired in Uganda, particularly spoken and written English skills, would later figure prominently in his role as Mau Mau leader in and out of prison. When Kariuki fought alongside Kenyatta against the "colonial potentate," he did not anticipate that Kenyatta himself would metamorphose into the "postcolonial potentate" under whose reign Kariuki would be assassinated. In his memoir *Mau Mau Detainee,* Kariuki apparently used his fingers that would eventually be severed from the body by Kenyatta's secret agents, to write plaudits about his political mentor:

Kenyatta is greater than any Kikuyu, he is greater than any Luo or Nandi or Masai or Giriama, he is greater than any Kenyan, he is the greatest African of them all. He knows no tribe, no race, he bears no hatred or malice for the past; he is human and yet wiser than any other human I have ever known. (211)

Contemplating Kariuki's apparent unreserved adoration for Kenyatta and hyperbolic estimation of Kenyatta's worth as a leader with the benefit of hindsight accentuates the sense of poignancy and paradox in his assassination. *Mau Mau Detainee* was penned on the eve of Kenya's independence and the concomitant euphoria and optimism of the time. Hence, the memoir, not only elides serious consideration of the political scenario in Kenya after Kenyatta, but fails to anticipate the yet to be experienced fallout between the two former freedom fighters, and the transformation of Kenyatta from mentor to nemesis, and from affable leader to assassin.

The discovery of Kariuki's mutilated body was the culmination of a tale of a body that suffered untold pain in both colonial and postcolonial times, leaving a profound and lasting imprint on the collective memory of the Kenyan peoples. In a sense the assassination may be regarded as a form of "ultimate incarceration," extermination in postcolonial Kenya of a firebrand politician who survived the colonial detention camp. If political assassination of the kind Kariuki suffered was in itself the ultimate incarceration from which there is no release, one could argue, the state intentionally or unintentionally thrust the evidence of the mutilated body to the public imagination as an object lesson in the dangers inherent in political dissent and dissidence. There is no space in this section to investigate in depth the suffering of Kariuki's body in the Kenyatta regime nor is such a venture probable, given that there is no evidence that Kariuki left any written record of his torture at the hands of state operatives before his body was found at the Ngong Hills. Much of what transpired between his capture at the Hilton Hotel and the discovery of his body in the thicket on the outskirts of the Nairobi remains up till now a matter of conjecture and speculation. But his prison memoir recounts in detail his horrific experience as a political detainee in the colonial era and how his body (and the bodies of others like him) was subjected to intense pain and torture time and again for his relentless writing of letters of protest and complaint. Kariuki's memoir, *Mau Mau Detainee* can thus be seen as a narrative about the writing hand and "body in pain," to borrow Elaine Scarry's phrase.

In his *Tell Me Africa,* James Olney dismissed Josiah Mwangi Kariuki's memoir *Mau Mau Detainee* as seriously lacking in literary merit (17). But most Western critics received the text with disdain and disgust, not so much because of its deficiency as a work of art but mainly because of its content. William H. Friedland criticized the memoir for apparently not revealing enough about the then dreaded Mau Mau movement and for simply focusing on the narrator. Friedland stated: "The title of this volume develops expectations which remain largely unfulfilled since this book deals mainly with the author's experiences as a detainee during the Mau Mau emergency in Kenya and only peripherally with the question of Mau Mau" (626-27). Other critics such as Roger Chance, cast aspersions at the veracity of Kariuki's account and admonished readers to verify Kariuki's claims by comparing them with official British colonial archives (76-77). Marjorie Perham's remark in the introduction of the memoir that the narrative was "substantially true" did not help matters since it also implied that part of the memoir was untrue (11). To be sure, Kariuki's characterization of Kenyatta as the "greatest African" exemplifies claims that are neither substantially true nor objective. However, the patronizing and paternalistic temperament that suffuses Perham's ambivalent introduction tends to diminish

Kariuki's credibility and authority (63). But if the life writing elicited unfavorable reviews, it also found favor among other circles of critics. For instance, Marguerite Ylvisaker described Mau Mau Detainee as "an outstanding memoir" which was "a revealing light into the motivations of Mau Mau adherents" (664).

In this chapter I go beyond merely revisiting issues of content and form in Kariuki's memoir raised by earlier critics. For instance, whereas Olney critiques the memoir for what he perceives to be its literary want, I seek not only to investigate the rhetorical strategies that Kariuki utilizes, but also whether literary merit is necessary or desirable for a text narrativizing confinement and brutality. Also, I discuss the interplay between the timing of the writing, memory, audience, and the motivation for writing, or what Olney appropriately terms the "narrative imperative" (10b). Equally critical to this study is the conflation of the singular "I" and plural first person "we" or, in other words, how collective experience is embedded in individual experience, particularly with regard to experiencing confinement, trauma, and torture and resisting through writing. Lastly, I plumb the implications of the memoirist's truth claims and the detractors' doubts.

The Narrative Imperative

The narrative imperative or motivation behind J.M. Kariuki's writing of *Mau Mau Detainee* should be deduced from considering the context of its emergence in the heart of the imperial center in Britain. Evidently, JM Kariuki's audience was predominantly European and especially British. It is significant that he wrote his memoir not only in the English language but also while in the metropolis in Britain and not the colony, a year after his release in 1960 from seven years in detention. At the time of his writing, the bulk of the Kenyan population had little or no literacy in English. Clearly, Kariuki intended first and foremost to address the imperial British audience. To be sure his book was later to be translated into Swahili as *Mau Mau Kizuizini* for the benefit of Swahiliphone Kenya readers. But there is no gainsaying the centrality of the imperial audience, which was eager to glean some information about a member of what they perceived as a "terrorist" group that had fought fiercely to dislodge Britain's colonial hegemony in Kenya in a lengthy and bloody struggle; to confirm their assumptions of Mau Mau barbarity and atavism. Kariuki mentions that while in England working on the memoir, the British editor Margery Perham, urged him to complete the writing process expeditiously, because "many people in England did not understand what had been happening" in Kenya during the Emergency period between 1953 and 1960 (213). At the same time there was a burning desire on the memoirist's part to affirm his humanity and the humanity of the Mau Mau movement to the imperial audience, which, it seems to me, was little more than a constellation of doubting Thomases. He seems to have been not only keenly aware of his European audience but also the challenge of making himself intelligible to them.

For instance, in describing his reaction to the news of his mother's death while he was still in detention, he states: "It is difficult to explain the quality of my feeling to the Europeans" (171). Throughout his narrative Kariuki goes to great lengths to "explain" the Kikuyu and African cosmology to his European readers, explaining issues that he would have otherwise taken for granted had he solely an African audience in mind. In furnishing evidence of the rationality and humanity of the Kikuyu, Kariuki frequently invokes their folk wisdom by quoting a motley of proverbs and generally presenting largely positive ethnographic insight into the nine Kikuyu clans. But more importantly, he sanitizes the Mau Mau movement by justifying its emergence, absolving it from charges of irreligiosity, profanity, and vindictiveness, and exposing British colonial brutality, inhumanity and barbarity. Therefore, Kariuki's principal motivation was to offer a counter-discourse to the distorted image of the Mau Mau movement in the British imagination. His story goes against the grain of the official colonial history, as most narratives of confinement in the colonial epoch do. In this regard, Kariuki states:

> The future historian of these times may well find it difficult to get our side of the story. Many documents vital to his task will be burnt before independence. But in my narrative of the camps and our strange life together inside them he may perhaps see some glimpses of truth and justice of the movement's unity, and he may begin to understand why we do not regard the soldiers of the forest as 'hard-core', 'terrorists', or 'murderers', but as the noblest of our fighters for freedom. (215)

Put differently, the memoir presents an intriguing encounter and disjuncture between the British audience's "expectations" on the one hand and JM Kariuki's own motivation on the other. When Roger Chance condemns Kariuki for raising "expectations which remain largely unfulfilled," he presumably speaks for the majority of imperial readers. Because the memoir did not say what the British audience, for the most part, wanted to hear about what it perceived as an "unacceptable, backward-looking face of African nationalism," it met with either trenchant vilification or enabled them to move from rejection to at least "partial understanding" of the movement (Clough 63).

Marshall S. Clough claims that the authority of Kariuki as author of a narrative about Mau Mau experience is undermined and undercut by his "limited experience of the war itself" (68). Kariuki himself candidly admits in the memoir: "I was never in the forest myself but I hope that the true story of the glorious fight of the armies in the Aberdares and Mount Kenya forests will soon be written by someone who was"(62). But from the standpoint of experiencing the brutality and ferocity of colonial incarceration, Kariuki's credibility is beyond all doubt. Kariuki hears about, witnesses, and personally experiences various forms of torture as he was shuttled between the fourteen detention camps from 1953 to 1960, making him something of an authority on torture. As mentioned above the interplay between resistance and torture is the story that is inscribed on Kariuki's body from colonial to postcolonial times. In his memoir, Kariuki demonstrates that writing protest letters while in detention was his form of resistance, earning him considerable bodily and psychic harm from the colonial administration. Further, his memoir is in itself a continuation of resistance, an indictment of the British colonial ethos that glossed over its own tyranny and only focused on depicting the Mau Mau as diabolical.

Torture as Human Rights Violation

Invoking a collective "we" identity, Kariuki writes in graphic detail about how the detainees were subjected to humiliating body searches: "We were ordered to remove our clothes and all parts of our anatomy thoroughly examined" (92). The act of being stripped and searched may not have had discernible physical pain but the psychic pain that the humiliating act engenders should not be downplayed. Maina Kinyatti, writing about incarceration during the Kenyatta regime in his *Kenya: A Prison Notebook,* provides even in much more graphic detail about the warders' seemly eroticized pleasure in torturing state captives and searching their naked body cavities, underscoring the depravity and dehumanizing nature of incarceration. In his dairy entry of September 17, 1987, Kinyatti writes: "This morning, before sunrise, three guards opened the door and forced me to strip naked for a body-search. Suddenly, one of the guards grabbed my penis and ruthlessly started pulling it. He stopped pulling it when I screamed in pain. The other two guards thought it was fun, they burst [out?] laughing. The pain . . . , I could not control my tears—thin, painful tears. Before they left the cell, the vicious guard tauntingly asked me: "why were you screaming, I thought I? was giving your penis a massage?" (221).

But beyond this strip search and physical torture, detainees were also subjected to rigorous interrogation, which as Scarry maintains in her *The Body in Pain*, is itself a form of torture (29). The interrogation was apparently intended to extract from the detainees confessions of taking illegal oaths and involvement in guerilla activities, although as Scarry further argues the real intention is to display power rather than to get information from the victim. Scarry's claim is borne out by Kariuki's observation in the memoir that the force of interrogation often resulted in any number of false confessions from himself and other detainees. On several occasions Kariuki himself was stripped completely naked and beaten severely and brutally for writing letters of complaint against the inhuman and inhumane treatment of prisoners, letters that were smuggled out of detention and posted to colonial administrators and liberal British parliamentarians. On the whole whenever confessions were not easily forthcoming the captives' bodies were subjected to horrendous beatings, deprivation, and abuse. Kariuki mentions the castration of detainees at Nyangwethu near Naivasha as one of the most atrocious method of extracting information that the colonists employed. He writes: "Kwa Nyangwethu was, however, particularly bad and was notorious not for mere beatings, but for castration" (68). His claims have been corroborated by historians such as Caroline Elkins in her *Imperial Reckonings: The Untold Story of Britain's Gulag in Kenya* (2005) and David Anderson in his *Histories of the Hanged: The Dirty War in Kenya and the End of Empire* (2005). Remarking on *Imperial Reckoning*, Mahmood Mamdani echoes Kariuki's claims of brutal torture in colonial detention camps: "As one reads through Elkins' extended description of the regime of torture, one is struck by its predominantly *sexual* nature. Male detainees were often sexually abused through sodomy with foreign objects, animals, insects, cavity searches, the imposition of a filthy bucket-system, or forced penetrative sex. A common practice during the interrogation was to squeeze testicles with pliers" (8).

Kariuki's experience at Langata detention camp under Camp Commandant Marlow is typical of the torture his body underwent with the occasions for beating ranging from 25 to 60 strokes at one go (96,104). He faced mock execution like Russian dissident writer Dostoevsky. Kariuki writes:

> Next morning Marlow (Camp Commandant) took me outside 'C' Camp to a place near the Forest and said he would shoot me unless I wrote

> down on a piece of paper that I would not send any more letters to England, that I would cooperate with the government...Although the thought of death was still not wholly desirable I refused. He then took from his car a piece of three-ply wood about three feet by two and told me to hold it above my head arm's length. He walked five yards away and said he was going to kill me if I did not agree to write the sentences. Still, not imagining he could be serious, I refused. To my horror he raised his gun and shot at me. I remember a tremendous noise and knowing that I was *now dead* and then nothing. He had in fact shot through the wood and I had fallen down with it. (105) [my emphasis]

Scarry has propounded the view that mock executions are an instance of an extreme form of torture (30). A mock execution enacts the illusion of death and the reality of survival in a manner that wreaks havoc on the victim's psychic and physical well-being. The victim is almost always convinced of his demise until the reality of this severe and crude form of a practical joke that is not a joke dawns on him. Mock executions are a crude play on the victim's body and psyche. Kariuki was brought close to what he truly believed was to be his end, thus his words, "I remember a tremendous noise and knowing I was *now dead*...", only for events to suddenly take a different direction altogether. There is a sense in which survival of death, whether actual or imagined can be traumatic. As Cathy Caruth has argued in her *Unclaimed Experience*, surviving death itself constitutes an abiding form of trauma. The effect on the victim may most certainly be traumatic. We can therefore safely say that Kariuki's mock execution accentuated the sense of shock and trauma that the carceral experience occasioned.

The effect of the torture on the body and by extension the psyche was so intense that sometimes it caused hallucinations and total disorientation. As Scarry maintains, the dissolution and "uncreating" of the victim's world is at the very core of the torturer's mission. Bound up with this uncreating mission is transforming innocuous things such as the furniture, doorknobs, or even the body or parts of one's body into weapons against the victim. That is perhaps the reason why Kariuki sometimes lost his sense of self and body and was floating in a world of phantasmagoria as the passage below suggestively indicates:

They gave me no food or water but fortunately someone had thrown a bucket of water on the floor to make it uncomfortable for me to sleep on. So for the first three days until it dried up I was able to lick wetness off the cement and during that time I could think straight and speak out aloud to myself. On the fourth and fifth days cold water started coming out of my skin in a sort of sweat...On the sixth and seventh days my eyes became heavy like stones and nightmares began. Turbaned Indians passed by all wearing red beards; different coloured stars got in and out of my eyes; old Kikuyu women were dancing and always there were people moving to and fro... On the eighth day I no longer realized where I was, nor did my body seem to be part of me. I felt like a human wheel turning round and round and then like a man falling through thousands of feet from a high mountain in a thick forest. (121)

Deprivation of basic necessities such as water and food heighten the ordeal of incarceration. Kariuki's world was virtually dissolved in successive stages. The floor is turned into an instrument of torture and so is the water that is poured on it to make it wet and thus "uncomfortable" for him to sleep on. That Kariuki is forced to lick the water on the concrete floor to quench his thirst is a measure of the fight for survival under extreme conditions of dehumanization. As the excerpt above indicates there is a progressive descent into "nothingness" that the torture seems to achieve. By the sixth day Kariuki's body was emitting water in unusual ways, while the eyes were heavy like stones, implying that at this stage the body and eyes had become, like the wet floor, weapons used to torment him. But the pinnacle of his ordeal is on the eighth day when the mind becomes disoriented and he is plagued by nightmares and hallucinations. Kariuki's remark "I no longer realized where I was, nor did my body seem to be part of me" encapsulates the essence of dissolution of one's sentience, one's sense of self, and reality. The British colonial regime would go to such lengths to exhibit its power.

At one point so severe were Kariuki's beatings that the memoirist claims a fellow detainee who witnessed it committed suicide. He writes: "The evening of my beating-up, a detainee hanged himself in Compound 4. His sleeping companion, Jimmy from Embu, told me that he had seen my treatment and has said he could not stand living in this hell any longer" (162). And yet it was still difficult to break Kariuki's indefatigable spirit of defiance. He could not resist the itch to write another letter because he believed he was suffering for doing what was right, which could be a defining theme of memoirs of political incarceration. Contrary to the expectations of the colonists, Kariuki maintains that more often than not the torture only served to radicalize him. He wrote; "When will people realize that such beatings only stiffen the resolve of the victim? Finally the authority's treatment was rapidly building me up as martyr which was contrary to their real objectives" (120).

The "I" and the "We"

Kariuki's incarcerated body in pain is the constant motif in his narrative so that we are bound to conclude that his body is metonymic of the ordeal of others who confronted their fate as detainees in the colonial detention camps. The suicide victim's choice of "hell" as a metaphor for detention reinforces the trauma and torture resulting from conditions in the colonial detention camps. Indeed, the collective story of the Mau Mau detainees is embedded in Kariuki's individual narrative, so that Clough could not have been more correct when he concluded that *Mau Mau Detainee* is both an individual and a collective narrative. There is a sense in which the boundary between the first person singular and plural is flattened and blurred. Olney's penetrating observation about African individuality that "individual experience is not individualized" is applicable to Kariuki's narrative of the detention experience (76).

Clearly, close-reading of Kariuki's text tends to discount Kwame Anthony Appiah's postulate that the "we" of the oral narrative is overtaken by the "I" of the print culture. It is not that Appiah's suggestion lacks validity, valency or veracity; but it does not seem to apply with equal measure to all printed works in Africa as Kariuki's memoir testifies. It may be prudent to avoid accepting uncritically the applicability of Appiah's assertion and let the texts themselves vindicate or discount it. In this case, *Mau Mau Detainee* goes against the grain of Appiah's thinking on the self-society nexus.

Yet it bears elaborating that in stating "we" Kariuki opens up various identitarian possibilities with the pronoun "we" implying any number of groups including hardcore Mau Mau as opposed to soft core, the Kikuyu as opposed to other ethnic groups in Kenya, the detainees as opposed to the agents of state, and occasionally Kenyans as a whole. Despite the manifold and sometimes ambiguous connotations of "we," it seems to me that the narrative privileges the "we" of the hardcore Mau Mau and then the Kikuyu. The title, *Mau Mau Detainee* proclaims and presents Kariuki as a synecdoche of the collective identity of the Mau Mau adherents, both soft and hardcore. But the opening sentence of the memoir, "I am a Kikuyu who was detained in fourteen of Kenya's detention camps between 1953 and 1960" situates him within the Kikuyu-centric "we" that tends to dominate the Mau Mau memoirs. Yet, when he mentions "Like many other Kikuyu families we also had a strain of Masai blood in us, a legacy of the old raiding days" Kariuki overtly undercuts the myth of ethnic purity among the Kikuyu (29).

It should be noted that Wambui Otieno, who wrote Mau Mau's Daughter, also claims multiple ancestry including Masai and Ndorobo over and above her Kikuyu roots. Also Kenyattta is said to have had Masai blood. My contention however, is that the dominant "we" of the Mau Mau memoir acknowledges the ethnic impurity but often insists on a certain Kikuyu-ness that is less inclusive than exclusionary in its collectivity. Kariuki's *Mau Mau Detainee* is not an exception to this rule.

Nonetheless, that is not to say that this is a narrative in which the self-evaporates completely into the collective. Following Stein and Volkan, Antoinnette Errante has argued that all narratives "are representations of reality in which narrators also communicate how they see themselves and wish others to see them" (16). Therefore, *Mau Mau Detainee* is as much about the collective experience as it is about how Kariuki saw himself and how he wished others would see him. Like Wambui Otieno in *Mau Mau's Daughter*, Kariuki presents himself as a team player in the liberation movement, but nonetheless one imbued with peculiar or intrinsic individual attributes. Kariuki stands tall over other detainees because, as he claims, he is more educated than most, and unlike most educated youths of his time, he chose to suffer with the illiterate masses, struggling alongside them and fighting for them through hazardous letter writing, and being instrumental towards initiating and establishing literacy classes for fellow detainees. Apart from portraying himself as a courageous and selfless leader in a time of extreme crisis, he also mentions that he was good at soccer and composing songs.

Further he projects an image of moral probity for himself and the Mau Mau movement in which homoeroticism and illicit heterosexual liaisons were frowned upon. He is also a teetotaler and helps impose a drinking and sex ban in the camps. In a way he portrays himself as central to the establishment of a parallel legislation to govern the life and death of detainees in the camps. Elsewhere he candidly admits that although he was Catholic, his faith waned over time and sometimes he felt, like Ngugi in his *Detained* twenty year later, that the colonists used Christianity as a ploy to dissuade or diminish resistance to their rule.

How do the British colonists view Kariuki? There is a telling portrait of Kariuki in the purview of the colonists that his memoir implicitly discounts and deconstructs. The officers at the camp parade him before the crowd of fellow detainees after a very severe beating and declare: "This is your leader, Mwangi. He is the most dangerous man and he spends his time writing letters outside the camp, an action that is against the law" (120). Yet, throughout the narrative Kariuki sees himself and would like to be seen as a victim rather than a "dangerous" villain.

Kariuki at once absolves himself from all blame and interrogates the mistreatment that his body undergoes at the hands of the British colonial authorities. Even when he confesses to writing those incriminating letters, he often insisted that there was nothing wrong, nothing illegal with that. Like most prisoners of conscience, Kariuki sees the detaining system itself as reprehensible and culpable while he stands on a high moral ground.

It is tempting to say that Friedland's critique of *Mau Mau Detainee* alluded to earlier, was premised on what he perceived as the narrator's narcissistic obsession with self. In Friedland's reading, the text is wanting because it is fundamentally a story about a single Mau Mau detainee rather than detainees. Friedland does not take into account the fact that it is inevitable for self to be foregrounded in almost all autobiographical instances from St. Augustine's *Confessions* to Barack Obama's *The Audicity of Hope*; from Nelson Mandela's *No Easy Walk to Freedom* to Kenyatta's *Suffering without Bitterness*. Friedland, therefore, ignores one of the salient characteristics of the autobiographical genre by insisting upon the diminution or elimination of the self. It is far more accurate to conclude that in its tempo and thrust *Mau Mau Detainee* captures the collective experience through individual expression; allowing neither the collective to suffocate the individual nor the individual to supersede the collective.

Scary has argued that in times of war and torture civilization is deferred. She adds that whereas war is "morally problematic," torture is an "absolute immorality" (Scarry 21). Kariuki's prison memoir captures the context of both the war of liberation and the colonial response; it narrativizes the African insurgency and the British counter insurgency. More importantly, it narrativizes what it meant to be detained by a colonial system that was hell bent on stifling or silencing any and every dissident voice. Scarry stipulates that in torture and war there is a sense in which the suspension of practices and tenets of civilization is legitimized by the participants. It becomes not only lawful to torture and to maim and to mutilate but also to kill. It is therefore a paradox that Kariuki would still believe in British statutes and the capacity of the British not only to observe their own laws, but also to respect basic laws of human decency. He therefore ceaselessly wrote letters of complaint in an attempt to prick an otherwise seared and dead British conscience. The British sensibilities were then generally at one with the actors in the counter insurgency. The British did not necessarily suspend their own laws; their laws justified their total involvement in what Charles Mills has aptly characterized as "expeditions of conquest" in far flung geopolitical entities of the world much in the same manner as the American and Arabian laws legitimized the capture of millions of Africans to serve as chattel slaves in the Americas and the Arab world. But more significantly, in the case of the Mau Mau, the colonists tortured, mutilated and maimed as a way of converting real pain into the fiction of power, as borne out by their treatment or more correctly mistreatment of Kariuki's body.

Torture, like Kariuki's, is then to be viewed as a political construct aimed at not only making the locale, contours, and conditions of incarceration a veritable "hell" or "a cage" as most victims characterize their captive state, but as Scarry postulates, it is also a means of "unmaking," "uncreating" or dissolving the world of the victim and showcasing the power of the perpetrator or the institution he stands for or purports to represent. The relentless inflicting of pain on Kariuki' body by the detention officials was, therefore, an attempt to disintegrate his world in a sadistic and savage exhibitionism involving the fiction of colonial power. His relentless writing of protest letters and the subsequent writing of his prison experience dramatize his attempt to re-create his world, uncreated or unmade by the colonial terror machine. If the British had perceived torture as enactment of absolute power, Kariuki saw literacy and education as liberating tools enabling the Africans to wrest power from colonists.

To understand why Kariuki's letters had little effect on the torturers and hence did little or nothing to change the material reality of both Kariuki and his fellow detainees, we turn again to Scarry's compelling theorization of the body in pain. For one thing, Scarry postulates that the torturer and the tortured are at two polar ends of the pain equation. There is the certainty of pain on the part of the victim and doubt about the reality of pain on the part of the victimizer. "To have pain is to have *certainty*; to hear pain is to have *doubt,*" Scarry elegantly puts it (3). Kariuki's pain and that of his fellow detainees was known only to themselves but remained for the most part a fiction, an impossible and improbable reality in the imagination of the colonists. The object of torture, Scarry points out, is to make the victim lose his or her world, voice and sense of self, precluding any possibility for empathy and sympathy on the torturer's part (35). Doubt, therefore, is key to the invisibility of Kariuki's pain in the colonists' vision. Also, although doubting the victim's pain, the colonist uses his self-conscious display of agency to convert absolute pain into the fiction of his power to which he intends Kariuki and company to surrender. It is hardly surprising that the initial general imperial response to *Mau Mau Detainee* is replete with doubt even from editor Margery Perham who was paradoxically more than eager to see the book roll off the press.

Truth Claims

There is no doubt that what we may call "imperial doubt" is the principal reason why Kariuki's truth claims about torture in the camps and the liberation struggle as a whole have come under intense scrutiny. As we mentioned earlier, Clough alleges that Kariuki's admission that he was not in the forest undermines the veracity of his claims. The imperial audience also found insufficient Kariuki's reliance on oral sources for narrating events he never witnessed. Roger Chance's admonition that readers check the veracity of Kariuki's claims against official records resonated with the imperial sensibilities of the time. What Roger does not concede is the rather obvious possibility of manipulation of official records and deletion of information found unpalatable to the colonial regime. Kariuki alludes to the apparent imperial predilection towards doubt regarding his version of events and the possibility of official distortion of history in a passage we quoted earlier in this chapter (215). To be sure there are certain obvious errors or inconsistencies in Kariuki's narrative. For example, as Clough points out Kariuki claims that he took the unity oath in December 1953 before his detention, whereas his detention began in October 1953(64). Also, there is an error in Kariuki's reference to Lake Victoria as the "sea" surrounding Saiyusi island, although one could argue that in this instance, it is the case of Kariuki's imprecise or inaccurate diction while using the language of the colonist as a medium of expression which leads to the failure to distinguish between sea and lake (27).

However, it has to be noted that Kariuki wrote the memoir too close to the events recounted to have forgotten significantly what needed to be remembered and to be narrated. So for the most part his account should be presumed reliable or "substantially true," to borrow Perham's qualification, but without Perham's paternalistic baggage. Recent scholarship in trauma studies has intimated that immediacy is in itself a hindrance to remembrance, that when the traumatizing event is too close in temporal terms to the victim, her or his memory of what happened is hampered. In light of this, it could be argued that at the time Kariuki wrote his memoir in 1960, he was too close to the trauma of detention to recall and to comprehend what transpired (see Cathy Caruth's *Unclaimed Experience* and also her edited volume *Explorations in Trauma and Memory*). There is however, no evidence in the narrative that Kariuki was too traumatized or petrified to remember "substantially" through narrative his ordeal and that of others. As Pierre Janet has opined, "Memory is an action: essentially it is the action of telling a story" (qtd. in Kolk and de Hart 175). The action that Kariuki takes in telling the story is in itself the substance with which memory is made and enabled. But this is not to say that Kariuki's account is absolutely true.

The relativity of autobiographical truth is a matter that has engaged a whole range of disciplines with a stake in the genre of autobiography; from literary criticism to sociology; from history to ethnography, from philosophy to psychology. The position I find tenable in this debate is the one advanced by Gusdorf, Spender, and Olney all of who argue that the propagation of historical veracity or absolute truth is not central to the autobiographical project. Spender concedes that "Everyone is a liar about certain things," an observation that implies a narrative is not necessarily a fraud simply because it contains certain elements of untruth (121).

Any lingering suspicion that Kariuki's apparent inaccuracies invalidate his whole account should be settled by considering Olney's statement: "Innacuracy is not a serious problem for the autobiographer" (19). In a sense Kariuki's "truth" is in consonance with the collective memory of the Mau Mau fighters as evidenced by the bulk of the Mau Mau memoirs. Secondly, his candor for example, in exposing the chinks in the Mau Mau hierarchy, highlighting cases of detainees raping fellow detainees, incidences of same sex sensual liaisons in the camp (which his moralistic self-frowned upon), African brutality against Africans in and outside the camps, all vouch for his honesty and desire to tell the truth as best as he could. And lastly, we should be attendant to the fact that Kariuki's writing is at once a political construct and a psychological adventure whose major objective is neither to record history nor to tell the truth. He is fundamentally trying to come to terms with the horrors of the period whose immediacy itself may be a barrier to both clarity and comprehension both to him and to his audience. This narrative of confinement is more of an affirmation of humanity, a therapeutic exercise or a psychic adventure, than an historical account, and thus those who demand historical veracity of it impose on it a weight it cannot bear. As I have argued throughout, Kariuki's memoir is preoccupied with the fact of his body in pain, the "emphatic presence of the body" to use Susanna Egan's expression, and his body as representative of others in the same or similar circumstances, and not with historical truth.

Further, Kariuki's own candor in stating that he lied while in incarceration opens certain possibilities about the truthfulness of his claims in this memoir. He states: "During the time I was in detention never once did I tell the whole truth as I am setting it down now, although six times screeners laboriously wrote my false confessions which had been forced out of me. There is a Kikuyu proverb, '*Njita Murume*,' which is to say that 'when you knock someone about even if you ask him to call you God, he will do so;' but the truth is that you are not God" (61). Kariuki suggests that truth telling is contingent on the circumstances of its being uttered. What Kariuki in effect means is that it is during the chronological "now" of writing his narratives that he tells the truth. The momentous now of his writing, the moment of truth telling refers to around 1960 soon after his release from detention. In other words the statement tends to imply that it was expedient to lie while one is locked in the colonial detention camp to avoid torture or further torture. One could argue that if Kariuki lied before, then he could lie again, thus casting shadows of doubt over his supposed truth claims in the memoir.

But the other possibility is that the candor associated with admitting having lied and the extenuating circumstances in which he told the lies project him as an honest person whose account *now* should be presumed to be true. Additionally, Kariuki underlines his honesty when he concedes ignorance regarding some details of the war: "I do not know" (61). Kariuki's admission of the limits of his knowledge has striking resemblances with Camara Laye's statements in his *Dark Child* (e.g. "I cannot remember exactly" and "I did not know") concerning his childhood and some of the esoteric elements of Mande culture, in that in both cases the admission at once functions as a self-effacing and authenticating enterprise (Laye 17, 19). It is in the light of this attempt to establish authenticity through a modest admission of ignorance that Kariuki's earlier statement:"I was not in the forest" should be taken; that is, he is not trying to say he was where he was not or that he knew what he did not know or that he was what he was not.

Issues of Style

Kariuki employs a wide range of stylistic devices without much sophistication. The stylistic and structural simplicity of his life writing is, however, not necessarily a weakness. In the ten chapters of his memoir Kariuki traces in chronological order his sojourn in the various detention camps by employing a wide range of rhetorical strategies including songs, allegory, Gikuyu proverbs with their English translations, and billingsgate (in which he belittles the oppressors). In what follows, I discuss some of these aspects of style.

Songs seem to have been integral parts of incarceration and tales of incarceration in colonial times in Kenya. In this regard, there is a striking resemblance between oral tales of confinement and the written incarceration narratives in that in both, songs play a significant role. In the story of Sela and Mwambu and the Liyongo epic analyzed in chapter 1, the characters sing songs that propel the plot, songs which the narrator is required to sing in turn during his or her narration to punctuate the ebb and flow of the story. I am also reminded of my own experience growing up in the rural areas of western Kenya where I often listened to my grandmother Sarah Kituyi Nabulyalya narrate tales that were spiced with song, the singing of which entailed enacting the characters' roles. Kariuki mentions how detainees forged bonds of solidarity and solidified their commitment to the struggle by singing. He writes: "we sang together in a hut [in the camp] at evening the Song of Africa and the Song of Kenyatta at Kapenguria" (177). Indeed Kariuki's memoir contains a number of songs, which detainees sung in colonial detention camps. As he indicates, while incarcerated at the Lodwar detention camp, he composed "*Rwimbo rwa Africa*" or "The Song of Africa" in collaboration with one Joseph Kirira to celebrate the occasion of Ghana's independence on 3 June 1957 (154). It is a song whose transcendences and racial identification with the rest of black Africa, one could argue, tends to obfuscate the immediate concern of the Mau Mau movement with the disruption and dissolution of the Kikuyu world.

Ngai aheire Andu airu
Thi-ino ya Afrika
Gocagai mwenye Nyaga
Tondu wa wendo wake

God gave to the black people
This land of Africa
Praise the God who dwells in
The high places
For his blessings

Thikiririai kiriro
Afrika ya muhuro
Tondu nimaranyarirwo
Ni mbari ya Nyakaburu

Listen to the sobbing
Of our brothers in South Africa
Where they are being tormented
By the tribe of the Boers

Tugakena muno muno
Andu airu twi hamwe
Tuthondeke ngwataniro
Uthamaki wa andu airu

We shall greatly rejoice
In the unity of all black people
Let us create in our unity
A United States of All Africa
(154-155).

"The Song of Africa" essentially articulates the desire for a United States of All Africa, echoing the Pan-African dream of Edward Wilmot Blyden, and later Kwame Nkrumah, Jomo Kenyatta, and Julius Kabarage Nyerere. The liberation struggle in Kenya was concurrent with the struggle of black Africans to free themselves from the shackles of the apartheid regime in South Africa, with the latter struggle continuing way into the 1990s. It is therefore easy to see Kariuki's eagerness to draw parallels between the repercussions of colonial counter-insurgence in Kenya in the 1950s and "*Kiriro Afirika ya muhuro"/* [the sobbing of our brothers in South/Africa/ Where they are being tormented]. Identification with black South Africans is therefore predicated on viewing them as fellow sufferers. This sense of solidarity with fellow suffers is commonplace. Kariuki mentions that when "Ghana became independent on 3 June 1957 there was great rejoicing among the detainees" hence the celebration for which Kariuki and Kirira composed *Rwimbo rwa Africa* (154). But as "Song of Kimathi" illustrates, the Ghanaian and South African experiences and others elsewhere, were important only to the extent that they resonated with the actualities of the colonial rocking of the equilibrium of the Kikuyu cosmos. Put differently, whereas the concern for the rest of Africa may not have been necessarily incongruous with Mau Mau interests, it is still sensible to conclude that the movement's primary concern was to reverse the particularity of the dispossession of Kikuyu *ithaka na wiyathi* (land and freedom).

"The Song of Kimathi" eulogizes Dedan Kimathi, regarded as one of the most iconic leaders of the Mau Mau movement. Kimathi is said to have led the Mau Mau forces in Aberdares Forests from 1952 to 1957. The British captured him and executed him in 1957 (Kariuki, 152). Here we examine three of the eight stanzas of the song that Kariuki incorporates in his memoir:

Ria Kimathi witu ambatire
Kirimaini ari wiki
Nietirie hinya na umiriru
Wakuhota nyakeru

When our Kimathi ascended
Into the mountains alone
He asked for strength and
Courage
To defeat the White men

Tukurira tondu turi andu airu
Natutiri nyakeru
Naturiri a kirathimo kiao
Ngai witu ari mbere

We are tormented because we are black
We are not like the White Men
We have not received their
Advantages
But yet is our God in front.

Mwihumbei ukiriria wake
Kunyarirwo kana gukua
Mukimenyaga mari a uthamaki
Wa Gikuyu and Mumbi

You must put on endurance

To face tribulation or death
Knowing that you belong to the Kingdom
Of Gikuyu and Mumbi (152-153).

The song is unambiguous in its revolutionary intent. It clearly has racial undertones as it establishes the distinction between the white colonizing entity and the colonized black. Yet the invocation of the Uthamaki wa Gikuyu na Mumbi or the Kingdom of Gikuyu and Mumbi tends to delimit the "we" of the song to the Kikuyu who claim ancestry from Gikuyu and Mumbi. That effectively excludes the rest of the Kenyan ethnic groups from the equation, a point that several commentators have alluded to in their insistence that the Mau Mau war was a purely Kikuyu affair (Daniels, 23). It should, however, be noted that Kariuki does not claim authorship of the song. He actually states that it "was composed in the forest" where, as we have already observed, he admits he never was (152). But as he further elaborates, it was "very well known in our country." The question to ask, therefore, is not whether or not Kariuki wrote the song because he clearly did not, but what function it serves in his memoir. For one thing, the song eulogizes Kimathi, one of the most influential leaders of the Mau Mau movement. Second, it espouses and epitomizes the ethos of the Mau Mau movement in its quest to recapture lands lost to the British imperial might. Third, the song punctuates the dominant prose of the text, creating variety and forestalling boredom. Fourth, the addition of this very well-known collective text to the prison narrative, is that not only does it enhance Kariuki's "we-feeling" with the Mau Mau rank and file, but it imbues his text with a sense of intertextuality or heteroglossia that is a salient feature of prison narratives.

It is instructive that both songs bear apparent religious undertones, even overtones, with several allusions to God or Ngai. (In *Thunder from Mt. Kirinyaga* Maina wa Kinyatti argues that the Kikuyu Ngai was different from the Christian God). Kariuki seems to also use the songs to consolidate his assault against the colonial conception of the Mau Mau as savage heathens. The line "*Ria Kimathi witu ambatire/Kirimaini ari wiki"/* [When our Kimathi ascended to the mountain alone] recalls Jewish prophet Moses with his solitary sojourn to Mt. Sinai where he received the ten commandants. It would seem, casting Kimathi in the role of Moses justifies Mau Mau. The song injects religious fervor into the bloody struggle. The messianic connotation in turn tends to absolve the song's inaccuracy in claiming that Kimathi ascended the mountain alone. The songs also exhibit a sense of syncretism, a mixture of Kikuyu indigenous precepts and aspects of Christianity whose core objective is mobilization of the people against colonial tyranny and terror. "The political songs," as Clough observes, "some of them reworked Christian hymns and others simply using hymn tunes with a completely different text, followed Mau Mau activists into the forests, and became an important element in evening observances" (144).

In his prison memoir Kariuki uses billingsgate, a narrative aspect that as Ioan Davies notes is a commonplace in prison writing. This aspect of style entails using disparaging terms to refer to what the incarcerated views as his or her foes. In this regard, on several occasions Kariuki uses coarse language to describe prison officers. He refers to Noah, the African prison officer who presided over the castration of detainees at Nyangwethu as "coarse-fibred, stupid" (163); he describes another officer, Chester of the Lodwar camp as "brutal and foolish"

(82), and officer Mansfield of the same camps as "lugubrious and foolish" (149); he refers to the officer in charge of Yatta camp as fit to be the "Chancellor" of a "University of Fools" (117).

Kariuki also uses allegory, for instance, to describe the ambivalent character of prison warders. He writes:

> It must be seem strange to an outsider that while warders would sell tobacco and newspapers today, tomorrow they would meticulously search our quarters on the orders of their superiors for the same tobacco and triumphantly haul us for punishment if they discovered anything. We say that when a man takes a dog out hunting a jackal, the dog will run far ahead out of sight and start playing with the jackal in a hidden place because they really are of thc same kind. When the man catches up with them the dog will straight away start barking fiercely and chasing the jackal again at a safe distance. This is because it is the man who gives the dog food which it will not get if it disobeys his orders. (102)

Almost inevitably Kariuki turns to the store-house of oral tradition to extrapolate on the contradictory conduct of the warders. In this allegory, the dog symbolizes the warders who secretly connive with the jackal, representing the prisoners while out of the sight of the man, figuring white colonial officers. If Kariuki draws from this common pool of orature to enrich his written text, it must also be stressed that it is perhaps the profusion of Kikuyu proverbs in the text that most imbues the texts with a Kikuyu flavor and particularity. To ensure that the reader is not left with any doubt as to the source of the proverb, he often prefaces his proverbs with "we Kikuyu have a proverb or say, a "we" that proclaims collective ownership of the often terse, immutable and compact oral text that reflects Kikuyu philosophy and metaphysics. These include, "Murimi ndaunagwo guoko" / (He who is working in the cornfield should be fed there) (34-35); "Mwana angiguikiria ruhiu nawe ndukoe umuikirie"[If a child throws a panga at you, do not throw it back because you will appear more foolish than the child, who may injure you with it] (61); "Ndiri njega ndiringanaga na muthi mwega"/ (A good pestle never has a good mortar) (78).

It is quite tempting to dismiss Kariuki's text as Olney does, as lacking literary merit and unworthy of readerly interest and attention. Yet, such a hasty conclusion would be unfortunate as it would be synonymous with throwing out the baby with the bathwater. It seems to me essential to consider Kariuki's narrative style in the light of the narrative imperative that is chiefly located in staging a counter-discourse to the British version of the Mau Mau. While Kariuki does not completely leave the "problems of style" in the "schoolbag," as Harlow would put, it is apparent that to him, as to most prison narrators, the content was more important than the form (Harlow, 10).

Writing on the abiding effects of the recurrent beatings in the detention camps, Kariuki remarks: "I failed to die but the scars on my knees and chest will always be with me and I still suffer severe attacks of pain in my abdomen and thorax" (162). The body in pain during the colonial regime that Kariuki's presents unwittingly is his own body that was later to be found assassinated in a thicket at Ngong Hills in the Kenyatta regime. Reading the text with the benefit of hindsight makes it possible for us to appreciate a number of things. For one thing, Kariuki was a supreme example of what Ioan Davies would characterize as diehard revolutionaries "dedicated to transforming a system which they believe is corrupt and immoral and to speaking the truth as they see it" (31). Being a revolutionary meant that to him activism was more paramount than art. At any rate not all prison writers or narrators aspire to or are able to attain artistic excellence. When the articulation of an ideological or political position is paramount in a prison text, it becomes necessary, as Harlow suggests, to keep problems of style and aesthetics in the schoolbag. What was more important to Kariuki was to give an account of himself and to elaborate his role in the struggle in and outside the detention camps. He projects himself as a selfless crusader for justice in colonial times who was willing to face the risks and dangers associated with following such a cours, a fact that is borne out my his eventual assassination. In alluding to the colonial regime's torture on his body as making a martyr out of him, one cannot help but notice Kariuki's unconscious prescience since in the end he paid the ultimate price of political martyrdom in Kenyatta's reign. Concerns about Mau Mau Detainee's form or content should not or do not therefore diminish the stature of a text penned by one of Africa's most committed political reformist about his suffering and the suffering of others in the infamous colonial detention camps.

Chapter 3: The Tenor and Genre of Ngugi's Prison Narrative

> Autobiographical texts may be a minefield for the unwary reader, but they can also be a field of play and an occasion for critical reflection on changing reading practices, audiences, and ethics
>
> —Sidonie Smith and Julia Watson, *Women, Autobiography, Theory: A Reader*

Leftist intellectual Ngugi wa Thiong'o remains one of the better known Kenyan writers in Africa and beyond. His fame rests solidly on his achievements both in the creative and critical realm. His impressive literary output belongs in the category of the most known titles from an African writer. *Weep Not Child* (1964), *A Grain of Wheat* (1968) and *The Devil on the Cross* (1982) were voted among Africa's 100 best Books. His other titles include, *Matigari* (1990), and *The Wizard of the Crow* (2006), not to mention his childhood memoir, *Dreams in A Time of War* (2010). His critical and often polemical essays include the much quoted *Decolonizing the Mind, Writers in Politics, Homecoming* and *Re-Membering Africa.* Perhaps Ngugi's most enduring legacy is his mid-stream disavowal of the English language and his zealous and impassioned promotion of indigenous African languages as the vehicle of artistic expression for African writers. Ngugi's disavowal of English was done mid-stream because it came as an afterthought, coming as it did long after his exemplary use of English as a vehicle of artistic expression had propelled him to tremendous international fame, taking him where Gikuyu alone would never conceivably have been able to take him. Moreover, English remains Ngugi's principal medium for intellection as the bulk of his critical essays demonstrates. My hunch is that by the time Ngugi declared his supposed divorce from English, it was already too late to make such severance really authentic enough.

I will return later to the lesson detention taught him about the use of his mother tongue instead of English, the language of the colonial master, thereby underscoring the status of confinement as a university of a kind. Suffice it to say here that apart from his intellectual and literary accomplishments, Ngugi's fame also stems from his run-ins with the Kenyan government particularly the Jomo Kenyatta and Daniel arap Moi regimes. Because of his activism and defiant political position Ngugi too almost inevitably found his name inscribed on the long list of Kenya's political detainees of the postcolonial era. Indeed any study of Kenyan prison narratives would be seriously incomplete if it did not include Ngugi's personal prison account.

This chapter examines Ngugi's personal prison account *Detained*, which he wrote because of his detention and partly while in detention, recording his thoughts, his experiences, and following the dictates of his rich imagination as he grappled with issues such as truth, torture and trauma. Principally this chapter discusses the genre and the tenor of his prison narrative. It would seem both the message of the narrative and the form it assumes are inextricably tied up together. In other words the chapter analyzes the interplay between content and form as useful way of unearthing what Ngugi's prison narrative is about. If there is a prison text that poses or answers the question; "Does genre matter?" then surely Ngugi's is one such, not the least reason being because of the many and varied readings the narrative has invited or induced. In addition, analyzing Ngugi's text sheds light on why leftist intellectuals were the target of both Kenyatta and Moi's vicious terror machines.

Ngugi's detention saga began on the night of December 31, 1977 when special security agents of the Kenyatta government arrested him at his Limuru home in the outskirts of Nairobi. He was never told the reason for his arrest. He was never arraigned before a court of law. He was detained without trial at the Kamiti Maximum security prison for nearly a year, until December 12, 1978. The closest the government deigned to explain the reason for his confinement, was presenting him, while he was languishing in detention, with a vague and elliptical detention order signed by then, Vice President Daniel arap Moi on December 29, 1977: "The detailed grounds on which you are detained are:- You are detained on the following grounds: 1) You have engaged yourself in activities and utterances which are dangerous to the good government of Kenya and its institutions. In order to thwart your intentions and in the interest of the preservation of public security your detention has become necessary" (204).

Clearly, the "detailed grounds" were anything but detailed. There is little to glean from the nebulous detention order as to the exact reason for the detention; not only is the official document terse, it is indicative of the government's inability or unwillingness to pinpoint Ngugi's specific "crimes." Hence for him, as is evident from his prison text *Detained*, it became expedient during and after detention, to only speculate on the possible motives for his detention, such as his involvement in the Kamiriithu community theatre, and the Marxist ideology informing his literary and critical output. In a statement to the Detainee Review Tribunal Ngugi wrote:

> I have not been charged or told so, but I am convinced in other words that I am where I am because I have written about and believed in a Kenya for Kenyans, because I have attempted to hold up the mirror through which Kenyans can look at themselves, in their past, their present and their future. I am here because a tiny section of that society—but more influential because of the political and ill—gotten economic power it wields over the laboring majority—has not particularly liked the image of its role in Kenyan history. They have therefore struck with vengeance at the hand that raised the mirror . . .(188)

Yet, by detaining Ngugi without trial, the "good government" of Kenyatta was not only acting within the law of the land, but was acting according to its own tradition of repression and suppression, demonstrating powerfully one of the various ways at its disposal, by which it consistently dealt with political opposition and dissent soon after independence from British colonial rule in 1963. Indeed there was a long list of political detainees before Ngugi, men and women who were detained without trial because the government found their political positions inimical to its interests. The hostile political ambience then forced Ngugi to flee his native Kenya soon after his release from detention and to remain in exile as a *negropolitain* writer in Europe and the United States for over two decades.[1] His return to Kenya from exile in 2004 with its attendant complications, including the rape of his wife and his robbery may form the subject of another paper, and should not detain us here.

Ngugi wrote part of *Detained* on toilet paper while in detention and completed the rest of it upon his release. The text encapsulates Ngugi's trenchant critique of and reflection on the conditions of incarceration, the legacy of imperialism and colonialism, the class chasm between the masses of "peasant," with which he identifies himself, and what he calls the "comprador bourgeois class." Besides narrating his dehumanization, deprivation, and degradation he confronted at the hands of state apparatuses in his individual capacity as a political detainee, Ngugi ponders his country's past, present, and future political economy and cultural milieu, as the excerpt above indicates. In sum, *Detained* may be regarded as a statement of Ngugi's highly revolutionary ideological stance. Written in the heyday of his Marxist ideology, the text has a partisan, defiant, revolutionary, and militant tone, making it appear to be the manifesto of Ngugi's private and public self as an intellectual then committed, as Janet Lyon would put it, to linking his "voice to the countless voices of previous revolutionary conflicts" (4).

Evidently, there cannot, and should not be only one way of reading *Detained*. The text is a highly hybridized mosaic, containing as it does, fragments of letters, official documents, newspaper excerpts, records of parliamentary debates, traditional and revolutionary songs, Christians hymns, parody of Biblical passages, poems, dramatic dialogue, references to historical documents, and bits and pieces from various memoirs and other literary works. In a way the text's "generic promiscuity," to use Dorothy Hale's phrase, legitimates any number of varied and variegated exegeses and classifications (449). Indeed Ngugi's life narrative has been the subject of much critical engagement since its publication in 1981, with any number of critics classifying it as a memoir, *consolatio*, autobiography, *testimonio*, historical document, and prisoner's diary.[3]

This study distinguishes itself by its emphasis on Ngugi's thematic preoccupation with truth, torture, and trauma and the manifesto as a genre that manifestly undergirds Ngugi's *Detained*. In what follows, I examine the thematization of truth and the portrayal of torture and trauma in Ngugi's prison text, before turning to the text's manifesto attributes.

Narrator as Harbinger of Truth

But how should we approach the question of truth in Ngugi's prison narrative? Should we regard his narrative as the "abiding" truth, even the absolute truth, of the circumstances surrounding his detention? In *Detained* Ngugi presumably sets out to outline his life and opinions in relation to political detention and its individual and collective ramifications. We get less of the details of his experiences and more of his interpretation of his own personal history as a committed writer, of his locale in the interminable continuum of struggle against tyranny, and of Kenya's own conception of itself as a nation. His "history of a kind" is not history as such but a certain interpretation of history. It is in the light of the predominance of opinion in Ngugi's incarceration text that we should approach our estimation of the author's truth claims. Yet like most participants in the autobiographical act, Ngugi tends to present his opinions as truth even when the evidence marshaled to anchor such truth claims appears somewhat inaccurate or tends to border on the mendacious. In some instances, what threatens the appearance or reality of truth is the writer's rather extravagant use of hyperbole.

Thus, subjecting Ngugi's narrative to close scrutiny may expose it to the risk of being adjudged unreliable, a move that may be altogether a classic case of being blown apart by the landmine of life writing as Sidonie Smith and Julia Watson warn in the epigraph at the beginning of this chapter. Here a few examples of unwarranted "scrutiny" would suffice. (1) Ngugi claims that Me Kitilili wa Menza, the female leader of the Giriama resistance to colonial rule, then old and weak, managed to escape from prison at Manyani and walked hundreds of miles back to the Kenyan coast. As Gikandi discloses in his book *Ngugi wa Thiong'o* (1988), a certain section of historians have disputed this truth claim. This calls to mind historian David Stoll's furious discounting of the claims of the Guetamalan testimonio, *I, Rigoberta Menchu* (1984).[2] There is an apparent contradiction in Ngugi's statements regarding the length of the colonial rule in Kenya. At one point he claims the period was "seventy years of destructive alien presence" (46). Yet earlier on he had referred to the duration as "sixty years of colonial culture of repression and mass terror" (29). So, did colonial rule in Kenya last for seventy or sixty years? (3) Ngugi claims that the Kamiriithu theatre group attracted so much interest that throngs of Kenyans "trekked on foot and in hired matatus and buses from all parts of the country" to come and watch its performance of the controversial *Ngaahika Ndeenda* (72). This could be taken as either hyperbolic or simply disingenuous because for one thing the play was performed in Gikuyu, a language which, unlike Swahili, is not, properly speaking, spoken in "all parts of the country." (4) Ngugi's remark: "To be wealthy in Kenya today is incomplete without land in Limuru" is also misleading and reductive because from before, during, and after the late seventies when Ngugi wrote, land in Limuru has not been the requisite measure of wealth in Kenya (74). He also claims that the "crime rate and drunkness in the village had markedly fallen for the duration of the play's run!" (80). One may contend that it is difficult to verify this claim, although certainly the memoirist's intent to project the positive results of the community theatre is obvious. The point is that we do not read life narratives such as Ngugi's *Detained* as instances of historical exactitude. What then becomes of Ngugi's truth claims?

Ngugi quotes a rather sympathetic prison superintendent at Kamiti Maximum Prison as asking him: "Tell me the truth, was the play really being acted by workers and peasants?" The play in question is *Ngaahika Ndeenda* widely believed to have been one of the reasons for Ngugi's detention. Like most other observers, the sympathetic prison officer was doubtful of Ngugi's claim that the actors in the play were not university students or professional thespians masquerading as the peasants and workers of Kamiriithu. In the conversation with the superintendent, as in the rest of his prison memoir, Ngugi insists that the actors were indeed peasants and workers, his pet expressions. But this conversation is also evidence of Ngugi's own deliberate thematization of truth, a leitmotif that we see running in any number of prison narratives, including the tale of Sela and Mwambu and the Liyongo Epic (see chapter 1). Ngugi foregrounds this thematization of truth by quoting famous Swahili poet Shabaan bin Robert's poem in the peritext,

> *Kweli itashinda namna tunavyoishi*
> *Kweli haihofu tisho wala nguvu za majeshi*
> *La uongo lina mwisho, Kweli kitu cha aushi*
> *Kweli itashinda kesho kama leo haitoshi*
>
> Truth will prevail in this life
> Truth fears neither threat nor military force
> Falsehood will cease, but Truth is abiding
> Truth will prevail tomorrow, if not so today. (Shaaban vi)

To insist upon asking whether Ngugi speaks the truth in *Detained* is perhaps insisting upon the wrong question, if not missing the whole point of the autobiographical act in which Ngugi participates in the fast place. The revolutionary ethos that drives his writing and defines his memoir in terms of political manifesto sees truth in terms of resistance to any and all forms of oppression and exploitation. Simply put, truth is equal to resistance to tyranny. Ngugi appropriates the concept of truth in Robert's poem in the peritext, representing "truth" that is mediated through leftist ideology, revolution, and counter-hegemonic writing. In a sense *Detained* is Ngugi's truth, abiding truth in Robert's terms, because it runs counter to the official narrative of detention. It is a kind of truth that is not defined by factual evidence but the willingness and ability to expose a system the harbinger of truth finds unjust and oppressive.

However, what most absolves Ngugi from charges of mendacity or distortion of reality is the view in life writing circles that autobiographical acts are not history or factual accounts per se. Georges Gusdorf has, for example, situated autobiography in the realm of art in which invention and innovation are more urgent than historical veracity. Ngugi's *Detained,* I think, carries far too many authorial opinions and ruminations to bear the weight of authority as a historical document. It is a case of life writing in which opinion outweighs preoccupation with narration of life. Yet even if the contrary were true, that is if narration of life outweighed expression of opinion, or even if the memoirist were to strike a perfect balance between narration of life and expression of opinion, *Detained* would still be an autobiographical piece for which factuality and veracity are not prerequisites. Also, to accuse Ngugi of falsity is to ignore the fact that autobiographical works are first and foremost works of art as Gusdorf asserts.

When the sympathetic prison superintendent's urged Ngugi: "Tell me the truth" he may have been echoing the general wish of readers of Ngugi's text. They hope to read the truth, to be told the truth. Indeed, the readers of Ngugi's memoir are told nothing but the truth, but it is the truth of art and should be best understood as such. The truth of *Detained* lies in its ability to harness aesthetic possibilities of art that make the art a powerful tool for speaking to historical events without being constrained by factuality.

Torture and Trauma

As Ngugi recounts in his memoir, nothing can prepare one for the foreboding sense of dislocation and disorientation that incarceration engenders. He exposes how the mental torture that the uncertainty over when or whether one would be released from detention takes its heavy toll on the victim. He writes:

For those who wait in prison, as for those outside prison, dreams of freedom start at the very minute of arrest...One of the cruelties of detention—unlike ordinary imprisonment—is precisely this *not* knowing when one will get out. For the ordinary convicted prisoner—we are not talking of the unfairness of the trial, the so-called justice involved—he knows the duration of his sentence and no matter how long it is, his emotions and intellect can adjust to it. Not so the political detainee: he can be released after an hour, a day, a week, or after fifty years! (147)

Ngugi writes about the pain of uncertainty, this "ignorance of when" from the point of view of one who does not merely depend on the carceral imagination but from an experiential point of view of the carceral (147). He speaks from experience as it were, making his description lucid and profound. He debunks the view that there is any conceivable or justifiable differentiation between detention and torture when he states: "Some ask: were you tortured in detention? But detention itself is torture" (147).

Ngugi loathed the humdrum prison routine describing it as "dull, monotonous, repetitious, tortuous in its intended animal rhythm of eating, defecating, sleeping, eating, defecting, sleeping" (117). Besides the de-individuating effect of being known by a number Ngugi reveals the use of disease as a weapon wielded upon detainees. Like the despotic regimes in Brazil and Argentina, *Detained* exposes the official intentional and callous denial or delay of medical attention to ailing detainees.[3] Ngugi himself recounts how it took a whole month for the prison authorities to accept his request to have his nagging toothache attended to. But when he stubbornly refused to be taken to hospital "in chains," he was left to heal on his own, which he did. Yet it is correct to conclude, following Elaine Scarry in her *The Body in Pain,* that when the prisoner's body is in pain, it is used as a weapon against him or her in the service of the torturer. In Ngugi's case, by aching, his tooth had become a weapon in the hands of the state to torture him from within the body. And by both delaying and denying him medical attention, prison authorities enhanced and ensured the use of the body as a weapon against the "self" inhabiting that same body.

Ngugi invokes the image of the "cage" or the "dungeon" in several instances in his characterization of detention to underline its degrading and traumatizing properties. Stripped of his sense of humanity, Ngugi felt he had been reduced to the status of an encaged dangerous animal or a slave in a dungeon. These expressions and images indicate the depth and breadth of trauma and torture that detention enabled and enhanced. He also depicts himself as wrestling "demons" or "dragons" in an effect to remain sane in the detention conditions aimed at, as he puts it, "turning his brain into a mess of rot"(9). The demons and dragons suggest the hell-like experience that detention felt for Ngugi. It is interesting that experience in the cage as a political prisoner motivates Ngugi to write what I term at once a political manifesto and an art manifesto. It is to this generic question of manifesto that we now turn.

Political Manifesto and Art Manifesto

Most scholarship on the manifesto acknowledges or affirms the affinity between modernity and the manifesto genre. In her *Manifestoes: Provocations of the Modern*, Janet Lyon theorizes on the close link between modernity and the genre of manifesto. The title of her text in itself implies the link she envisages between manifesto and modernity. Manifestos are therefore perceived as a consequence of modernity and exhibit modernity's political or revolutionary temperament. Art manifestos such as Tristan Tzara and others' *Dadaist Manifesto*, for instance, are associated with the avand garde movement that arose in the era of modernity and intended to revolutionalize the theory and practice of art (music, painting, writing etc). But there are also other kinds of manifestos, ranging from disciplinary manifestos (e.g. Basarab Nicolescu's *Manifesto of Transdisplinarity,* really a manifesto of quantum physics), and cultural nationalist manifestos (e.g Molefi Asante's *An Afrocentric Manifesto* and its emphasis on black cultural nationalism) or ideological manifestos (e.g. Karl Marx's *Communist Manifesto*). It bears clarifying that these categories are to be taken heuristically since in practice there are frequent overlaps between them. Also, it would seem there is often an underlying shock effect, tension, and political thrust in most manifestos. In this regard Lyon views manifesto as "an emblem of political combat," arguing that "to write a manifesto is to participate symbolically in a history of struggle against dominant forces"(4). She draws attention to the stylized use of the pronouns "we," "us," and "them" in manifesto. In her description of manifesto, Lyon states: "The manifesto participates in a reduced understanding of heterogeneous social fields, creating audiences through rhetoric exclusivity, parceling out political identities across a polarized discursive field, claiming for "us" the moral high ground of revolutionary idealism, and constructing "them" as ideological tyrants, bankrupt usurpers, or corrupt fools" (3).

It is important to stress that I am less interested in either the apparent negativity in Lyon's definition than in what the definition does in characterizing the nature of the voice and tone of manifesto as a genre. As Lyon posits, there is in manifesto a Manichean dialectic between "us' and "them;" with "us" representing those struggling against the dominant forces on the one hand, and "them" representing tyrannical agents of the dominant forces on the other. Manifesto does not aspire to an ecumenical or universal message that would have appeal to all and sundry; it includes and excludes audiences through its rhetorical strategies, implying that by what it says and how it says, it almost explicitly defines its audiences. It may be cogent to use Leigh Gilmore expression the ""you" and "we" who will listen and respond," in characterizing audiences that the manifesto creates (707). The narrating "I" in the autobiographical manifesto is far from apolitical; it is implicated in a political enterprise that links it to the collectivized and politicized "us" or "we."

Martin Puchner in his The Poetry of Revolution links the manifesto genre to revolution and elucidates upon the political and ideological underpinnings of the genre. Puchner alleges that although Marx and Engles's Communist Manifesto was not by any means the first manifesto ever, it not only became a socialist/ communist icon but gave tremendous impetus and direction to the genre of manifesto: "Even though the Manifesto became the single most significant manifesto, the text that defined for many subsequent writers what a manifesto should be, Marx and Engels did not create these genre alone; the manifesto has a history or prehistory before the Manifesto" (11).

Puchner further states that it is Engels who suggested the title "manifesto" for their collaborated work after coming to the conclusion that what they were working on was more than simply a credo as they had initially conceived of it. To Engels credo was suitable only for presenting a set of precepts, but the work of the kind they were engaged in their joint venture, called for a genre oriented to a "narrative" form. Puchner identifies a close affinity between the manifesto genre and the history of socialism and communism, demonstrating how as Puchner asserts, "manifestos weave together social theory, political acts, and poetic expression" (2). Manifesto, he concurs with Lyon, is obsessed with "changing the world" and even stages "history as revolution" (21).

Puchner also identified "impatience" as an important attribute of the genre: "Throughout its subsequent history, the manifesto would be defined by its impatience, by the attempt to undo the distinction between speech and action, between words and revolution" (22). He however draws attention to the emergence of the art manifestos particularly in the 1960s and 1970s, resulting from what he terms the intrusion of the genre into the realm of art (20). Puchner conceives of the resultant "art manifesto" as "an art forged in the image of the manifesto: aggressive rather than introverted, screaming rather than reticent; collective rather than individual. Radical modernism and avant-garde art must therefore be regarded as an art not based on the doctrines or theories proclaimed in the manifestos but on the formal influence of the manifesto, its poetry, on art" (6).

One could add that there is perhaps often a very thin line between the political manifesto and the art manifesto in that both adopt a "screaming" and "aggressive" tone and voice in not only addressing their subject matter but in their insistence on changing the world. These two categories, I should reiterate, are essentially created for heuristic purposes. It is well to say the art manifesto is often not entirely apolitical. It may well be that, particularly in the case of Detained, it is not tenable to distinguish between political manifesto and art manifesto. When Ngugi declares and narrates in Detained his divorce from English as a medium of artistic expression and his marriage to Gikuyu, his narrative takes on the characteristics of the art manifesto. He exhibits the combative spirit of cultural nationalism and stubborn insistence on the use of indigenous African languages that he would fully expound on in his post-detention intellectual works particularly, Decolonising the Mind and Writers in Politics. In a passage parodying the cultural insight of an illiterate "Muugikuyu warder," Ngugi counters the cultural war that the European hegemony wages against African culture and values: "Have you ever heard any European calling himself Mutiso, Kamau, Onyango, Kiplagat or Simiyu? Have you seen Europeans bothering about your languages? . . . What have Europeans done to you people so that you follow them like dogs their master? What have they done to you that you despise your own tongues and your own country?" (129-130)

It is instructive that the warder's lesson on culture and patriotism is presented directly without quotation marks. There is a sense in which Ngugi's cultural consciousness is conflated with that of the warder who comes across as an unlikely source of such deep knowledge that we can today safely characterize as truly Ngugian. The warder's sentiments strike a chord with Ngugi. The prison warder's series of questions suggest the extent to which the indigenous Africans have been duped to loathe themselves, their languages and names. Ultimately, the warder's lesson on culture has the trappings of an epiphany or pseudo-epiphany for the writer because, as he claims, his idea of writing a novel in the Gikuyu language then crystallizes and is subsequently actualized. Ngugi writes: "That night I sit at the desk and start the story of Wariinga in the Gikuyu language. It flows just like that, and for the first time since my incarceration, I feel transports of joy. That which I have toyed with but feared—writing a novel in Gikuyu—is happening before my own eyes, and I have government toilet-paper for writing material, and a government-paid warder as a consultant. I am willing to learn" (130).

The passage draws attention to a number of paradoxes namely; 1) the paradox of prison as the site for writing; 2) the paradox of prison as a university; 3) the paradox of the prison warder as a cultural professor; and 3) the paradox of using toilet paper as the material upon which to write. On the whole prison, prison warder and toilet paper are subjected or subject themselves to unlikely uses, uses not officially sanctioned or intended by the incarcerating authorities. A lot could be said for the political implication of writing in prison with the unwitting "assistance" of the prison warder. But it seems to me that the crux of the message in the passage above is Ngugi's disavowal of English as a medium of literary expression and his embrace of his own Gikuyu tongue. The result was his historic novel, Caataini Mutharaba-ini, which was subsequently translated as The Devil on the Cross, a novel that marked a linguistic watershed in his literary oeuvre. The passage is, in this regard, an instance of the presentation of Ngugi's art manifesto, a forceful declaration or demonstration of how he was determined to change the world of his literary expression and possibly of others as well, by ditching English and clinging tenaciously to his mother tongue as an artistic carrier of lived and imagined human experience.

Ngugi had, without any shadow of doubt, not heard of the potency of the mother tongue for the first time in the "prison university." As he mentioned his Decolonizing the Mind, he attended the historic 1961 conference of African writers of English expression at Makerere University, Kampala and had been disturbed by the exclusion of African writers who wrote in African languages, particulary Fagunwa who wrote in Yoruba and Shabaan bin Robert who wrote in Swahili. Ngugi was privy to the fierce and animated debate of the 1960s between Obi Wali and Chinua Achebe over the language of African imaginative projections. Wali had sparked off the debate when he alleged that African literature in European languages had reached what he saw as a "dead end" as the title and thrust of his famous essay, "The Dead End of African Literature" indicated. (330). Ngugi was aware of Achebe's rebuttal that English had the capacity to carry the burden of African experience in the imaginative realm. Yet there is no tangible evidence that, as a writer and an intellectual Ngugi took a decisive position on the matter then. At any rate he continued writing in English and made no public declaration whatsoever on the question of language, until after his epiphany in the prison university.

It is imperative to reiterate that I draw on Puchner's and Lyon's characterization of manifesto as a generic classification to read Detained as manifesto. Yet it bears clarifying that reading Ngugi's text as manifesto does not imply it is only a manifesto.[4] But it seems to me that approaching Detained as a manifesto enables us to enter an interpretative frame that best explains what underpins and underwrites the necessarily combative, tendentious tone of the text. There is ample evidence that Ngugi's text displays attributes that conform to the generic conventions of as propounded by Lyon's and Puchner. In other words, reading Ngugi's Detained as manifesto enables us to make more sense of the polemics and partisanship of his prison writing, and the "high moral ground" from which he speaks against what he considers the reprehensible political leadership of his country and its foreign partners in crime.

Therefore, broadly speaking, reading *Detained* as manifesto entails, first and foremost perceiving it as emblematic of Ngugi's Marxist political combat with the dominant capitalist forces in Kenya. In the text, Ngugi constantly identifies himself with the patriots and peasant masses. It is instructive that he suggests that his detention was predicated on the Kenyatta's government displeasure with his involvement with the peasants of Kamiriithu in organizing community theatre. Moreover, he frequently calls himself the "son of peasants." Hence the politicized narrating "I" of Ngugi's *Detained* is an attempt, as Gilmore would put it, to "weld the personal to the collective and posits an international "you" and "we" who will listen and respond" (707). These pronouns "you" and "we" allude to individuals within and without the Kenyan frontiers, who make up the audiences that Ngugi addresses with the manifestly "rhetorical exclusivity" of his prison narrative. What he writes and how he writes it inevitably excludes, and alienates those it critiques. Those excluded include individuals that Ngugi describes in the opening sentence of the preface as powerful and wealthy and responsible for his detention (xi). In other words, the manner in which his text includes and excludes audiences through its rhetorical devices, particularly the distinction it draws between the patriots, laborers, workers and masses of peasants on one side, and the comprador class, the colonial agents and the despots in power on the other side, is beyond any shadow of a doubt. Speaking from a "high moral ground" Ngugi vilifies those who he regards as "ideological tyrants" both in pre-independence and post-independence Kenya, or what Achille Mbembe would call the "colonial potentate" and the "postcolonial potentate" respectively (292).

The manifesto is thus decidedly polemical and combative in its representation of historical 'reality' and its articulation of political ideology, operating as it does on the "moral high ground of revolutionary idealism." Ngugi exhibits these polemical and combative tendencies in *Detained* as he riles against the inadequacies and injustices of colonial and postcolonial eras in Kenya. Lyon's theorization of three distinct characteristic of manifesto is particularly illuminating in apprehending the genre that she claims is an "undertheorized genre" (1). Lyon postulates that manifesto often manifests itself through: first, a foreshortened, impassioned, and highly selective history which chronicles the oppression preceding the "present moment of crisis"; secondly, the enumeration of grievances against a group; and thirdly, the using of epigrammatic, declarative rhetoric that challenges the oppressor and calling the audience to action (3).

Some characteristics of a manifesto are exhibited in *Detained* by the way in which Ngugi chronicles Kenya's long history of tyranny and oppression from colonial to post-independence eras, as exemplified by his unexplained incarceration; he presents a litany of President Jomo Kenyatta government's errors of omission and commission, and ultimately exhorts his Kenyan readers to continue without letup in the struggle for just rule, despite enormous sacrifices by some, such as incarceration or death. I argue that Ngugi's message to the audience is not to awaken them to a new struggle, since in his purview the struggle is already always in force.

Far from being fortuitous or gratuitous, the foregrounding of ideology as a guiding principle in this chapter is based on an awareness of Ngugi's unambiguous Marxist leanings (but filtered through the lens of Kenya of the 1970s and 1980s), which motivated and molded his political activism and intellectual activities for decades leading up to his detention without trial in 1977. Ngugi's novel *Petals of Blood* (1977) and the play he co-authored with Micere Mugo, *Trials of Dedan Kimathi* (1981) exemplify the Marxist zeitgeist that pervaded his writing then. The period of Ngugi's detention and the writing of *Detained* was characterized by the emergence of a number of leftist intellectuals disenchanted with the postcolonial situation in Kenya, most of who embraced Marxism, particularly its antithetical attitude towards capitalism and ever-increasing gulf between the poor and the rich. On the other hand the government demonized Marxism and viewed it to be tantamount to treason, hence the heavy crackdown and imprisonment and detention of intellectuals with Marxist leanings. Ali Mazrui's summation of the actions and attitude of the Moi regime during the cold war era sheds light on the dangers and risks that then dogged Kenyan leftist intellectuals. Mazrui writes,

The government of Kenya was co-opted into the Western camp, sometimes at the expenses of Kenya's own citizens. Being socialist or left-wing as an intellectual became a political hazard. All sorts of laws and edicts emerged about subversive literature. My own nephew, Dr. Alamin Mazrui of Kenyatta University, was detained without charge by the Moi regime for more than a year for being a left-wing Kenyan academic in the company of such other left-wingers as Ngugi wa Thiong'o and Micere Mugo. Intellectual opposition to capitalism in Kenya became increasingly a punishable offence. Lives of socialists were sometimes in danger, as in the case of the relatively powerless Pinto, who was assassinated. (59)

In what follows, I show specific examples of how Ngugi's text displays the three elements of the manifesto, namely a foreshortened history of oppression; a list of grievances; and a call to the audience for action.

Foreshortened History of Oppression

It needs to be stressed here that central to Ngugi's Marxism was the notion of Kenya's history. Patrick Williams has accurately underscored the primacy of history in Ngugi's ideological orientation. Williams remarks, "[p]erhaps the single most important terrain of intellectual struggle for Ngugi is history: in general, the history of imperialism; more locally, the (African) histories of Africa and Kenya; most precisely the history of the resistance of the Kenyan people, with Mau Mau as its high point" (210). By devoting more than half his prison memoir to a particular history of the country, Ngugi locates himself, and his fellow detainees, within the trajectory of victims of state repression. In other words, we encounter here the staging of "history as revolution" in Puchner's words, using history as a basis for undoing and redoing an unjust world. The history to which Ngugi gives so much primacy is in essence a counter-history, counter-hegemonic, as is his entire prison-writing project, involving *Caitaani Mutharaba-ini* and his Gikuyu novel, later translated as *Devil on the Cross* (1981). Ngugi places the present moment of his detention in a "foreshortened history of oppression," a history of oppression which began in the colonial period and continued unabated, after Kenya gained independence from Britain in 1963.

Ngugi's engagement with a particular history of his country is an appropriate point of departure for locating his version of a foreshortened history of oppression as an integral strand of the manifesto genre. In a highly poetic moment of Ngugi's prose, he states towards the last half of his life narrative:"Life in prison is not all endless confrontation and 'profound' meditations on history" (116). However, even a cursory examination of his text shows that although his representation of detention does not depict it as being endless brooding on history, a history of particular kind is central to the thrust of his self-narrative. In fact this "foreshortened history of oppression" dominates his text, tracing oppression from colonial to postcolonial times. Ngugi's "'profound meditations on history," his preoccupation with Kenya's history suffuses his text, as to give it the semblance of a historical document. Indeed for Ngugi, contemplating Kenya's past is more than idle engagement with historical curiosities; it is both necessary and desirable for apprehending the legacy of oppression culminating in and emblematized by his detention. In other words, Ngugi seems to maintain, that it is only by historicizing the "present moment of crisis" that we may fully grasp the nature and scope of the crisis or as he puts it himself, a way of "know[ing] why we are where we are" (55).

Ngugi situates the genesis of the repressive and exploitive ways of the then current regime to colonial occupation in Kenya, the period he calls "the seventy years of destructive alien presence" (29). It bears stating that positing the British colonialists as "aliens" implies the apparent distinction between alien and indigenous, and suggests the polarized dichotomy between "them" and "us" that is typical of what Lyon terms the "rhetoric of exclusivity' of the manifesto genre. Ngugi's engagement with history focuses on exposing what "them" (the British) did to "us" (Kenyans). "Pillage, plunder and murder," writes Ngugi. "[It] was the British way" (46). The history of oppression consists of the wanton and relentless "plunder" and "pillage," of Kenya's indigenous human and natural resources, including the expropriation of land. But Ngugi also associates the colonial regime with the "murder" of Kenyans, particularly those who stood up for their rights. Ngugi recounts the exploits of the "long line of resistance heroes" who died at the hands of the colonial government such as Nguunju wa Gakeere, Dethan Kimathi, Koitalel arap Samoei, Waiyaki, Menza wa Mekitilili, Arap Manyei, and victims of the Muranga massacre (46). Seeing himself as part of the concatenation of resistance in Kenya's history, Ngugi finds it necessary to present a foreshortened history of resistance and the ruthless state response, which preceded the Kenyatta regime.

Apart from painting the colonial government as murderous, Ngugi suggests that in fact, detention was part of the colonial legacy: "Detention was an instrument for colonial domination. In its origins and purposes, it is clearly a colonial affair" (44). British colonialists, Ngugi opines, left the effective example of how to deal with dissent and opposition by enacting and enforcing detention laws (43). Ngugi is, therefore, interested in "origins," the root of the problems plaguing postcolonial Kenya, not the least being detention legislation, which he terms "obnoxious," and which he identifies as being the brainchild of the colonial dispensation (50). Under these colonial laws not only were Africans detained without trial, but they also were kept under inhuman conditions about which KANU, the future governing party, but then a people's movement, lamented vehemently before independence (50).

Ngugi's historical account also faults the British for not only demonizing freedom fighters who principally belonged to the Mau Mau movement, but also devaluing indigenous African culture, elevating white bourgeoisie culture, and creating tribalism as part of the divide-and-rule stratagem. Ngugi states: "Thus, the famed traditional rivalry between the Agikuyu and the Luo people was clearly a later colonial invention. The fact is that, right from the beginning, the two nationalities had the biggest working class elements. The unity of the Muugikuyu worker and the Jaluo worker (because of their numbers) was always a threat to imperialism in Kenya . . . They had to create artificial rivalry" (82).

At the same time as Ngugi presents the portrait of heroic Kenyans he also draws attention to Kenyans who were complicit in the suffering of their compatriots, by dint of their collaboration with imperialist agents. In this category belong Kenyans who were collaborators through and through and those like Harry Thuku and Kenyatta, who were initially exemplary freedom fighters, but metamorphosed into turncoats, in order to serve the interests of their colonial and imperialist masters upon release from detention. Also culpable in Ngugi's historical account of suffering is the Christian Church for teaching "[o]bedience of the oppressed to the oppressor" (42). Ngugi views the Church in colonial times as serving the same purpose of subjugating the masses as the brute force of the police, albeit insidiously. He writes: "[T]hese were the ultimate aesthetic goals of colonial culture carefully nurtured by nailed boots, police truncheons and military bayonets and by the carrot of a personal heaven for a select few. The end was to school Kenyans in the aesthetic of submission and blind obedience to authority…" (42).

Ngugi further argues that the subjugation of the indigenous population entailed inhibiting or thwarting indigenous efforts at cultural expression. Ngugi highlights the paradoxical situation illustrated by the efforts of the British to erect the Kenya National Theatre at the heart of Nairobi city, where it is inaccessible to Kenyan nationals, and in which no Kenyan plays were allowed to be staged. Ngugi observes: "The institution of British theatre in Kenya in the 1950s was a reactionary response to the resurgence of a popular dance and theatre following the return of Kenyan soldiers from the European-generated Second World War" (67). As a result the colonial administration made frantic efforts to start British theatre clubs in all the major towns in the country, to oversee cultural performance in schools and ensure the elevation and promotion of British cultural values and practices. For instance, Ngugi notes that at his former school, Alliance High School, it became customary to stage Shakespeare's plays "attended by colonial governors and applauding administrators" in line with the apotheosis of the so-called British high-brow culture (67).

Ngugi is at pains to clarify that whenever and whatever acts of oppression and human rights violations were inflicted upon people perceived to be a threat to the interests of the ruling colonial elite in Kenya's past, they were not isolated incidents, but they indeed were instead systemic and normative. He writes that, "acts of animal brutality were not cases of individual aberration but an integral part of colonial politics, philosophy and culture. Reactionary violence to instil fear and silence was the very essence of colonial settler culture" (38).

List of Grievances

Having considered Ngugi's account of the crisis, at this point I turn to his list of grievances. I consider as grievances, what he cites as the immediate and direct causes of the "moment of crisis," the culture of despotism in postcolonial Kenya in general and the injustice of his own incarceration during the Kenyatta regime in particular. Most of these grievances, although not all, are therefore contemporaneous with the moment of crisis and/or the moment of writing. Ngugi's grievances may be divided into two, individual and collective where the collective signifies the peasant masses, although I must concede that these two sets of grievances are inextricably tied to one another. In his narrative, Ngugi himself tends to frequently collapse the binary between his individual experience and the collective experience. Even when the grievances appear to affect him in his individual capacity, there is a sense which he foregrounds the relational or collective significance of his suffering. The aggrieved and politicized "I," which necessarily speaks from a "high moral ground," almost always becomes the synecdoche for the collectivized "we."

On the whole in *Detained,* Ngugi levels complaints against several institutions and systems such as neo-colonialism, imperialism, the executive arm of government, intelligentsia, law enforcement officers, and legislators, as well as specific individuals. He presents a list of grievances against the Kenya postcolonial state, and its bourgeois henchmen. He criticizes the "comprador bourgeoisies" led by President Kenyatta, for betraying the dreams of independence. "The comprador bourgeoisie," he charges, "which had been growing in the womb of the colonial regime desired to protect and enhance its cosy alliance with foreign interests" with a view to exploiting the Kenyan masses and perpetuating the colonial legacy (53). He therefore depicts post-independence Kenya as a reincarnation or resurrection of colonialism; hence his repeated use of the metaphor of "colonial Lazarus" in characterizing his country. Ngugi implies that like the Biblical character Lazarus whose death was nullified by being raised by Jesus Christ, the symbolic death of colonialism at independence was rendered null and void by embracing of colonial ethos, values and systems by the postcolonial Kenyan state. In other words, the return of "colonial Lazarus" in the garb of African nationalist leaders, translated into a repetition of the cycle of repression, human rights violations, oppression, and exploitation of the Kenyan masses. Following in the footsteps of their colonial predecessors the Kenyan ruling elite followed the ethos of "pillage, plunder and murder"(46).

Ngugi harshly criticizes Kenyatta's obsession with self-aggrandizement, and a reenactment of the quintessential colonial culture of exploitation of the masses. Ngugi believes the greed of the few "comprador bourgeoisies" which motivates them to work in cohorts with their imperial allies, is what consigns millions to poverty. The ethos of "pillage, plunder and murder" inspires revolutionary statements such as JM Kariuki's famous line, which Ngugi quotes to reinforce his indictment of capitalist greed: "We do not want to create a Kenya of ten millionaires and ten million beggars" (95). Like their European settler predecessors, who were "parasites in paradise" (29). Ngugi describes the new political dispensation as a "dependant class, and a parasitic class in the *kupe* sense (56). The image of 'kupe,' the Swahili word for 'tick,' accentuates the notion of dependency of this class upon the sweat and blood of the peasant masses. Ngugi singles out JM Kariuki as "one of the bitterest critics of the post-independence betrayal of the Kenyan people" who was assassinated because he stood up against these rapacious "lucky few," who impoverished the masses with their greed (95).

Apart from outright elimination of opponents, Ngugi inevitably lists the government's inheritance of colonial inhuman detention laws as a grievance. It was a salient part of the great betrayal of independence and had direct ramifications on him in his individual capacity as a political detainee. At independence, only few inconsequential terms were amended in the law of the land, Ngugi correctly notes, leaving the detention laws intact and open to abuse by the nascent KANU governing party. Ngugi observes that it was still within the government's legal right to waive the "normal democratic assumption of a Kenyan's guilt for crimes of thought and intention" (51). Ngugi faults the KANU government for retaining and consolidating "all the repressive colonial laws" and continuing to keep its citizens in detention in conditions as bad if not worse than the ones it complained against in the colonial era. He quotes one of his fellow detainees, Wasonga Sijeyo, as making the following telling statement on the state of detention between 1977 and 1978 in Kenya: "I have been in colonial detention for five years. I have been in this compound five years. But these two years have beaten all the previous twelve years" (127). Things were getting worse rather than better. The KANU regime had intensified the suffering and deprivation of detainees by including various forms of torture. Ngugi writes:

> "The detaining authorities are not of course content to just inflict the wound: they must keep on twisting hot knives into it to ensure its continued freshness. This takes various forms: physical beating with the possibility of final elimination; strait-jacketing to ensure bodily immobility; sleeping on cold and wet cement floors without a mat or a blanket so the body can more easily contract disease . . ." (100).

In his individual capacity as a detainee, Ngugi suffers the de-individuating consequences of being known merely by a file number namely, K 6, 77 (3). Ngugi writes: "From Saturday 31 December 1977 I had died to my name Ngugi. Henceforth I would answer to a lifeless number on a file among many files" (19). Simon Gikandi has cogently expounded upon how galling and devastating such de-individuation was to a writer of Ngugi's stature, who was already remarkably famous, both nationally and internationally at the time of his detention (198). The same de-indivituating capacity of detention is highlighted in any number of prison memoirs across Africa such as Malawian Sam Mpasu's *Political Prisoner 3/75*, Nigerian Wole Soyinka's *The Man Died*, and his compatriot Kunle Ajaide's *Detained for Life* as well as Kenyan Wanyiri Kihoro's *Never Say Die*.

In *Detained*, Ngugi claims that the aim of the confinement was to "teach [him] a lesson in submission" (xi). This included being denied privacy, with the prison authorities imposing upon him 24-hour surveillance even on matters such as attending to the demands of nature. He was denied of freedom to receive and send information, the freedom to write freely, and even access to the radio or newspapers. Upon release from detention several months after Kenyatta's death, the state still continued to consign Ngugi to pariah status. He was trailed by secret police; he was charged for drinking after hours; he is denied reinstatement to his faculty position at the University of Nairobi; and even after attending an interview where he beat all candidates, he was not offered a new position at the same state-run and state-controlled university.

The other grievances Ngugi holds against the Kenyan government involve its imitation of the colonial mentality of denigrating and disparaging indigenous cultural expression. The Kenya National Theater continued to stage foreign plays, while the government banned the performance of Gikuyu plays of the Kamiriithu Theatre Group with which Ngugi was associated. The ruling elite continued to ape the "white bourgeoisie" culture by developing and maintaining aversion for local names and languages, things which otherwise epitomize what he terms "authentic" indigenous Kenyan culture (59).

It is reasonable to speculate that for the political establishment of the time foreign plays in a foreign language would appear safer to stage since they were presumed to be too far removed from the grim local realities. These local realities were best left untouched, unarticulated and unreflected in local languages since this would potentially cause disaffection against the ruling elite. But quite frankly, this allure of the "safe" foreign artistic productions is ludicrous since it assumed the gullibility of the Kenyan masses and oddly celebrated Kenya's negation of its own rich and diverse indigenous cultural heritage. In other words, the government then assumed that Kenyans were absolutely incapable of "gleaning" something regarding their own myriad of predicaments from the menu of foreign plays particularly the corruption of the rulers. But even importantly, by negating its own indigenous cultural wealth, Kenya unwittingly, in Ngugi's view, effectively took the odious option of suicidal self-negation.

Calling Audience to Action

Having painted such a bleak picture of Kenya's conception of itself as a nation, of the rotten leadership and the history of injustice, of the Kenyan postcolony making itself a clone of the Kenya Colony, what does Ngugi then suggest is the way forward? Quite inevitably, Ngugi does not want Kenyans to fold their arms and watch their country crumble and crash. He is quick to offer solutions to salvage the situation, to call his audience to action. In her theory of the manifesto, Lyon cites the ending of Franz Fanon's *Wretched of the Earth* (1969) as a classic example of a call to the audience for action: "Come, then comrades, it would be as well to decide at once to change our ways. We must shake off the heavy darkness in which we were plunged and leave it behind. The new day which is already at hand must find us firm, prudent, and resolute" (Fanon quoted in Lyon 29).

In what way does Ngugi call the audience to action in *Detained*? In responding to this question, it is necessary first of all to identify who is Ngugi's intended audience. In his statement to the Detainee Review Tribunal, Ngugi addresses the Tribunal as his intended audience. It is tempting therefore to say that the chairman and other members of the Tribunal constituted his audience for that particular fragment of his text. But the inclusion of the document as well as others like it, in the published text is an index of Ngugi's desire for the details of his detention and the depth of his reflection on detention, and his country's history, to be read by a larger audience. When Ngugi declares in the statement that he always wanted a "Kenya for Kenyans," there is little doubt that he wanted the Kenyan masses to read this text and its collection of fragments (188). Ngugi's vision of a Kenya for Kenyans is necessarily exclusionary, particularly when considered in the light of his countless attack on alien and alienating institutions and influences on his native country. He exhorts his audience thus: "Kenyan people, wherever they were, under whatever circumstances, had to keep on insisting on certain irreducible democratic and human rights. If we do not do this, if we succumbed to the culture of fear and silence, Kenya would have merely moved from a colonial prison to a neo-colonial prison" (112).

Ngugi exhorts his audience not to succumb to the "culture of fear and silence" and thereby let their independence become a transformation from one symbolic incarceration to the next. It is noteworthy that Ngugi invokes the collective and politicized pronoun "we" also present in Fanon's text (23-26). It is this collectivized "we" that Ngugi appeals to for action. This is the "we" of the "moral high ground" of the manifesto genre and is in tandem with the "rhetoric of exclusivity." Obviously excluded in this implied "we" is the "comprador class" that suffers the brunt of Ngugi's sustained attack. Ngugi issues a caveat earlier in the text that suggests the exclusion of this category of people; "There is no way I could have written this prison memoir without treading on some sensitive toes" (xi). These include Kenyatta and his henchmen.

It is important to exercise caution in determining whether Ngugi calls the Kenyan masses to a class struggle pitting the poor against the wealthy. It may be more germane to conclude that Ngugi merely exhorts the masses to *continue* with a class struggle that is always already underway. We can deduce this from Ngugi's negation of claims that his play was "calling for a class struggle in Kenya" (188). "How" asks Ngugi, "could the play call for something that was already there? (188). But rather than completely disavow the "class struggle," it appears Ngugi simply endorses and encourages it in his impassioned message. Sustaining the resistance spirit and staying the course is Ngugi's call to the audience for action.

In *Detained* therefore Ngugi locates himself within the context of a longer history of struggle and detention (even assassination) of others like him, before him and in his time. It is a story of the I within the matrix of a wider collective "we" which consists of several other is beyond the narrating I, some of whom are separated temporally and spatially. It is a kind of history that inevitably and necessarily runs counter to the official narrative. It is a foreshortened history, selective, and subjective, a history that fixes its accusatory gaze on the excesses and oppression of successive regimes in Kenya, and their zealous efforts to silence real "patriots" like him. It would seem to Ngugi, patriotism, like truth, is synonymous with resistance to oppression and exploitation in colonial and postcolonial Kenya.

In short, Ngugi uses history as a tool to contextualize the oppressive regimes in Kenya and to underscore the necessity for embracing the ethos of resisting and removing such regimes. Ngugi's invocation of a foreshortened colonial and postcolonial history, his enumeration of sins of commission and omission, and his call for action in *Detained,* suggest an attempt at pinpointing the diagnosis and prognosis of Kenya's symbolic national illness and proposing a peasant-led revolution as the radical surgery needed to ameliorate the condition. The political ideology of changing the Kenyan world that informs Ngugi's intellectual and political activities is at play in *Detained.* Lyon's statement about the nature of manifestoes is applicable to his art and activism: "Laying their finger on the pulse of the new world—"the moment of social transition"—the manifesto's revolutionary artisans mark the artistic praxis that will create the new world" (16). *Detained* is therefore at once a political manifesto and an individual and collective record of the truth, torture, and trauma of detention.

Indeed, it goes without saying that genre matters, and therefore classifying *Detained* in whatever generic taxonomy tends to shift the emphasis in the interpretation of this important text. Whereas the text lends itself toward multiple classifications, misclassification is the first sure step towards misreading. The revolutionary ideal, the passion to change the world of Kenyans that informs Ngugi's text could be lost if we did not read it as a manifesto. *Detained* is therefore a manifesto of a leftist intellectual who creates himself as a son of peasants driven by the revolutionary ideal and a burning desire to undo an unjust system of things in the country of his birth.

Chapter 4: Doing Things with Words in Prison Poetry

> [C]an words alone bring down the tyrant?
>
> —Kunle Ajibade, *Jailed for Life*

In March 1969 Kenyan Swahili poet and political activist Abdilatif Abdalla appeared before a Mombasa court on sedition charges. The magistrate found him guilty and sentenced him to eighteen months in prison for the offence. But the attorney general Charles Njonjo successfully appealed against the sentence, claiming the magistrate had been too lenient. Abdalla's sentence was accordingly doubled to three years. The sedition case thrust Abdalla, then aged 22 and described in a section of the media as a "revolutionary young man," from relative obscurity to the national limelight in post-independence Kenya.[1] Writing retrospectively in the preface to his anthology of prison poems, *Sauti ya Dhiki,/* 'Voice of Agony,' Abdalla would state with unequivocal candor, that he was imprisoned because of being found guilty of writing and distributing in a number of towns on the Kenyan coast, a pamphlet entitled "*Kenya Twendapi?"/* 'Kenya: Where are we Headed?' (xiii). Abdalla's anti-government activities had not gone unnoticed, and he was therefore compelled to feel the full force of the Jomo Kenyatta regime for rubbing it the wrong way.

However, would the prison term tame the revolutionary fervor of young Abdalla? Would it silence him? Upon his release in March 1972, Abdalla presented to Oxford University Press the manuscript of *Sauti ya Dhiki* (Voice of Agony), his collection of poems for which prison was the site for writing. Its publication the following year marked the first appearance in print of the post-independence literature of incarceration Kenya.[2] Clearly, the revolutionary young man imprisoned for sedition had continued to do things with poetical words while incarcerated, doing things with poetry that the incarcerating state did not sanction or approve of. For one thing, the poems deconstruct and disrupt the official national narrative of President Kenyatta as the benevolent and caring founding father of the nascent Kenyan nation. The poet uses the poems not only to give a poetic account of his prison experience, but also to reconstruct himself and his shattered world. Put differently, the incarcerated revolutionary seeks to tell his own story, on his own terms, and to be heard, despite what we may call the silencing intent of imprisonment. Hence, in incarceration and as in freedom, Abdalla sticks to his revolutionary stance. One could say Fredric Jameson's characterization of the third world intellectual who "produces both poems and praxis" is, therefore, befitting of Abdalla (25).

It is, therefore, imperative to conclude that the political engagement that implicated and imbricated Abdalla in what the Kenya government viewed as seditious activities was not in the least extinguished by his prison experience. On the contrary his incarceration seems to have instead further radicalized him, heightening his urge to continue marrying art and political activism. Indeed for Abdalla, art and activism appear more or less like Siamese twins, as the examination of his thematic concerns in *Sauti ya Dhiki* bears out. On the whole Abdalla's *Sauti ya Dhiki* could be seen as a manifesto of his political ideology, capturing as it does the vicissitudes and injustices of imprisonment, and indicting Kenyatta's autocratic regime and the apparent impunity with which the regime broke independence promises. His poetry is therefore necessarily tendentious. That Abdalla would muster the courage to mount such a trenchant critique on Kenyatta's government within prison walls at a time when writing against the government was tantamount to committing suicide is an astounding feat. One may speculate that perhaps by sustaining a stance antithetical towards the government while within prison walls, Abdalla was being true to his character and nature. And yet the various explicit and implicit ways within which Abdalla expresses his iconoclasm and militancy are an index of the multiple poetical voices with which he resists oppression from state apparatuses.

Like Soyinka's famous poem "A Shutttle in the Crypt" and prison memoir *The Man Died* as well as Ngugi wa Thiong'o's *Detained*, Abdalla's *Sauti ya Dhiki* was written on toilet paper behind prison walls. This collection of poems stands as Abdalla's response to what he perceived as the government's criminalization of dissent. It encapsulates the many and varied moods and affective states that engulfed him as he figuratively journeyed in the psychic landscape that the prison ambience fostered. The poet evinced and expressed a wide range of emotions including bitterness, defiance, confidence, regret, and self-doubt as he "traveled" under the conditions of deprivation and dehumanization that this figurative prison journey occasioned. As Soyinka stated regarding his prison poetry, "the poems are a map of the course trodden by the human mind during the years of incarceration" (qtd. in Afejuku, 21). Soyinka's conception of prison poetry as a map suggests that in such poetry readers are able to trace the inmate's mental, psychic or philosophical journeys. As a map would consist of any number of details and destinations, prison poetry contains a whole range of mental or psychic courses or journeys. The prisoner as poet is also impelled to speak in multiple tongues, to paraphrase Sidonie Smith and Julia Watson, whose conception of self as well as Bakhtin's idea of speech variability inform this analysis.

The Multiple "I" and Speaking in Tongues

In what follows I investigate how Abdalla speaks in many tongues as he engages with issues of self- representation, self-narration, and incarceration. I am interested in exploring how the poetical intentions of the poet interact with the narrative perspective, and how the prison context influences the content and form of the text. Additionally, following J.L. Austin's concept of "doing things with words," I examine the various voices and guises that the poet adapts and adopts to do things that help remake his world unmade by the prison experience. I argue that the poet's "I" appears in many guises and is heard in multiple voices as to problematize the notion of a stable, unitary self.

As Sidonie Smith and Julia Watson have remarked the very notion of a stable unitary self has increasingly come under attack in recent autobiographical criticism. Smith and Watson assert that focusing on "autonomous" individuality or "the sovereign self" is one of the ways in which seminal readings of life narratives in the West have notoriously "narrowed the range of vision" (Smith and Watson, 128). They see as misreading initial interpretations of the "I" which hinged on the presumption or assumption that the concept of individuality was sufficient as a determining force in life writing. They observe: "But if we recall the diverse modes of life narrating by marginalized, minoritized, diasporic, nomadic, and postcolonial subjects throughout the history of life writing, the concept of individuality is insufficient as a determining force (129). Smith and Watson call for a more nuanced reading of the "I" in life narratives, a reading that goes above and beyond the facile fascination with an "I" exclusively bound to an autonomous and concrete individuality. They state that James Olney in his *Metaphors of the Self: The Meaning of Autobiography*, exemplified such nuanced reading when he shifted the terms of debate from "self" to the concept of "subjectivity." Experimental life writing such as Roland Bathes's *Roland Bathes,* and Michel Lieris's *Rules of the Game,* has amplified the conundrum of the "I."

Indeed the idea of a fragmented self or subject has lately become commonplace, and so is the complicated and often conflicted interplay between subject and object. One could perhaps claim that as early as the early 19th century W.E.B. Dubois was well aware of the instability of the "I" when he conceived of the "double-consciousness" of the African American experience. Smith and Watson posit the existence of at least four types of the "I"; (1) the historical; (2) the narrating; (3) the narrated and; (4) the ideological "I"-s. Thus in their purview, the traditional approach which focuses upon studying the "I"- then and the "I"-now is also inadequate in making sense of the manifold manifestations of the pronoun.

As Smith and Watson further state, the historical or real "I" is a person located in a particular time and place, whose story the autobiographical act enacts or narrates but whose life is far more complex and transcendent than the story can possibly fully contain or fully embrace. One could think of the autobiographical mode as offering only a small portion of that life while other portions exist elsewhere (e.g. in the archives of the police, hospital, schools, churches, family album, or in the malleable memory of others). Nevertheless, this "I" that lives in the real world, they posit, is unknown and unknowable. In other words the "I" representing the real historical Abdalla is much more complex than the one presenting the prison imagination and experience of the late 1960s and early 1970s. The real Abdalla is scattered in the public and private archives of his native Kenya and the countries of his exile (e.g. the schools, airline manifests, payrolls, mosque registers, family albums, prison and court records, conference panels) and cannot be fully represented by the "I"-s or personae of his poetry.

One could argue that even the media's characterization of Abdalla as a "revolutionary young man" in 1969 is but a symptom and a consequence of a shifting interpretive impulse, which does not adequately capture the quintessence of Abdalla's authentic historicity. Are we, then, left with no viable option but to cling to the "agnostic" belief that despite or because of his poetry Abdalla's real "I" is both unknown and unknowable?

It would seem what the readers encounter is the narrating "I," the one telling the story whose range of vision is limited and remains within the confines of the story and lacks the broader experiential history of the historical "I." Yet this narrating "I," though knowable and known is equally complex. Smith and Watson assert that the narrating "I" is neither a unified nor stable subject; it is "split, fragmented, provisional, multiple" (60). Invoking Bakhtin in elucidating further on this fragmented subject, always in the process of coming together and of dispersing, they note, "We can read, or "hear" this fragmentation in the multiple voices through which the narrator speaks in the text. In fact, an "I" speaks in tongues or heteroglossia, to paraphrase Bakhtin. These voices can include the voice of publicly acknowledged authority, the voice of innocence and wonder, the voice of cynicism, the voice of postconversion certainty, the voice of suffering and victimization, and so on" (60).

The narrating "I" in Abdalla's *Sauti ya Dhiki* speaks in many voices, "speaking in tongues" as it were. The narrating "I" of the preface written in the Tanzanian commercial capital Dar es Salaam on February 22, 1973 where the poet was newly exiled upon release differs markedly from the various narrating "I"-s or voices of the poems written in prison. Presenting the poet as a political exile in a neighboring country, the "I" of the preface consists of a candid, if tacit, recovering of the memory and deciphering of the meaning of a just ended carceral experience. It is characterized by a detached prose at once commenting on and summing up the substance of the prison poetry that preceded its writing. It is "writing about writing" that is self-reflexive and explanatory. It is the narrating "I" that comes in the form of a historian of self, writing the history after the fact, and a critic of one's own earlier literary productions, produced under different circumstances. On the other hand it would seem the poet crafts each poem such that it has its one or more of its own grammatical narrating "I"-s, speaking in multifarious voices and exhibiting any number of colors and coming in different guises (e.g. defender of truth, political activist, prisoner, potential martyr, sage and agent of change, self-doubter and neophyte, unborn fetus, disinherited kin, patriot, Panafricanist, brother, friend, philosopher, consensus builder, etc).

It bears noting that, following Francoise Lionnet, Smith and Watson distinguish between the narrating "I" and the narrated "I" by viewing the former as the subject of history and the latter as the agent of discourse. In other words the narrating "I" is the speaking subject while the narrated "I" is the object, the protagonist of the narrative. The narrated "I" is a version of the self that the narrating "I" projects to the readers. Yet like the narrating "I" the narrated "I" is also multiple, fragmented, and heterogeneous. The similarity between the tags of the narrating and narrated "I"-s does not imply that they are one and the same thing. The similarity of the tags mainly is in the fragmentation the "I"-s embody. Yet there are still differences because the narrating "I" comes across as, for example, the philosophical or disenchanted storyteller, while the narrated "I" is the philosopher or disenchanted character whose story is told.

Lastly, the ideological "I" is to be seen, Smith and Watson argue, as the definition of self that is contingent on prevailing ideological, cultural, and historical notions of personhood during one's own time. In other words, the cultural and historical situatedness of the autobiographical narrator is determined by the particular moment in history in which he or she lived or lives. The overarching ideological concept of self, of one's relations to society or estimation of what is evil or good; all these factors are, therefore, present in the autobiographer's time and space and influence his definition of personhood. In this poststructural perspective, it is possible to read Abdalla's ideological self, particularly his Marxist temperament, as a product of the cultural context that shaped and molded him. Abdalla had been exposed to and enthused by Marxist literature and ideology that became a crucial catalyst in his political activism.[3]

Also relevant to our discussion here is what Smith and Watson term "alternatives to an individual self" in the postcolonial world of which Abdalla's poetry is part. They write,

Calling Western norms of identity into question, these writers, at diverse global locations, produce self-narrations through which they call attention to their status as the West's former "Others" and seek to be heard in different terms, to be accountable, to count. For such autoethnographers the emancipatory dimension of contemporary autobiographical practices and cultural work is primary, as they creatively inquire into histories of their own cultural erasure in the name of civilizing missions and employ modes of oral storytelling. (131-132)

These alternatives to the individual self-challenge or dismantle the Enlightenment idea of a unified selfhood, a universal "I" that defies time and location. In essence Abdalla, "seeks to be heard in different terms, to be accountable, to count" as Smith and Watson would put it.

Why Write?

The account Abdalla seeks to give of himself, one could argue, is a self-study that attempts to extrapolate upon the carceral experience and imagination with the tools of poetic prosody, and Kimvita, a dialect of Kiswahili that the British hegemony in East Africa minoritized and marginalized. One could argue that Abdalla's use of Kimvita is not only an indicator of cultural nationalism or autoethnographical tendencies, but represents, in its intent and intensity, a resolute counter-hegemonic endeavor. Yet, the postcolonial context of Abdalla's writing and incarceration means that the thrust of his counter-hegemony is, in the main, leveled against not a colonial autocrat but a postcolonial autocract, in Achille Mbembe's terms. The context is, therefore, both different and the same: the transition from the Western or colonial autocrat to the indigenous postcolonial autocrat did not change the reality of autocratic rule. In both situations the incarcerated individual feels inhibited, dehumanized, demonized, and deprived, and is probably driven by the emancipatory impulse to narrate herself or himself into being, to tell her or his own story, to count. By writing *Sauti ya Dhiki,* Abdalla may be said to be trying to claim subjectivity, to create himself from the passivity of an "object" as the prison system intends for him, to a speaking rational "subject." In other words, subject formation or creation is an integral part of the things Abdalla does with poetical words.

It is instructive that Abdalla does not state explicitly that he wrote the anthology of prison poems in order to transform himself from object to subject nor does he present any other overall objective. In the preface Abdalla states the reason for his incarceration i.e. that he was imprisoned for sedition, but not the overall reason for his writing while incarcerated. He only singles out six poems the context of whose writing or the identity of whose audience he reckoned needed some clarification. For instance, he states that he wrote "Tuza Moyo"/ 'Take Heart' in response to a poem he quotes from a sympathizer who he does not name; he wrote "Zindukani"/ 'Wake Up' for the coastal people; "'Sikakawane na Kimya"/ 'Don't be too Quiet' for his elder brother Ahmad Nassir; and "Kwa heri"/ 'Bye bye' for his fellow prison inmate Israel Otieno. On the whole therefore, Abdalla leaves it up to the reader to decipher his motivations for writing.

His summation of the collection of poems is largely ambiguous when it comes to the overarching motivations of his writing. He states: "Mashairi yaliyomo humu yanahusiana na yaliyonifika hata ikabidi nifungwe; kifungo chenyewe; niliyokuwa nayo moyoni; imani yangu na maoni yangu kuhusu yaliyokuwa yakitendeka nje ya kuta za gereza."/ 'The poems in this collection are preoccupied with the circumstances of my imprisonment; the experience of imprisonment, my inner most thoughts, my beliefs and opinions on things that transpired beyond the prison walls' (xvii). Abdalla's summation, therefore, does not categorically specify why he wrote the poems. Embedded in this statement of content, is an implied narrative imperative that is perhaps not explicitly articulated. Nonetheless, the import of this statement is that in it Abdalla calls attention to the very act of narrating itself, underlining the need or desire to narrativize or narrate self. To unlock the answer to the question: "Why?" we have to look beyond the poet rather than look up to him. Granted he states, regarding the poem "Moyo Iwa na Subira," that it was motivated by the need to comfort himself after hopes of being released from prison on Kenyatta Day October 20, 1971 were dashed (xiii). But if we bestow undue authority to this selective authorial statement, we may fall into the snare of concluding that it is the only poem the poet writes to console himself.

Conversely, we would miss the point if we entirely ignored what the poet says about his motives or motivation for writing. For one thing, the poet drops telling hints over and above the ones discussed above, hints connected to prison as the reason and site for writing that we cannot afford to overlook. He states, "[P]engine nisingeyatunga mashairi haya kama nisingelikuwa nimefungwa"/ '[P]erhaps I would never have written these poems if I was not imprisoned' (xiii).

Roland Bathes's introduction of the notion of the "death of the author" and W.K. Wimsatt and Monroe Beardsley's idea of "intentional fallacy" tended to debunk any tangible basis for the author to claim he or she had this or that intention for writing whatever they write. However Barthes' proposition of the death of the author, or Wimsatt and Beardsley's intentional fallacy shouldn't be accepted uncritically or wholesale. The onus should rest only on the critics to surmise the writer's motive. I propose that in trying to extrapolate upon the authorial intentions, we should neither ignore entirely what the author says are his motives nor exclusively dwell on what the work does not say about itself. It would seem readerly inference (and not intuition), that takes into account the context and the text is perhaps the more appropriate option in explaining the motivation for writing. To reiterate staking a claim on "subjectivity" and counterposing a different mythology of oneself or offering a counter-hegemonic account of oneself, seems to be possible and plausible reasons for Abdalla's prison poetry. So is seeking comfort which Abdalla reductively applies only to one poem, yet the therapeutic or scriptotherapeutic properties of his entire collection of poems is self-evident as is the very act of writing itself. Again, these are not the only possible reasons why Abdalla composed his prison poems, but further debate on the question of motivation should not detain us here.[4]

The "dialogic reverberations" in Abdalla's poems in *Sauti ya Dhiki* necessitate extending the frame of reference for the idea of heteroglossia and dialogism beyond the novel genre, contrary to Bakhtin's earlier configuration of the concept (Bakhtin 499). It is also important to be attentive to the way in which Abdalla participates in a social dialogue in his poetry, both taking and giving at the same time so that in Bakthin's terms, his word "in language is half someone else's." There are in *Sauti ya Dhiki* fragmented, multiple, and heterogenous "I"-s that imbue it with a sense of unmistakable multivocality. In other words, in his collection of poems, Abdalla speaks in tongues, in different languages and accents to articulate the feelings and imaginings of multiple "I"-s. Pinpointing the multiplicity of languages at play in the social heteroglossia, Bakhtin wrote,

Thus an illiterate peasant, miles away from any urban center, naively immersed in an unmoving and for him unshakable everyday world, nevertheless lived in several language systems: he prayed to God in one language (Church Slavic), sang songs in another, spoke to his family in third and, when he began to dictate petitions to the local authorities through the scribe, he tried speaking yet a fourth language (official –literate language, "paper" language). All these are *different languages*, even from the point of view of abstract socio-dialectological markers. (506) [emphasis in original]

Abdalla's poetry too, has the "illiterate peasant's" capacity and tendency to speak "different languages" by different "I"-s that the poet parades to us in an attempt to narrate himself, to orchestrate different themes, to serve his various "semantic and expressive intentions"(498). The difference in utterances and voices accounts for the varying subjective positions and subjectivities that are embodied in the "I" of Abdalla's poetry.

Bakhtin specifically locates the dialogic aspect of artistic expression in the genre of the novel. He bases his analysis on the concept of heteroglossia (linguistic variability), which typifies the novel, and as a consequence tends to set it apart from the other genres. Bakhtin argues that the novel is more prone to intertextuality, since it has the capacity of entertaining a multiplicity of social voices and a wide range of "links and interrelationships." Bakhtin's assessment of the stylistic elements of the novel is keenly attentive to the lack of uniformity in the novel, pointing to what he aptly describes as the "dispersion into the rivulets and droplets of social heteroglossia (485). Further, he argues that the novel contains a number of voices, which may be also seen as different languages that come to bear on the formation of the literary entity. A novel therefore consists of languages that are both varied and at the same time internally variegated. Based on his notion of the novel as a meeting point for these voices and languages, Bakhtin gives us his definition of the novel as: "a diversity of social speech types, sometimes even a diversity of languages and a diversity of individual voices, artistically organized" (484).

In sum, Bakhtin's notion of the dialogic and heteroglossia captures the various voices that emerge in Abdalla's prison poetry as evident from his style and thematic concerns, and how prison as a writing site impinges on the writing. This chapter bring to the fore the multivocality of his poetry and to demonstrate how it speaks to Bakhtin's concept of dialogism. In this regard, the title *Sauti ya Dhiki,* loosely translated into English as 'Voice of Agony,' is not one singular voice, but is perhaps better interpreted as multifarious voices of agony or anguish expressed by the one prison poet (Ohly 82). The multiplicity of voices is evident not only from the diversity of themes that preoccupy Abdalla, but the various stylistic and linguistic strategies he employs in his anthology. Moreover, Abdalla purports to speak for others—the underprivileged and deprived—in expressing disillusion with the illusion of prosperity in post-independence Africa in general and Kenya in particular. His *sauti* or voice is hence a synthesis of many voices, not a cacophony, but a polyphony through which readers can hear vicariously the unspoken agonies of the silent fellow sufferers or unspeaking others. But let us briefly make forays into the Swahili prosodic tradition in which Abdalla's poetic oeuvre belongs.

Swahili Prosody and Poetry as Autobiography

Sauti ya Dhiki is a collection of 40 stanzaed poems that Abdalla wrote in the period of his incarceration between September 1969 and December 1972, with only one poem,"N'sharudi" (I am back), being written after the completion of his prison term. All the poems adhere strictly to the rules of Swahili prosody. In one of his lectures at the University of Dar es Salaam in the early 1970s Abdalla explained the reason for his insistence on prosody: "watalaamu wa ushairi wa Kiswahili kwa umoja wao wamekubaliana kuwa shairi la Kiswahili ni lazima liwe na vina na mizani. Vitu hivi viwili ni kama roho ya shairi la Kiswahili." / 'Scholars of Swahili poetry have unanimously agreed that the Swahili poem must have rhyme and metre. These two things are like the soul of the Swahili poem" (Chacha, 34). It is not entirely true that *all* scholars of Swahili poetry concurred then or concur now with that view, unless by "all" Abdalla implies all prosodists.

Clearly, Abdalla's assertion demonstrates how much premium poets like him attach to adherence to Swahili prosody. But this seeming protectionism emanates from construing Swahili poetry as a heritage handed down from generation to generation amongst the Waswahili people. It is therefore appropriate to situate Abdalla's poetry within the Swahili prosodic convention, which also entails the tradition of using poetry as a vehicle for protest and resistance. I shall return to the question of poetry as resistance shortly, but at this point it is necessary to give an overview of Abdalla's poetry within the matrix of Swahili prosody.

As Abdalla's remarks above show Swahili prosodists consider *mizani* (metre) and *vina* (rhyme) not only as the mainstay of Swahili verses but mandatory as well. In their view, reckless deviation from this norm would render a poem *guni* (defective or deficient) resulting in the devaluation of the artistic composition (60). Sheikh Amri Abeid, (1954) William Hichens (1962), Lyndon Harries (1962), J.W.T. Allen (1967), and Shariff (1988) attempted the explanation of these highly rigid and clearly defined prosodic conventions. However, as Mohamed H. Abdulaziz in *Muyaka: 19th Century Swahili Popular Poetry* (1979), and Gudrun Miehe and others in *Kala Shairi* (2002) show, the classifications are often problematic in many ways, not least among them the tendency to conflate *utendi* and *mashairi,* which are two distinct poetic genres with the former consisting of longer narrative or epic poems, while the latter consists of poems that are relatively short and may be lyrical. In his discussion of Muyaka's poems, Abdulaziz cogently cautions: "At the purely metric and rhyme level the *mashairi* forms give one an impression of a highly rigid framework that would be bound to give rise to artificial diction and the reducing of the whole poetic work to mere versification" (48).

But Abdulaziz's rigorous analysis of Muyaka's verses reveals the poet's outstanding artistic astuteness within the confines of prosodic conventions, an astuteness that made Muyaka a model to look up to by his 19th century contemporaries and future generations of Swahili poets, including Abdalla. If Muyaka's mastery of prosody enabled him to successfully merge form and content to produce verses of considerable appeal across generations, Abdalla too succeeds in debunking the myth of empty artificiality and insipid versification in his poetry. Abdalla's prison poetry, one could say, operates within the figurative prison walls of Swahili verse prosody but without allowing his artistic productions to lose the saliency of their beauty and vibrancy. In chapter five I discuss at length how Abdalla's prison poetry differs significantly from that of Alamin Mazrui, another Swahili prison poet in this regard.

But suffice it to say here that Abdalla's poems in *Sauti ya Dhiki,* like Muyaka's, belong to the *mashairi* subgenre. In the volume his shortest verses such as "Tuza Moyo," (6) "Tendekezo," (62) and "Kokoiko," (64) have only one stanza of four lines each while the longest poem, "Kutendana" has 147 strophes. The bulk of the poems are short, roughly under eight stanzas each. The Swahili quatrain *tarbia* is made up of four lines with two hemstiches each with eight vocal syllables to the hemistiche and a rhyme pattern ab, ab, ab bx. Therefore the total number of measured syllables in each stanza is 64. As Abdulaziz aptly argues, Muyaka was instrumental in popularizing this syllabic measure and rhyme pattern (50). One other important aspect of *mashairi* as a poetic subgenre is the last line in the first stanza, called *kituo,* which acts as a refrain and is often repeated in all the subsequent stanzas for emphasis and musical purposes. The centrality of the musicality is underscored by J.W.T. Allen's observation that "[a]ll Swahili verse form was and almost all is composed to be sung" (179). Abdalla's own brother Ahmed Nassir (Juma Bhalo) is an accomplished *taarab* music composer and singer while Abdalla himself has recited his poems in various places and times in accordance with the tradition of performance in Swahili poetry (82).

However, it must be mentioned that Abdalla does employ a wide range of styles within the *mashairi* genre. He uses 8 main poetical patterns and another 17 minor ones (Ohly 83). Besides the predominant *tarbia* or quatrains, he also uses *tathlitha*, a verse with three-lines in each stanza as in "Nakumbuka,"/ 'I Remember,' (11) "Mamba,"/ 'The Crocodile' (10) and "Watiliye Pamba"/ 'Do not Listen to Them' (61).

Since all the poems are dated chronologically, I concur with Ohly who describes this anthology as a kind of "poetical diary" that registers Abdalla's varying moods, his feelings and thoughts, while he languished behind prison walls so much so that we can follow them "month by month" (87). Additionally the presentation of these various moods, feelings and thoughts, could indeed be seen as instances of self-creation and self-narration whose outcome is the re-enactment of the poet's various selves. The poems trace in almost chronological fashion the wide range of thematic concerns that preoccupied the poet, therefore accentuating the polyphony of his prison poetry. I will shortly be returning to the question of multivocality. But let me mention here that Ohly's characterization of the collection as a form of "poetical diary" suggests its affinity with or proximity to what Sidonie Smith and Julia Watson term genres of "life writing" such as autobiography or memoir. Regarding autobiography William Howarth succinctly remarks that it is an attempt by individuals to "carve a public monument out of their private lives" (92). The interplay between the private and the public sphere is quite pronounced in *Sauti ya Dhiki* as this collection of poems constitutes Abdalla's imposing "public monument," at once attracting critical acclaim and raising condemnation within and without literary circles. Yet, what is foremost in the content and context of *Sauti ya Dhiki* is the spirit of defiance and resilience as an examination of the wide range of themes in the volume would reveal. In other words, Abdalla's poetry comes across as a form of resistance to what he perceives as tyranny and bad governance in post-independence Kenya.

Resistance and Truth

Undertaking an ambitious and powerful construction of self as a paragon of virtue and truth is one of the principal things the poet does with words. He projects himself as the fearless voice of truth in his anthology that abounds with poems bearing overt political overtones. The very first poem in the collection "*N'shishiyelo ni Lilo*"/ 'I am unshakeable' is a supreme example of Abdalla's self-creation or self-presentation within the matrix of truth. The presentation of his ostensibly uncompromising position at once thematizes and politicizes the "truth" as he rails against the rulling elite in Kenya:

Walinena walimwengu, wa zama zilopisiye
Kwamba kweli i tungu, kwa yule aambiwaye
Nami haya ndugu yangu, sasa niyaaminiye
Asojua nasikiye, apeleleze ajuwe

Kweli naifahamu, haipendwi aswilani
Kwa mja hiyo ni sumu, mbaya iso kifani
Mwenye kuitakalamu, hapendezi katwani
Sasa nshayaamini, ni kweli haya ni kweli

Kweli imenitongeya, kwa kuinena mwendani
Wale nilowaambiya, wamenitiya dhikini
Wameniona mbaya, kumshinda Firauni
Kweli,sasa naamini, si wangi waipendao

Kweli naliwaambiya, wakuu wa nti hini
Haeleza moya moya, kwa wanati wa ntini
Kuhusu walofanyiya, upande wa Upinzani
Sasa kuwamo tabuni, nalipwa kwa hiyo kweli

Kweli lilipowatoma, kama dasturi yake
Wao wakaona vyema, afadhali wanishike
Wanishike hima hima, hima ndani waniweke
Ngomeni n'adhibike, nijute kusema kweli

Mno wanganiadhibu, adhabu kila namna
Na mangi yanganiswibu, ya usiku na mtana
Hayatakuwa sababu, ya kuniasa kunena
Kweli nitapoiyona, tanena siinyamai

Mateso yao yangawa, nda kuumiza mtima
Hayatakuwa ni dawa, ya kutonipa kusema
Ni bure wajisumbuwa, nilipo nnasimama
Si 'mi wa kurudi nyuma, kweli ilipo 'tasonga

Kweli naitiya tamma, nikuage ndugu yangu
Kweli si mwenye kukoma, kuwambiya walimwengu
Kweli si'yati kunena, katika uhai wangu
Nami kwa upande wangu, hi'yambiwa 'takubali

So said the people of the world, of times past
That truth is bitter, for the one being told
As for me, my comrades, I have come to believe so
May the one who does not know, seek to know

Truth is not at all palatable, this indeed I know
For man it is poisonous, dangerous beyond compare
Whoever says the truth, does not become popular at all
Now I believe this, it is indeed so

Truth has imperilled me, for speaking it, my friend
Those to whom I spoke, subject me to anguish
They view me as evil, more evil than Pharoah
Now I know the truth, is not loved by many

I spoke the truth, to the leaders of this country
I recounted one by one, to the citizens of this country
How they had been deprived, in their opposition ranks
Now being in trouble, is the price I am made to pay

When truth seared them, as it was wont to do
To arrest me, they deemed it fit
To arrest me speedily, to incarcerate me speedily
To make me suffer in the fort, so I may regret speaking the truth

However much they punish me, punishing me in whichever way
Whatever hardship I undergo, in daytime and night-time
I will not be dissuaded, I cling to my utterances
Whenever I see the truth, I will speak [it], I will not keep mum

Even if their torture, is heart-wrenching
It would not be the antidote, for stopping me from speaking
They are wasting their time, [as] I am immovable
I am not the sort that retreats, where the truth is that is where I go

Let me stop here on matters of truth, to bid you farewell brother
I will not stop telling the truth, to let the world know
I will not abandon the truth, in all my life
And I will accept the truth, when someone else tells me. (1-4)

The poem opens with reference to the ancient sages, who stated "kweli i tungu"/ 'truth is bitter.' Invoking the wisdom of *wahenga* or ancient sages is not uncommon among the Waswahili and most other African communities. This invocation is in effect a reference to a shared and common text from the collective linguistic and literary fund that is recognizable to a wide spectrum of East African Swahili speakers. Bakhtin's assertion that "the word in language is half someone else's" is proven here as Abdalla attributes the axiomatic statement to 'the people of times past' and puts the borrowed words to his own use (504). Quite appropriately Abdalla uses an archaic expression "wa zama zilopisiye"/ 'of times past' rather, than a more contemporary expression as "zama zilizopita," to at once ensure there is harmony in the metre and rhyme, with for instance the last word in each line in the stanza ending with the syllable 'ye,' and also to emphasize the antiquity of the sages and hence the depth of their wisdom and the veracity of their views. Abdalla makes a shrewd choice of words to reinforce his argument on the necessity and the hazards of speaking the truth.

These images (notwithstanding that they may be somewhat trite) target the sense of taste, compelling the reader to imagine or experience mentally the taste of bitterness and to envision the danger of truth as something with ominous fatal potentialities, namely poison, in the purview of those in power. In the sixth stanza the poet appeals to our sense of touch when he says "Kweli lilipowatoma, kama dasturi yake" / 'When the truth seared them, as it was wont to do', imbuing truth, like fire, with the burning or searing capability. In appealing to our sense of taste and touch, the poet reifies and concretizes an abstract a term as truth.

In this poem, Abdalla comes across as an inexorable purveyor and defender of the truth. As the voice of truth, the poet knows he must remain steadfast and unflinching in the wake of state repression. The final stanza is very emphatic on this, using the repetition of "kweli"/'truth' in every line to drive the point home. He is cognizant of the fact that the "[t]ruth is not at all palatable,'' and yet he is firm in his determination to speak it. The poem is quite explicit in pointing to those he told the truth; namely the Kenyan political leadership, and the Kenyan population.

Masking the Message

Yet, there are also instances in which Abdalla uses his poetic ability to do things with words that intentionally mask his message. One could add that whenever this masking occurs, the reader is hard pressed to untangle the truth of what the poet is doing with the words. This calls for delving beneath and behind the surface to decipher the underlying meaning(s) and implications. In such instances, the poet comes across as an astute riddle maker who cleverly metaphorizes human experience and challenges the audience to untangle the riddle. In this regard his poems serve multiple purposes including being; (1) interactive entertainment (e.g. crossword or jigsaw puzzles etc) which fully engages the intellect and attention of the audience for realization of the complete range of meaning; (2) a testament to the poet's creative ability and ingenuity; and (3) a decoy that may camouflage both the message and the intent of the poet. For Abdalla the third purpose of riddle making is especially important, given the prison environment in which he wrote and the prevailing curtailment of freedom of expression during the heyday of the Kenyatta presidency. Abdalla's poem "Mamba,"/ 'Crocodile' is a classic example of the use of metaphor as a stratagem for critiquing a regime he found wanting, immoral, and rotten.

However, the recourse to metaphor as a weapon of critique is hardly new across Africa. For instance, under the totalitarian rule of President Kamuzu Banda in Malawi, the country's poets Felix Mnthali, Frank Chipasula, Jack Mapanje, and Lupenga Mphande and others used metaphor as a weapon to undertake the hazardous task of criticizing the regime. As one report shows overt mention of the president and his cronies would have proved suicidal because it was common knowledge that Banda detained, assassinated, or fed to the crocodiles of Shire River any and all perceived critics of his rule. Therefore, the report, continues, many metaphors were developed to refer to the principal characters and issues in Malawian politics. For example, references to "dawn" or "cockerel" were metaphors for the Malawi Congress Party, whose flag contains a symbol of sunrise. President Banda proclaims "*Kwacha*" (dawn) at the beginning of all speeches and the kwacha and tambala (cockerel) are both the units of currency. "Chingwe's Hole," a cleft in the rock of the Zomba plateau is used to refer to detention.[5]

In harmony with the practice of using metaphor as a subtle tool for deconstructing and disrupting the status quo, Abdalla wrote:

Nami nambe, niwe kama waambao
Niupambe, upendeze wasomao
Niufumbe, wafumbuwe wawezao

Kuna mamba, mtoni metakabari
Ajigamba, na kujiona hodari
Yuwaamba, kwamba 'taishi dahari

Memughuri, ghururi za kipumbavu
Afikiri, hataishiwa na nguvu
Takaburi, hakika ni maangavu

Akumbuke, siku yake itafika
Roho yake, ajuwe itamtoka
Nguvu zake, kikomeche zitafika

Afahamu, mtu hajui la kesho
Hatadumu,angatumia vitisho
Maadamu, lenye mwanzo lina mwisho.

Let me also speak, so I can be like those who speak
Let me adorn the poem, and make it appealing to the readers
Let me compose a riddle, that those who can may untangle [it]

In the river there is a crocodile, highly conceited
He brags, and regards himself as invincible
He claims, he will live forever

He is a braggart, thumping his chest foolishly
He imagines, his might will not dissipate
For indeed pride, is before a fall

He should remember, when his day comes
He should know, his spirit will leave him
His might, will reach its end

Let him know, no one knows about tomorrow
He will not last forever, even if he uses threats
As what has a beginning, must also have an end. (10)

In this poem written in the *tathlitha* genre, (three lines in each stanza), Abdalla presents the riddle of a rapacious and supercilious reptile, the crocodile, deluding itself with the possession of an illusory and elusive immortality. He openly challenges the readers to unravel the riddle. The oral performance involving an artist presenting riddles (especially those with comparisons with animals) to audiences and challenging them to unravel them is not uncommon in the African oral tradition. It is instructive that in declaring his intention in the beginning of this poem, Abdalla uses the contraction of "niambe" namely "nambe" literally meaning "I speak" rather than "niandike"/ 'I write,' reflecting consciously or unconsciously the orality within which riddles are usually encoded and decoded. The relative brevity of the poem harmonizes with the nature of the genre of *mafumbo* in the Swahili oral tradition; just long enough to provide clues for the audience to respond to the conundrum. The power of riddles lies in their indirectness and the figurativeness. The power and beauty of metaphor is a distinguishing feature of riddles.[6]

On the surface the riddle in Abdalla's poem gives the impression of the simply ludic, even childish pastime. Yet unraveling the tenor represented by the vehicle "mamba'' or crocodile in this poem would hardly have been "pleasing" to the ruling regime in Kenya. Therefore, the poet's use of metaphor is a stratagem in which he assails Kenyatta's arrogant leadership and false sense of security and fake immortality. Kenyatta is the *mamba* or "crocodile" of Abdalla's cryptic poem.[7] The point of the poem, is that no matter how powerful Kenyatta may be and no matter how long he holds the reins of power, using or abusing his power to violate the human rights of countless subjects, there is bound to be an end to his rule and his life. Abdalla reminds Kenyatta that as a mortal man his time to expire must surely come, sooner or later.

Abdalla, yet again turns to the authority of the ancient sages and invokes a famous Swahili proverb "Hakuna lenye mwanzo lisilokuwa na mwisho"/ 'There is nothing with a beginning that has no end.' However, apparently, due to the dictates of metre and rhyme, the poet paraphrases the proverb and renders it as "lenye mwanzo lina mwisho"/ 'what has a beginning, must also have an end.' Although the received synctatic structure of the proverb is altered in the poem, the substance remains the same, i.e. it aptly carries the Swahili and Islamic worldview on transience or impermanence as quintessential attributes of human life on earth. The metric pattern in the poem is 4+8 with the second hemistiche seeming to at once complement and to respond to the first one in each line, evoking the enactment of a real exchange between the artist who presents a riddle and the audience which attempts to figure out the solution.

The four-syllable first hemistich is contrasted with the eight syllable second one, with the first one showing the reality of the shortness of human life, whereas the long one shows the appearance of longevity or eternity. Further, the overall brevity of the poem, apart from situating it within the tradition of performance of riddles, also accentuates the brevity of human life and the inevitability of death. In other words, Abdalla attempts to imagine the demise of Kenyatta, and the end of tyranny in Kenya. Thus the crocodile of Abdalla's poem is synonymous with what Achille Mbembe calls the "postcolonial potentate" or "postcolonial autocrat" who is blinded by a rather warped attitude toward mortality and his own subjectivity. As Mbembe argues, the autocrat's ostensibly absolute subjectivity is hallucinatory, fake and empty. Its facticity lies in caricature only: "The absolute does not exist in reality" (165). Given the autocrat's imagined and imaginary immortality and invincibility, it takes considerable courage for an imprisoned poet to even think about the autocrat's death; it is tantamount to imagining the unimaginable or thinking the unthinkable. As a matter of fact to have the audacious imagining of the crocodile's end or the President's death as Abdalla does in this prison poem was considered as treasonable at the time of its writing as the literal killing of the President. In a sense, therefore, Abdalla uses poetical words to "assassinate" the tyrant and perhaps gets away with such an audacious action. It goes without saying that artistic taunting and imaginary killing of Kenyatta the postcolonial potentate, is made possible by what words at the disposal of a consummate wordsmith can do in spite of or because of the actuality of incarceration.

This bold poem at once aptly represents Abdalla's angst and anger and anticipates Kenyatta's death, an eventuality that came to pass on 22 August 1978, eight years after the poem was written. It signifies the "killing" of Kenyatta before his actual death. The thrust of the poem also recalls the rise and fall of the Pate dynasty on the Kenyan coast as captured by Sayyid Abdallah Ali bin Nasir in his classical *utendi* (long narrative poem) titled *Inkishafi* (Revelation) in which the ruling elite are depicted as having lolled in luxury and pomp but ultimately expired and were interred and forgotten. "Mamba" is therefore the apogee of Abdalla's iconoclastic outlook on Kenyatta's rule. Following Mbembe's characterization of the representation of the autocrat in popular culture, it is appropriate to conclude that Abdalla wrests "from the state the power to represent itself and to publicly exhibit the autocrat" (160). In the Kenyan case Kenyatta was the autocrat. Abdalla makes words to "publicly exhibit the autocrat" as a beastly mortal capable of dying like the victims of his tyranny. The poet therefore demonstrates that he did not have the fear and inhibition that plagued even the bravest critics at the time.[8] It could then be said the question Kunle Ajibade, the

Nigerian prison diarist raises; "[C]an words alone bring down the tyrant?" could be answered in the affirmative, at least figuratively (87). In other words, the poet's words brought down the tyrant when the poem was penned in 1970.

A Range of Miscellaneous Voices

Nonetheless, the fact that the voices of dissidence suffuse Abdalla's collection of poems does not preclude the presence of other voices with which the poet speaks or imagines and represents his various real and imagined selves. Doubt and didacticism, for example, seem to be strange bedfellows, but in Abdalla's poetry they go hand in hand. This synthesis of points of view that seem antithetical to each other recalls Bakhtin's proposition that an individual does not have one single point of view, but he or she inhabits multiple "worldviews" through the various social discourses he or she speaks (450). As mentioned earlier Abdalla's marriage of art and activism lends itself to arousing the readers to action. It is therefore in harmony with this rabble-rousing stance that we encounter poems calling upon the masses to awaken from their slumber and to act against tyranny, such as in "Wasafiri Tuamkeni,"/ 'Travelers, Let us Arise,' "Zindukani"/ 'Wake Up!' "Jana na Leo na Kesho,"/ 'Yesterday and Today and Tomorrow,' "Semani wenye Kusema,"/ 'Speak those who can,' and "Kokoiko!" whose onomatopeic filiation to the crowing of a rooster renders it almost untranslatable.

Chacha Nyaigoti Chacha describes Abdalla's *Sauti ya Dhiki* as a collection of poems aimed at "kufundisha umma wa ulimwengu wa tatu"/ 'teaching the third world public' (65). Yet a closer examination of the poems betrays the poet's intermittent feelings of inadequacy, such as in "Telezi,"/ 'Slipperiness' "Wasiwasi Enda Zako,"/ Dread, Go Away' "Moyo Iwa na Subira,"/ 'Oh! Heart, be Patient' and "Njia Panda"/ 'Crossroads.' In what follows, I argue that Abdalla's didacticism contrasts with his expressions of doubt to create voice diversity or polyphony that undergirds the writing of his poetry.

Abdalla is averse to figurative slumber, which can be interpreted to mean acquiescence and quiet acceptance of totalitarianism. In a number of verses he calls on the public to awaken from this state of acquiescence and confront their own destiny. In typical didactic fashion he says in "Kokoiko!"

Kokoiko! Kokoiko! Awika jimbi awika
Vitandani muliyoko, namuanze kurauka
Asoitika mwito, atachelewa kufika
Yule aliyekutwika, ndiye atayekutuwa

Kokoiko! Kokoiko! The rooster is crowing
Those of you sleeping, start getting up quick
The one not heeding the cockerel, will be late

The one who put the load upon you, is the one who will unload it from you. (64)
As hinted earlier "Kokoiko! Kokoiko!" is onomatopeic imitation of the crowing of a rooster. Perhaps it is Abdalla's infusion of such dramatic effects in his poetry that impelled Ohly to make the rather extravagant remark that "Abdilatif is attracted by the theatre" (88). Needless to say in this poem we hear the voice of a rooster, a non-human entity acting out in the human drama. Reading polyphony in

the imitation of crowing in the poem should not be perceived as ascribing undue significance to a tangential detail of the poem. But it should be borne in mind that the crowing of the rooster signifies that the time has come to wake up and to act, "Vitandani muliyoko, namuanze kuamka"/ 'Those of you sleeping, start getting up quick time for action.'' It is therefore quite apparent that the philosophy actuating Abdalla's poetry privileges the dynamism of political activism rather than the statis of acquiescence.

Despite Abdalla's outright militancy and iconoclastic writing, as a prisoner of conscience he could not help but engage in soul-searching. Chacha alludes to this internal conflict when he discusses what he calls the poet's "mjadala na nafsi"/ 'dialogue with his soul' (66). *Sauti ya Dhiki* is not then merely a testament to the poet's venting of his anger at the jaded political landscape, economic disparity, human rights abuses, and bad governance; it accords him an opportunity to scrutinize himself critically. Whereas there is no doubt about Abdalla's commitment to political engagement and the struggle for change in Kenya, there are poems in the anthology that show moments of vicious self-blame and self-doubt that this self-scrutiny engenders. For instance, in the poem "Telezi"/ 'Slipperiness,' the poet interrogates, not his role in the struggle but his approach. He writes:

Japo hivyo zilikuwa, ndiya hazipitiki
Bali mimi haamuwa, kwenenda japo kwa dhiki
Kumbe vile nitakuwa, mfano wa samaki
Ni mfano wa samaki, kuiendeya ndowana

Zikanibwaga telezi, sikujuwa kuzendeya
Ningekwenda kwa henezi, yasingenifika haya
Lakini tena siwezi, mwenendo huu kutumiya
Sitawata kutembea, ila tabadili mwendo

Though that is how the paths were, they were impassable
Yet I decided to proceed, despite the hardships
Little did I know, I will be like a fish
Like a fish, taking itself to the hook

I fell on slippery ground, I did not know how to walk on it
I should have been more cautious, to avoid whatever befell me
But I will not ever again, walk in that fashion
Though I will not stop walking, I will change my approach. (23)

In the poem, Abdalla likens himself to "samaki"/ 'a fish' that foolishly lets itself to the hook, oblivious of the danger the hook poses to its survival. This is a self-deprecating image that exhibits the poet's awareness of his folly, but awareness that only surfaces after the harm is already done. So in this poem we witness the voice of regret and self-blame, underscoring the multiple voices with which Abdalla presents his poems. In this instance it has dawned on the poet that his approach was somewhat imprudent and flawed. Abdalla arrives at the moment of what Ioan Davies describes as the "reformulation of [revolutionary] ideas in such a way that they [would have] profound implications for the direction of the political movement" (54). It would seem self-interrogation then becomes a necessary step for the incarcerated poet to recreate his uncreated world, to make sense of his incarceration and remake his shattered world.

Embedded in this poem therefore, is also a heavy sense of regret for trusting the wrong person and trusting too much. He had learned his lesson as the poem shows, so that he expresses his intent to change the "approach," rather than completely abandon the journey.

The Journey Motif

At this point it is perhaps appropriate to examine further the preponderant metaphor of the journey in Abdalla's poetry. In other words, one of the things the poet does with poetical words is to traverse any number of stages in his psychic journey, stages that readers may subsequently map out. The journey as a metaphor is particularly exemplified in the poems "Ndiya Panda"/'Crossroads' and "Wasafiri Tuamkeni"/ 'Let Us Arise, Travelers.' Needless to say, the metaphor emanates from the recurrent journey motif in both religious and secular literature. For example, the Qu'ran contains journeys made by Prophet Muhammed, and shares core aspects of the journeys made by Jewish patriarchs Abraham and Moses. Regarding the journey metaphor and the Bible, Floyd V. Filson observes that "the journey narrative is one of the dominant literary patterns of the Biblical story" spanning from the nomadic wanderings of the patriarchs from Ur to Haran to the missionary journeys of the apostles (68). In both the secular and spiritual spheres, many are the times when life itself is perceived as a journey. But it is probably the journey or pathway to just a world—as Mari J. Matsuda would put it—that should be given primacy in an explication of these poems since this is Abdalla's principal preoccupation in his art and activism (8).

In utilizing the journey as metaphor Abdalla's poetry lends itself to intertextuality and thus speaks to Bakhtin's concept of dialogism. In other words as Bakhtin postulates with regard to the novel, there is, in Abdalla's poetry, the tendency for borrowing utterances from others and infusing whatever is borrowed with one's own idiosyncrasies. Further, the echoes of Abdalla's own poems can be discerned in the subsequent poems of other poets. In line with Kimani Njogu, I reiterate yet again that dialogism and heteroglossia (linguistic variability) are not limited to the genre of the novel merely on the basis of what Dorothy Hale describes as the novel's "generic promiscuity" in her explication of Bakhtin's social and linguistic theory (449). It may well be that dialogism itself exhibits a certain level of "promiscuity" that makes it applicable beyond the novel.

In the poem "Ndia Panda"/ ' Cross Roads' Abdalla expresses his dilemma of choice and indecision as he faces the challenge of which way to go in the journey. The voice we hear is that of a desperate and lost traveler as the excerpt below demonstrates:

Safari naloiyanza, bado ningalimo kwenda
Sitawata kujikaza, isipate kunishinda
Nataka kuimaliza, ndivyo nipendavyo tenda
Sasa niko njia panda

Ilipofika safari, silijuwi la kutenda

Nimekwisha kufikiri, lakini limenishinda
Nawatakanyi shauri, nijuwe ndia ya kwenda
Mojawapo ya ndiya panda

I am still on the journey, the journey I began
I will not relax, so as not to be vanquished
I want to stay the course, that is what I want to do
Now I am at a crossroads

When the journey began, I had no idea what to do
I have pondered about it, but I find no answers
I implore you for guidance, so I can know where to go
Which one of the crossroads [to take]. (79-80)

This poem is an index of the incarcerated poet's crisis of confidence. In the line "Nimekwisha kufikiri, lakini limenishinda,"/ 'I have thought about it, but I find no answers,' the poet concedes that as a traveler he is unable to successfully navigate the place and space that the journey demands of him. Determined to stay the course, Abdalla seeks for the readers' help to navigate his way in the labyrinthine journey with the words "Nawatakanyi shauri, nijuwe ndia ya kwenda" / 'I implore you [in plural] for guidance, so I can know where to go.' The title "Njia Panda"/ ' Crossroads' is a fitting image of a tortured and divided self. This voice of hesitation, indecisiveness, and self-doubt is another of the multiplicity of voices that emerge in *Sauti ya Dhiki*.

Voice of the Unborn

The poem "Usiniuwe"/ 'Don't Kill Me' (51) in which the poet adopts the voice of a foetus to accomplish certain things with words merits some consideration. A superficial reading of the poem would see it, as most critics have, as protest against abortion, as the narrating and narrated "I" is a foetus pleading with the mother to spare his or her life. The questions to ask are: Why should a political prisoner write about abortion? Why does he use words to impersonate an innocent foetus facing imminent extermination? There could be any number of answers to these questions. But to me it is the prisoner's quest for a kind of solidarity with the foetus that is the conscious or unconscious impetus behind this poem. I find striking resemblances between the unborn threatened with abortion and the incarcerated; they are both confined for given terms in their "prisons"; they are both helpless, and unloved. In a way the political prisoner regards himself as innocent as the fetus at the mother's mercy. I tend to think the womb in Abdalla's poem symbolizes prison while the mother symbolizes the imprisoning, human rights violating, and loveless state. In the 18th stanza the persona states:

Sitakosa mlimwengu, ambaye atanileya
Anionee utungu, kama tulo damu moya
Si kama wewe mama, usonisikitikiya
Nasikiza ombi langu, mamangu nihurumiya

I won't lack someone, who will take care of me

> Someone who will empathize with me, like a blood relative
> Unlike you mother, who feels no compassion for me
> Listen to my pleas, be merciful to me mother. (53)

Therefore, the foetus recognizes the mother's callous and heartless attitude and hopes to find mothering and nurturing elsewhere. The mother's callousness is analogous to the callousness of the Kenyan state under Kenyatta, which had little regard for prisoners of conscience such as Abdalla who, like the fetus, regarded himself as "innocent." The recourse to or desire for compassionate nurturing from a surrogate mother elsewhere is a symbol, I think, of the poet's propulsion towards exile as an antidote to the tyranny in his "unmotherly" mother country. Thus, the poem points to the extent to which Abdalla knowingly or unknowingly binds himself up in a strong bond of solidarity with other political activists for whom exile is an expedient option to initial or further imprisonment or something worse like assassination. The prescience embedded in the poem should not be overlooked. It is a fact that since his release from prison in the early 1970s Abdalla has been living in exile, in Tanzania and in United Kingdom and, at the time of this writing, in Germany. The countries of his exile have served as surrogate mothers in the wake of the lack of figurative maternal love from his native Kenya. It is reasonable to speculate that in pleading "Usiniuwe!"/'Don't Kill me!" Abdalla was meditating on the possibility of his political assassination by agents of the Kenyan government. The thought or memory of death or being killed pervades his poetry and underlines the trauma of incarceration (e.g. see "N'shishiyelo ni Lilo" (1); "Mamba" (10); "Muosheni" (75); and "Leo N'singekuwako".

Yet it is the individual memory of his experience within the collective memory of his coastal people and Kenyans at large that Abdalla would like to situate the record of his incarceration or more accurately the record of his affective response to incarceration. Clearly, Abdalla essentially sets out to etch his poetry in the wide collective memory, carving out for himself an enduring public monument. *Sauti ya Dhiki* then, embodies a private and public memory tied up together. Written under incarceration and surveillance against a system that imprisoned him for his writing in the first place makes Abdalla's *Sauti ya Dhiki* one of the bravest and most vocal voices of protest against despotism to come from Kenyan prisons. Abdalla marries art and activism, lending his poetry a political engagement that is laced with multifarious voices. It is clearly evident he is one of the writers who Ioan Davis describes as "dedicated to transforming a system which they believe is corrupt and immoral and to speaking the truth as they see it" (31). Already a poet prior to his incarceration, Abdilatif Abdalla captures his affective responses to the ontological and existential reality of the debilitating conditions without losing sight of the writing in prison as a daring act of recalcitrant defiance; or, put differently, a bold reaction to the imprisoning action of the postcolonial potentate. And in reading his prison poetry we embark on an exploration or mapping of his psychic journey as we "listen" to his articulation of a wide spectrum of voices whose fulcrum is the denunciation of the postcolonial autocrat. The multiple voices do things with poetical words that not only help remake the prisoner's unmade world but also undo the world of the imprisoning state apparatuses. Emerging from prison as a site for writing, *Sauti ya Dhiki* is, therefore, a supreme example of how prison literature can and does counter-hegemonic things with words.

Chapter 5: The Quest for the Right To Be Human in Prison Poetry

> The question remains for us to see in what ways postcolonial Africa continues to be complicit in a prison experiment that uses a logic of revenge, and does little to restore hope or humanity.
>
> —Mechthild Nagel, "I Write What I Like"

This chapter is a meditation on a poetics and a politics of pain and relief in Alamin Mazrui's prison poems titled *Chembe cha Moyo* (1988), (Arrow-head in my Heart). If the poems in *Chembe cha Moyo* capture the anguished perception of tragedy and trauma that detention signified for Mazrui, it also underlines the love-hate relationship between the poet and his Kenyan state. Like Abdilatif Abdalla's *Sauti ya Dhiki* (1973), *Chembe cha Moyo* as a text is centrally situated within the context of incarceration and political struggle for change. *Sauti ya Dhiki* and *Chembe cha Moyo* are both collections of prison poems that essentially grapple with issues of personal and collective dignity and freedom in the wake of human rights abuses, despotism and decay in the postcolonial or neocolonial moment. They represent rare collections of poems in Kiswahili that have emerged from prison in the colonial and post-independence period. Abdalla wrote *Sauti ya Dhiki* in prison while serving a jail term for sedition in the Kenyatta era in the late 1960s and early 1970s while Mazrui wrote the play *Shadows of the Moon* (1991) and *Chembe cha Moyo* (to which this chapter now focuses) while he was locked up as a political detainee in the Moi era in the 1980s.

By the time of his detention, Mazrui had already burst onto the Kenyan literary scene in a powerful way. His literary oeuvre had begun with *Kilio cha Haki,* a pre-detention play that placed him among the leading East African playwrights, principally because of its superior aesthetics and anti-capitalist stance. The publication of *Kilio cha Haki* would become both a blessing and a curse; imprinting indelibly Mazrui's name in the canon of Swahili literature and rising the ire and mire of the paranoid Moi regime. Moi's attitude and actions towards talented intellectuals like Mazrui is almost an exact replica of King Mringwari's raging paranoia towards Liyongo's extraordinary talent and growing fame (see Chapter 1). One could say Mazrui's detention seems to have been essentially linked to the regime's displeasure with the publication and popularity of *Kilio cha Haki.*

Mazrui's poetry of incarceration *Chembe cha Moyo* has not elicited as much critical attention as his pre-incarceration play *Kilio cha Haki.* Critical responses to *Chembe cha Moyo* are few and far between. Critics who have analyzed it such as K. W. Wamitila in *Uhakiki wa Fasihi* (2001), Kimani Njogu and Rocha Chimera in *Ufundishaji wa Fasihi* (1997), and Florence Ngesa Indede in "Mabadiliko katika Umbo la Kiswahili na Athari zake katika Ushairi wa Kiswahili"(2008), tend to concentrate on the stylistic and linguistic elements and do not attend at all or enough to the context and themes of the text.

This chapter intends to bring to the fore not only Mazrui's thematic preoccupations, but also the ethos underlying his prison poetry in *Chembe cha Moyo* in contrast to Abdalla's *Sauti ya Dhiki.* Among the questions I examine are: What is the connection between the text of Mazrui's poems and the detention context within which they were written? How and to what extent does he thematize truth? What is the place or role of the "I" pronoun in Mazrui's poetic world? Does the "I" enter the stage in multiple guises as expressions of the poet's various ways of self-narration? How is the "I" related to the "we" of the collective identity? The study also addresses the questions of trauma as they are related to the text and context of the carceral imagination and experience.

Alamin Mazrui was born on March 10, 1948 in Lamu, on the Kenyan coast. As his last names suggests, he belongs to the famous Mazrui family, once a powerful dynasty that has had tremendous influence on the cultural and political history of the Kenyan coast. He was born and bred in a highly religious milieu. His father was the Kenyan Chief Kadhi in the 1960s and so was his grandfather before him. But young Mazrui's calling was never to be one in the religious realm of his father and grandfather. He was to take after his uncle Professor Ali Mazrui, who blazed the trail in secular education and has attained iconic stature, as exemplified by his being named one of the top hundred public intellectuals of modern times.[1] Alamin Mazrui's academic journey began at Kizingo Primary School, then Khamisi High School where he completed his A-Level education in 1968. After a brief stint as a chemist for STS, a chemical testing firm in Mombasa, Mazrui moved to the United States for higher education. He joined Rutgers, State University of New Jersey, where he obtained a Bachelor of Science degree. But he later pulled out of a Master's Degree in Food Science at Rutgers after developing asthmatic complications that hindered his participation in laboratory sessions. He was subsequently forced to make a drastic shift in his academic career by taking a Master of Art degree in Applied Linguistics. He later joined Stanford University from where he graduated with a PhD in Linguistics in 1980.

He was teaching at the Kenyatta University in Nairobi, Kenya and served as the university's representative in the University Academic Union (UAU) at the time of his detention in 1983. Like Abdalla, Ngugi, and Micere Mugo, and other so-called dissident intellectuals, Mazrui found Kenya under Moi uninhabitable and was forced into exile after his release from detention in May 1984. After a brief teaching stint at Port Harcourt University in Nigeria he moved to The Ohio State University in the United States where he was between 1989 and 2007. At the time of this writing he teaches at his *alma mater* Rutgers, State University of New Jersey.

Njuguna Mutahi and Mugo Theuri state in *We Lived to Tell* that when Moi ascended to power in 1978 he vowed to follow closely in his mentor's footsteps, hence his *Fuata Nyayo* (follow the footsteps) clarion call"(1). When Moi released Ngugi wa Thiong'o, Adam Mathenge, and Martin Shikuku who Kenyatta had detained, it almost looked like he was contradicting his promise to follow his predecessor's path of tyranny, suppression, and human rights violations. But the veneer of populism in the nascent Moi regime waned fast. Moi started a spirited campaign to ban numerous organizations such as the Kenya Civil Servants' Union, Students Organisation of the University of Nairobi (SONU), and Universities' Academic Union (UAU) to which Mazrui was an official. Hot on the heels of this ban of organizations was the return of detention without trial.

Mazrui was dragged from the classroom in March 1983 during the first round of detentions in the Moi era under the Prevention of Public Security Act, Cap.57 of the Laws of Kenya. He joined the long list of officials of the newly proscribed university faculty union who were detained such as Dr. Willy Mutunga, Kamoji Wachira, Prof. Edward Oyugi, Maina Kinyatti, and Mukaru Ng'ang'a.[2]

Where and Why?

One of the most salient aspects of *Chembe cha Moyo* is the apparent silence in the blurb and in the introduction on detention as the place of writing. The blurb vaguely dwells on generalities, merely stating that "*Chembe cha Moyo* ni mkusanyiko wa mashairi yenye mdundo wa kisasa kututongolea hisia za ndani zinazotokana na mazingira mapya katika mataifa ya Ulimwengu wa Tatu."/ '*Chembe cha Moyo* is an anthology of poems with a modern resonance revealing inner feelings that emerge from a new environment in the Third World nations.' Either the blurb does not say whose "inner feelings" are at stake or it presumes that those feelings are typical of all individuals in the Third World! Neither does it account for the presumed newness of the environment in the Third World. This calls to mind Chacha Nyaigoti Chacha's characterization of Abdilatif Abdalla's *Sauti ya Dhiki* as an indictment of misrule in the Third World in general without as much as attempting to allude to the specificity of the Kenyan situation. I want to argue that in the context of literature of resistance and the turbulent 1970s and 1980s in Kenya both Chacha and the blurb writer were probably using Third World as shorthand for Kenya.[3]

The loudness of the silence regarding the "Where" of *Chembe cha Moyo* writing is accentuated by the militant tone of the poems in the collection, which pull no punches about where they were written. Yet it is difficult to surmise the "Why" of the writing of *Chembe cha Moyo* without also unearthing the "Where" of its being written. It is, I think, in unraveling the connection between where and why that we can come close to fully understanding the interplay between context and text in Mazrui's poetry. Mazrui has disclosed that he had indeed discussed unequivocally the question of why and where in his original introduction of the anthology.[4] Nonetheless, fearing that such candid revelation would short-circuit the book's distribution and sales, the editorial team at the Nairobi office of Heinmann publishers decided to elide it altogether. The introduction that remained in the published version is, therefore, a mutilated vestige of the original manuscript, dwelling as it does on the "safe" stylistics and aesthetics of Swahili poetry in general and making no mention about why and where Mazrui wrote his collection of poems.

This apparent reticence contrasts starkly with Abdalla's preface in *Sauti ya Dhiki* in which he mentions that he wrote the poems as a prisoner jailed for sedition. Although we can characterize Abdalla's explanations for writing as rather nebulous and imprecise, the candor in the paratext is self-evident. What accounts for this difference? For one thing Abdalla and Mazrui were incarcerated and wrote and published under different circumstances. It should be noted that Abdalla's editor at Oxford University Press was his own brother Abdillahi Nassir and therefore perhaps hardly a disinterested participant in presenting the context of and site for the writing of his brother's poems. But more significantly, it would seem, the attack on books, writers, and intellectuals was presumably much more pronounced in the Moi regime under which Mazrui's *Chembe cha Moyo* emerged. Thus, while as a writer Mazrui may not have been afraid of revealing detention as the site for writing, his publisher was much less inclined to risk the ire and mire of the Moi terror machine. The publisher seems to have reckoned that he had taken some risk already in publishing the poems in the first place, and was able but unwilling to go any further.

However, although the peritext succumbs to the culture of silence that the Moi regime perpetuated and perfected, it is still not impossible to speculate about the motivation for Mazrui's poems. For one thing the bulk of the poems are preoccupied with incarceration with some of them being quite explicit in this regard. The first poem "Niguse"/ 'Touch Me' is a case in point.

Nitokapo Kizuizini
Nitamwomba yeyote mwendani
aniguse
taratibu
pole pole
lakini
kwa yakini

Niguse tena
Unijuze tena
Unifunze tena
maisha yalivyo
maisha yaonjavyo
ladha yake ilivyo

Nipo hapa nimekukabili
Niguse tena tafadhali
Niguse!
Niguse!

When I come out of Detention
I will beseech any of my beloved ones
to touch me
softly

slowly
but
surely

Touch me once again
Let me know once again
Instruct me anew
about how life is
about how life tastes
the taste of life

Here I am facing you
Please touch me once again
Touch me!
Touch me! (1)

From the very first line of the first poem, Mazrui foregrounds the reality of incarceration, alluding to the moment "Nitokapo Kizuizini"/ 'When I come out of detention." The plea "Niguse" in the title and that is repeated throughout the poem underscores the deprivation of human contact, human rights in general and in particular, the denial of human touch that the speaker in the poem has experienced in the detention. The plea is indicative of the speaker's desperate yearning for the human touch and contact, literally and figuratively, and envisions the momentous and joyous moment of release that would make such contact both possible and probable. The reference to "Kizuizini"/ 'Detention' is overt not tacit, amplified as it were, with the upper case initial "K". And yet this allusion to the condition of detention in particular and incarceration in general is not isolated but indeed suffuses *Chembe cha Moyo* far too much to assume that it is accidental.

Since the silence on the facticity of detention in the introduction and blurb deprive us of potentially useful tips as to the motivation for writing, we are left to speculate from what we can glean from the poems themselves. Thankfully, the poems do not disappoint as such in this regard, as "Niguse" illustrates. Other poems that explicitly mention or thematize incarceration include; "Kifungoni"/ 'Incarceration' (14); "Kizuizini"/ 'Detention (27); "Nayeyusha Pingu"/ 'I am Melting Handcuffs' (33); and "Hakuna Yeyote"/ 'Alone' (40). Mazrui wrote both *Shadows of the Moon* and *Chembe cha Moyo* under the depressing conditions of detention and against the wish of the prison authorities. Prison generally tends to be anti-books and anti-writers. As Mechthild Nagel cogently notes, religious books such as the Bible seem to be the only "innocuous" texts one is allowed to access while behind the bars.[5] Prison, like the boarding houses across most of Sub-Saharan Africa, is home to dog-eared copies of the Bible, presumably reminding inmates of their sinfulness and/or their proximity to sin as well as their need to make peace with their Maker. One could argue that for the political prisoner the presence of the Bible in the cell is an implicit message that by sinning against the state he or she sinned against God and should therefore make amends.

That is not to suggest that prisoners find the religious text antithetical to their ideals. As Ethiopian political prisoner Taffara Deguefe's prison diary *A Tripping Stone: Ethiopian Prison Diary* illustrates, the prisoner's quest for solace from religious texts and tenets is sometimes integral to maintaining sanity or coping with the trauma of incarceration. In his diary Deguefe repeatedly recounts how a pattern of prayer and sermons sustained him and other believing detainees in the early 1970s after the fall of Ethiopian Emperor Haile Selassie. In his diary *Detained*, Ngugi too records how religiously inclined fellow detainees turned to religious activities as a means of coping with the trauma of incarceration.[6]

If the presence of the Bible was meant to woo Mazrui towards a spirit of repentance and contrition, to lead him towards submission to secular authorities, it perhaps achieved little or nothing in this regard. And yet the Bible made possible Mazrui's search for solace in ways that the prison authorities least expected or desired. Mazrui was least interested in simply reading and imbibing the wisdom of the Bible; instead he used the margins of the Bible that he was given by the prison authorities to scribble his poems and play. Also, he had to resort to stealing pens from prison warders and once from a pilot, to be able to write. On the whole the write-and-hide game he had to play indicates that it needed more than the simple will to write to be able to write under prison conditions.

Writing then appears to have been a compulsion, something that needed to be done in spite of or because of the prevailing anti-writing detention surroundings. In answering the question concerning the "where" of the writing, one should take into account the fact that the locale was the most unlikely. So why write from such an unlikely locale? As the title of this chapter suggests, I think seeking solace in writing was an important motivation for Mazrui's prison writing. The therapeutic properties of writing seem to play a crucially important role in the writer's motivation, particularly in the genre of poetry that lends itself towards free release of pent up feelings and emotions. But this self-expression also enables and enhances self-narration, albeit in the somewhat incoherent and circuitous poetic form. This brings us to the grammatical "I" of Mazrui's *Chembe cha Moyo*.

I contend that there are multiple "I"-s in Mazrui's prison poetry that reflect and refract the poet's self and reality as a real historical person detained for political reasons. Or perhaps to put it more accurately these "I"-s project the poet's wide spectrum of invented selves. They range from the optimistic to the nihilistic, from militant to the resigned, from the devout to the almost irreligious, from confident to the doubting, from the cultural nationalist to the Pan-Africanist, etc. In "Niguse," the "I" refers to an incarcerated but yet optimistic self. There is optimism, if cautious optimism, because the yearned for desire for the authentic human interaction is now more than just a remote possibility due to the apparent prospect of freedom. In this opening poem, Mazrui presents a self that needs to learn to be human again as the second stanza suggests:

Niguse tena
Unijuze tena
Unifunze tena
maisha yalivyo
maisha yaonjavyo
ladha yake ilivyo

Touch me once again

Let me know once again
Instruct me anew
about how life is
about how life tastes
the taste of life

This is an "I" whose selfhood hangs on to a receding sense of *being* but which takes refuge in the knowledge of the real possibility of *becoming* human again, of belonging yet again in the human fold, of enjoying one's unalienable human rights once more. Through the desperate tone of the narrating and narrated "I" Mazrui compellingly reveals how life in detention and outside detention is worlds apart. The experience in detention has almost erased the speaker's memory of what it means to be free outside the prison walls. His experience is similar to that of Moroccan political prisoner Abdellatif Laabi whose prison memoir, *Le chemin des ordalies,* demonstrates the extent to which the "spatial configuration of the prison yard itself affects the narrator [Laabi] to his very core. It affects his physical relationship to the world around him.... Again the moment of release is both a time to rejoice, and a time of trepidation; it is a move from the known to the unknown" (Elinson, 294). For the incarcerated inured to being treated as non-human, release signifies a new learning experience in the business of normal human existence. Indeed incarceration had taught Mazrui to forget what it meant to be truly a free human agent. Clearly, by using the "I" in transition from non-being to human being, the poem reveals profoundly the magnitude of dehumanization that detention may wrought on individuals.

The same sense of cautious optimism is expressed in the poem "Nitangojea"/ 'I will Wait" (8) in which the narrating "I" projects itself as exercising patience and looking forward to reunion with a beloved one. Yet expressing or representing oneself in terms of the possibility of release and relief in the foreseeable future despite the present moment of crisis, accords with the search for refuge in poetry that underwrites the ebb and flow of *Chembe cha Moyo*.

Dissipation and Disappearance of Hope

But the optimistic "I" is sometimes replaced by a doubtful, even a nihilistic "I" in the range of poems in the anthology. In "Mtabiri"/ 'Seer' (52) one encounters an "I" presenting itself as a prophet of doom bereft of any iota of hope for a better future.

The speaker in the poem predicts assertively:

sauti tishi zimenijia
kusudi kunitabiria
hatari zilotukalia
na kutukamia

fearful voices have come to me
warning me of what is yet to come
about the danger we are bound to face
dangers that are about to engulf us. (52)

The narrator then lists a host of oddities that according to his predictions are set to occur (e.g. a female goat bearing through the mouth a grotesque offspring that is neither completely goat nor sheep; a human mother giving birth to a deformed child with a wound in place of the eyes; and the human population being pounded by the "mvua ya mauti"/ "rain of death" etc.) The speaker concludes by suggesting that the upheaval in the system of things shakes even angelic hordes:

Ndimi mtabiri
Mwona Mbali
Nami naogopa

I am the prophet
The far-sighted one
And I am fearful. (53)

It is possible to perceive this tremor or transformation of the social equilibrium as an emblem of social revolution, the kind envisioned by political activists who are not contented with folding arms and watching their societies crumble under tyranny and misrule. The leftist ideology that underpins Mazrui's entire literary output in general seems to lend credence to this supposition. However, the grotesque and unattractive images of the changes that ensue undercut the possibility of the prediction of an expedient revolution whose outcome is positive change. The speaking self in the poem is overwhelmed with fear, ending the poem with little or no hope of a bright future as the lines "Naogopa"/ 'I am fearful' clearly indicate.

If in "Mtabiri" the poet predicts impending doom and gloom in the not-distant future, he is not any more sanguine in his estimation of the present in "Mashindano"/ 'Contest'. The poem opens with the persona describing a tireless porter toiling to fend for himself and countless dependants:

Nimuonapo hamali mwenye tumbi ya midomo
yote yataka kulishwa
Huona mja asukumaye jabali liso kikomo
juu ya mlima usokwisha
Kwa kujikaza hulisogeza kidogo
Shubiri baada ya shubiri ilonyumbuka
Na chini ya kivuli cha huu mzigo
Humwona amejikita kwa tambo liloumbuka

Mishipa huvimba na kuiva rangi
Damu ikakimbilia usoni kwa wingi
sasa akishindwa
sasa akishinda
akishindilia vidole katika ardhi yenye mashaza
kimya kimetanda
roho inampaa
moyo ukimdunda
Katika muda huu wa hatari
muda wa kifo na nusuri

Ole wangu wee! ...
jabali hili litamshinda huyu mpweke
limvuruge chini ya nguvu zake
likititimka kurudia kwenye kiza cha mauti?
Kimya... mashindano yaendelea
ya wawili katika ndoto

Whenever I see a porter with many mouths
All needing to be fed
I behold a person heaving a limitless boulder
Towards a limitless mountain
He exerts himself to move it a little bit
Inch by inch he moves it
And in the shadow of this burden
I behold him standing erect with a disfigured figure
Veins swell and his color darkens
Blood rushes to the face
Now he wins
Now he loses
He digs his finger into the shell covered soil
There is quiet everywhere
He is distraught
His heart pounds
At this perilous moment
The moment of life and death.
Oh! Woe unto me! ...
Will this boulder conquer this loner
Will it crash him under with its might
As it tumbles back to the darkness of death?
Silence ... the contest continues
between the two in the dream. (31)

It is the risk, danger, and futility of the porter's onerous task of moving a huge boulder uphill that the persona foregrounds. And yet the porter is undeterred in doing the impossible and perhaps profitless job of heaving the boulder uphill; he is impelled by the plight of the countless mouths that depend on him for food. The narrator poses the disturbing question; Will the boulder crash the porter to death? If the question appearing at the end of the poem remains unanswered it also diminishes the need for the question of wages that may accrue from the task. In other words the possibility of death supersedes the issue of whether or not the porter gets paid or not. Clearly, in "Mashindano"/ 'Contest' (31) the poet reenacts the Greek narrative of Sisyphus who continually rolls a boulder up the hill only for the boulder to come down tumbling. Although the speaker in the poem alludes to a third person struggling to heave the rock up an endless hill, one is bound to discern that the person in question is indeed the narrating self from the line "Ole wangu wee!"/'Oh! Woe unto me!' in the final stanza. Also, although the rock is not directly said to be rolling back in "Mashindano," the sense of futility that pervades the poem suggests such possibility.

It is tempting to read this poem as being primarily concerned with the economic imperative, to interpret it as a classic case of a hardworking porter trying to make ends meet in a thankless economic system that has perfected depriving and denying workers. Given Mazrui's leftist orientation, such interpretation may seem plausible. While not altogether discounting the plausibility of such an interpretation, I think, being attentive to the context of the poem points towards Mazrui himself as the porter and hence suggesting that the task of heaving the stone uphill symbolizes activism against the Moi regime. As Ioan Davies has aptly argued incarceration allows for self-scrutiny for the revolutionary, enabling him or her to take stock of their individual role in particular and the general direction of the struggle.[7] Like Abdalla's poem "Telezi" in which he admits being initially tactless in the struggle against the Kenyatta regime in Kenya, Mazrui seems to acknowledge the enormity of the task at hand. In this poem Mazrui creates a self that is a "loner" or "lone ranger" thrust into loneliness and solitude through the isolation concomitant with detention. He may strive to push the boulder of Moi's tyranny up the mountain, but the danger of it rolling back and crashing him looms large. The exclamation "Ole Wangu"/ 'Woe unto me' is therefore applicable to Mazrui the political detainee pondering the "perilous moment" of detention and being uncertain of his release, much less the success of the revolutionary struggle for which detention has made him an ineffectual lone ranger. Or is he that ineffectual? One could say that Mazrui heaves the boulder of the Moi tyranny fundamentally and solely through writing while incarcerated. At the "perilous moment" of detention he continues writing without knowing whether or when these works of literature created in captivity would see the light of day. He has no clue at that moment whether prison authorities will find his resistance literature and confiscate or destroy it, crashing him and his precious prison oeuvre. But now with the benefit of hindsight we know that he indeed succeeded to publish his two prison works, *Chembe cha Moyo* and *Shadows of the Moon*.

The Female and Parental Selves

In *Chembe cha Moyo* the poet has also created female "I"-s that both identify with and articulate the position and condition of being female and a parental "I" who serves as a source of comfort, counsel, and solace. Given the context and reality of the poet's incarceration it is not at all surprising that these selves are implicated in the poet's attempt to make sense of his own condition and the condition of struggle against tyranny and capitalistic greed. In "Ninakwenda Nairobi"/ 'I am going to Nairobi' (29) the speaking self is a woman who candidly reveals to her male lover her intention of going to Nairobi to peddle her flesh as a prostitute due to poverty. She consoles him, assures him of her love and tries to make him understand why her recourse to prostitution is a necessary evil. The economic imperative that drives her to prostitution, risking her relationship with her lover and reducing her to a disposable and commodified sexual object, is at the very core of Mazrui's historical materialist ideology. Mazrui seems to be interrogating the oppressive economic system driven by capitalist ethos that would compel individuals to forego their humanity in order to survive economically. The poem presents an acute sense of self-demolition or self-immolation in what we may call the female condition. Whether "Ninakwenda

Nairobi" is a demeaning image of womanhood or not it represents one of the multiple "I"-s that inhabits the universe of Mazrui's poetry.

Another example of a poem in which there is a female "I" is "Bega kwa Bega"/ 'Shoulder to Shoulder' (4). In this poem the "I" does not refer to a whore in the making as in the case of "Ninakwenda Nairobi," but to the supportive wife of a freedom fighter in the colonial period in Kenya. She declares assertively:

> *Lakini kumfuata mume wangu naendelea*
> *Nchi yangu kuipigania*
> *Utu wangu kujirudishia*
>
> But I will continue to follow my husband
> In the struggle for my country
> To reclaim my personhood. (4)

The wife of the freedom fighter is at one with her husband in the struggle for freedom. Her female condition, the traditional female chores in the household, and her role as mother do not dissuade her from participating fully in the war of liberation. The female "I" in "Bega kwa Bega" is a classic example of a ball juggler, anticipating the modern career woman who has a fulltime job both at home and away. But more importantly she epitomizes countless courageous Mau Mau women fighters who supported their male counterparts in waging war against British colonial rule in Kenya.

Mazrui's invocation of the voice of an unknown and unnamed female freedom fighter excavated from Kenya's collective memory of the Mau Mau phenomenon may seem on the surface pointless. After all he was writing and living, albeit in detention, in the postcolonial moment. Yet it is the underlying continuity between the colonial and postcolonial moments that is crucial in this invocation. For one thing, the postcolonial dispensation resorted to detention without trial as a weapon to deal with political dissent in exactly the same way as the colonial dispensation before it. Jack Mapanje aptly captures the essence of the post-independence condition in Kenya within which Mazrui wrote when he alludes to the undying colonial character of legislation and leadership: "The Kenyan predicament manifested itself in almost every independent African country, where variants of colonial legislation were never substantially revised; instead they were extended to sustain African leaders' programmes of corruption, nepotism, imprisonment, exile, torture and elimination of political dissent" (xvii). It is therefore plausible to conclude that Mazrui found solace in ruminating about the continuity of relentless opposition to misrule in the postcolonial period as in the colonial one. He could identify with this female imaginative "I" of yester years, because her voice of dissent in the colonial past was like the voice of countless other dissenters, him included, in the postcolonial present. Thus the "I" of "Bega kwa Bega" may also imply an unstated "we" that is trans-historic and "transgender" in nature. This sense of solidarity that links political prisoners, real and potential ones, across time and place, is a typical motif in prison literature.

In "Nasaha ya Mzazi" (54) / 'Parental Admonition' the narrating "I" is a parent admonishing and consoling his or her own son who has become a victim of travesty or miscarriage of justice.

Lakini usiwe ni wa kushutuka
'Siwache machozi yakakudondoka
Yako ndiyo haki isiyo shaka
Yenye kukuvua joho la lawama

But do not be alarmed
Do not shed tears
Yours is an incontestable right
That strips you of the gown of blame. (54)

The poems invokes the detainee's inalienable right to freedom, to life, to being human and as such absolves him from blame for the victimization that the state has wrought upon him, hence the two concluding lines, "Yours is an incontestable right/That strips you of the gown of blame."

Given the fact of Mazrui's detention without trial, one could conclude that he is himself the principal audience or addressee of the poem. But he is also the source or creator of the parental voice that relays the never-give-up or never-say-die message in the poem, dispelling as it does any lingering doubts or regret over the detainee's political ideology, attitude, or actions, past or present. Thus in a way the poet utilizes the "I" in the poem to transform himself into his own fictive parent and counselor, to boost his own morale. In other words poetry enables Mazrui to create himself in the imaginative and affective image of his father or mother and through that to proclaim his innocence and his victimhood. He speaks to himself consolingly through the parental "I" as a way of coping with detention. This reinforces the proposition that the poet deliberately embraces poetry as a vital source of comfort in the face of the melancholy and despondency that detention presents.

Disavowal of Ideology

However, in trying to present various versions of the "I" that tend to reflect and refract his selfhood, Mazrui does not always tend to foreground the ideological at the expense of the essentially human. The sense of being or becoming human that his various "I"-s in *Chembe cha Moyo* aspire to or despair aspiring to is not obscured by a quest for ideological abstractions. This is so despite or because of the poet's manifestly Marxist stance. Granted Mazrui's uncle Ali Mazrui has aptly characterized his nephew, as a Kenyatta University instructor "who was detained without charge by the Moi regime for being a left-wing Kenyan academic" (60). Also, certain poems in this collection are unequivocal in their advancement of socialist or communist ideals (e.g. "Chungu"/ 'Ants' (18) in which the poet admires the cohesion and cooperation that epitomizes the "socialism" of ants and "Taji la Wema"/ 'The Crown of Virtue' (26) in which the speaker calls for socialism in the line "Basi upisheni ujamaa"/ 'Give socialism a chance'). But in the poem "Mimi ni Mimi"/ "I am Me" (12), there is ostensibly a vehement disavowal of ideologues and the ideologies and ideals with which they identify themselves or are characteristically identified. The narrating "I" refuses to be branded in accord with any ideological orientation:

Waniita mkomunisti
Waniita mkapitalisti
Na mimi ni binadamu tu,
Kwani hilo halitoshi?

They call me a communist
They call me a capitalist
And yet I am just human
Isn't that enough? (12)

The narrating "I" in this poem conceives of a selfhood that is not mediated through opposing ideological branding or paroxysms. Ideologies or ideological branding whether accurate or inaccurate glosses over the quintessential human attributes embodied in the self. Furthermore, emphasis on ideological differences tends to overlook our common humanity, or that we are fellow passengers in the train of life, to paraphrase Charles Dickens in *A Chrismas Carol.* As the next stanza shows, nations globally face challenges so similar as to make fiery arguments over ideology or ideological identification and differentiation count for little or nothing;

Nchi zinajiwakia
    Mamama wakiomboleza, wakilia
Tumbi ya watoto wakiumia
na maneno yote tunayotumia
    kuuana na kuangamia

Nations are burning
    Mothers mourn and cry
Countless children are hurt
by every word we use
    To kill and annihilate one another. (12)

What is needed, the poem seems to suggest, is a quest for pragmatic solutions to human problems, not engagement with empty ideological differentiation or the needless fomenting of animosity based on real and imagined ideological differences. The poet is acutely aware of the capacity of words to do things; not only do words enable dividing people according to ideological differences, they are also the tools with which humans "kill and annihilate one another." Chapter 4 dealt at length with the illocutionary acts of poetic language as exemplified by Abdilatif Abdalla's *Sauti ya Dhiki,* extrapolating upon the capacity of words to even "kill" as Abdalla figuratively kills president Jomo Kenyatta in "Mamba." It would be superfluous to rehash the argument here. But suffice it to say here, Mazrui's allusion to the power of words to kill has both a figurative and literal meaning. The role of hateful speech on radio as a catalyst for the Rwandan genocide in 1994 or the bloody post-election violence in Kenya in 2007/8 is a supreme example of this destructive power of words to kill in quite a direct sense.

If, as the voice in the poem suggests, "every word" we utter enables us to kill and annihilate one another, it could well be because of the definitions we create, and the meanings and connotations we ascribe to the ideological "us" and ideological "others," the boundaries we are all too eager to draw at the expense of our shared common humanity. That makes the speaker's words, "And yet I am just human/Isn't that enough?" even more compelling, because they stress this shared sense of human oneness. The poignancy of this assertion lies in the fact that almost all incidences of discrimination, conflict, battle, war, make nonsense of the unassailable truth that we are all human, all belonging to the one human family. For most victims of the atrocities that characterize human history, it has not always been enough to claim "I am just human" to avert their unhappy destinies at the hands of their fellow men and women. To be categorized as white or black, male or female, Christian or Muslim, Catholic or Protestant, Suni or Shi'ite, citizen or alien, straight or gay, capitalist or communist has often been more important than merely laying a claim on belonging to the human family.

But by tending to reject ideology and invoking his sense of humanity, the speaker in the poem may be said to be seeking solace in a fundamental truth that humans have flagrantly trampled upon throughout history. The detaining authorities do not fully appreciate and acknowledge the humanity of the detainees as they do their own, otherwise they would not subject them to extreme dehumanizing condition as they often do. Mechthild Nagel's allusion to the overriding "logic of revenge" in the postcolonial African prison industrial complex in this chapter's epigraph underscores this negation of humanity.[8] When and if my humanity is denied or negated as now, the self in Mazrui's poem seems to be saying, it behooves me to console myself with both the declaration and the knowledge that I am still human. The poem is therefore, the poet's attempt to stake a claim on subjectivity as opposed to being regarded as a mere object. Only that staking a claim on humanity appears to come at the expense of repudiating something held dear.

The apparent disavowal of ideological identification or taxonomy in the poem, including that of the leftist variety that undergirds Mazrui's activism, should, only be accepted with a caveat. The poet creates an image of a self that renounces ideology; rather it is a self that values the fundamental sense of just being human. Yet there is a level of inherent contradiction or irony in this self's disavowal of ideology since the disavowal itself is based on ideology, the ideology of devaluing ideology. At the same time by deigning to claim he is not to be branded a communist and any number of ideological tags, the self seems to point to the "rehabilitative" propensity of detention, its capacity to reform a detainee hitherto corrupted by hated and dangerous ideology. The Kenyan state would not have been more pleased than to hear a detained leftist intellectual recanting any and all ideology, including his leftist stance. It is supposedly a true measure of the success of the prison system. Nonetheless, I think, the disavowing self and voice in the poem is only a ploy the poet employs to hoodwink the authorities that he has reformed. As Barbara Harlow states in *Barred: Women, Writing, and Political Detention*, "penal institutions aim to function as part of the state's coercive apparatus of physical detention and ideological containment"(10). And the tenor and thrust of Mazrui's poem tends to delude the state into celebrating its victory over the poet. But is the state really triumphant in this regard, earning for itself this ostensibly double success of effecting upon Mazrui both "physical detention and ideological containment"?

One discerns in the creation of this self an attempt by the poet to appear to say what the Moi government wants to hear whereas the opposite may be what still holds true; Mazrui was, and perhaps, still is, a dyed-in-the wool Marxist intellectual. There is, therefore, the irony of Mazuri's own defiant adherence to leftist ideology behind this veneer of the image of an ideology negating self imbued with a somewhat redolent humanist impulse. Being attentive to the underlying paradox or deception in the poem and being cognitive of the context of its writing and the poet's ideological stance, leads us to read the meaning of the poem as a negation of its apparent negation of ideology. The negation of ideology is, therefore, a camouflage that could and should, in fact, be read as an affirmation of ideology.

Trauma and Tragedy

Implicated in this humanist impulse in Mazrui's poetry is an acute awareness of personal tragedy and trauma. It is true that some of the poems are concerned about the global village, about humanity and about the disenchantment with the postcolonial situation in Africa and other all-encompassing issues that affect larger collectivities or entities. But *Chembe cha Moyo* is more than a chronicle of the faceless "inner feelings" of the Third World as the writer of the blurb purports; it is also, if not more, about what the blurb and the introduction do not say, namely meditation on the personal trauma and tragedy of incarceration. The poems in the anthology amply demonstrate how incarceration, isolation, torture, and trauma are inextricably bound up together. Therefore, poems like "Niguse"(1), which thematize incarceration do not only locate detention as the site for writing, but also bring to the fore the extent of the site's traumatizing potential. Apart from "Niguse," there are a number of poems in the anthology that underwrite this sense of trauma in Mazrui's poetic narration of self and confinement. For example, in "Kifungoni"/'Incarceration' (13) the speaker relates both the desolation of his sense of self and the dissipation or disappearance of hope for recovery:

Kwa kuangalia juu mbinguni
Na kulia sana kwa matumaini
Samawati imeingia
Mwangu machoni.

Kwa kuota mahindi mashambani
Na kulia sana mahuzuni
Manjano imeingia
Mwangu machoni.

Waache majemadari waende vitani
Wapenzi waende bustanini
Na walimu mwao darasani
Ama mimi, tasbihi nipeni
Na kiti cha kale, cha zamani
Niwe vivi nilivyo duniani:
Bawabu mlangoni
Katika kingo ya maumivu ya ndani
Maadamu vitabu, sheria na zote dini

Zitanihakikisha mauti
Nikiwa na njaa au kifungoni

Because of looking up in the heavens
and weeping so much with optimism
The color blue has entered
into my eyes.

Because of the sprouting of corn in the fields
and weeping so much with sorrow
The color yellow has entered
into my eyes.

Let the commanders go to war
Lovers to the park
And teachers to their classrooms
As for me give me prayer beads
And an ancient chair, an old one
So that I can remain the way I am in the world
A Sentry at the door
On the banks of inner pain
So long as books, the law and every religion
Will ensure my death
In my famished or incarcerated state. (13)

The speaker's "kulia sana kwa matumaini"/ 'weeping so much with optimism' in the opening stanza is not a mark of optimism, but a post-optimism re-evaluation of his state as an incarcerated individual. At any rate that weeping has borne no tangible benefits. To the contrary, his eyes have turned blue, for nothing, one could say, because the much hoped for divine intervention from above has not materialized at all, much less changed his material reality. It is instructive that the initial "weeping with optimism" soon turns into "kulia sana kwa mahuzuni"/ 'weeping so much with sorrow.' The trauma is intensified by the knowledge that while one languishes in detention; other people such as army generals, teachers, and lovers, go about their duties as if there is nothing amiss.

But for the speaking "state guest" incarceration is never business as usual because of the attendant traumatizing deprivation of basic human rights and agency that it causes. The recourse to "tashbihi"/ 'prayer beads' is not driven by optimism or deep religious devotion but a resignation to one's despondent destiny. The speaker in saying "maadamu vitabu, sheria, na zote dini/ zitanihakikishia mauti"/ 'So long as books, the law and every religion/ Will ensure my death' is fundamentally a *death wish.* When the speaker alludes to "inner pain" he seems to imply the deep psychological trauma that gnaws at him in his incarcerated state. This inner pain is certainly related to what the blurb writer terms "hisia za ndani"/ 'inner feelings' except that the inner pain here points to Mazrui's imaginative projection of the trauma of detention rather than the hazy and faceless Third World to which the blurb points.

Other poems that thematize trauma include "Kizuizini"/ 'Detention' (27) in which the speaker is a beloved child narrating to the mother his ordeal of anger and mistreatment in detention; "Mfukuzwa,"/ 'I am a Reject' (15) and "Hakuna Yeyote"/ 'There is No one,'which narrativizes crippling solitude and isolation; "Chuo"/'School of Liberation' (2) which highlights trauma as part of the costly price of the liberation struggle; and "Hisia"/ 'Feelings' (3) which parades the wound on the psyche that detention inflicts upon individuals such as feelings of self-blame or self-hate.

Comparing Mazrui's and Abdalla's Prison Poetry

There is a sense in which Mazrui's *Chembe cha Moyo* is thematically and stylistically similar to and different from *Abdalla's Sauti ya Dhiki*. Mazrui wrote his poems in the early 1980s while in detention in the Moi era, almost a decade after Abdalla had written his *Sauti ya Dhiki* as a convicted seditionist in the Kenyatta regime. Nonetheless, the political motivation behind both Abdalla's imprisonment and Mazrui's detention need not be overemphasized; both were incarcerated for political reasons because they were perceived as representing a real or imagined danger to the respective regimes. Also, not only do these prison poets have similar roots on the Kenyan coast, having been born and bred on the Kenyan coast in an essentially Arabized and Islamicized Swahili socio-cultural milieu, but Marxist thought also substantially influenced them. The thrust of the poems that narrate their carceral experience is for the most part as political as the reasons for their incarceration. In unraveling the signification of *Chembe cha Moyo* and *Sauti ya Dhiki,* therefore, it is imperative to adopt an interpretive frame that takes into account the texts' political contents, contexts, and connotations.

Abdalla and Mazrui's literary styles are seemingly worlds apart. Their poetic styles seem to be governed by different aesthetic principles with the former strictly adhering to *arudhi* (traditional Swahili prosody) while the latter in the main adopting *mashairi huru* (free verse). Abdalla made manifest his poetic manifesto in a discourse at the University of Dar es Salaam in the mid-1970s when he declared: "Watalaamu wa Kiswahili kwa umoja wao wamekubaliana kuwa shairi la Kiswahili lazima liwe na vina na mizani. Vitu hivi viwili ni kama roho ya shairi la Kiswahili." / 'Swahili scholars have unanimously agreed that the Swahili poem must have rhyme and meter. These two things are like the soul of the Swahili poem' (quoted in Chacha 34).

On the other hand, Mazrui's introduction to *Chembe cha Moyo* constitutes his poetic manifesto: "Nafikiri kauli ya sawa zaidi ni ile isemayo kuwa ilhamu ya washairi hawa wapya imeamshwa na hali nyingine tu ya mazingira, kwamba mdundo wa ilhamu yao unatokana na ngoma nyingine, kwamba katika maisha yao wamekumbana na bahari nyingine za ufasaha ambazo mawimbi yake yamewapeleka kumudu mbinu nyingine za unahodha wa fasihi."/ 'I think its more cogent to say that these new breed of (Swahili) poets are inspired by different environmental conditions, that the resonance of their inspiration emanates from other sources, that in their lives they have encountered another sea of virtuosity whose waves have made them masters of a different set of techniques of literary aesthetics.' (ix)

Mazrui counts himself among this new crop of Swahili poets who do not follow the prosodic conventions. In his principles of poetry, he therefore, rejects the insistence on rhyme and meter that Abdalla espouses. But rejecting adherence to prosody does not mean he does not employ these aspects in his poems. To the contrary there is tremendous evidence of rhyme and meter in Mazrui's *Chembe cha Moyo*, which almost all attempts at translation from the original Swahili texts unfortunately and inevitably fail to capture. What one notices though in Mazrui's principles and practice of poetry is a deliberate attempt to create a synthesis between the antithetical *wanaarudhi* (prosodists) and *washairi huru* (proponents of free verse). Mazrui uses aspects of prosody but without being slavishly bound to or by its dictates. So while Abdalla comes across as a prisoner of prosodic style, Mazrui frees himself from the chains of convention without completely abandoning convention. In other words, although rhyme and meter may be said to be as prevalent in *Chembe cha Moyo* as in *Sauti ya Dhiki*, Mazrui's poems cannot be easily classified or pigeonholed in specific conventional Swahili poetic subgenres such as *tathlitha, tarbia, takhmisa, msuko, or malumbano* as Abdalla's.

Moreover whereas Abdalla writes principally in the Kimvita dialect of Mombasa, Mazrui's poems are more oriented toward *Kiswahili Sanifu* or Standard Kiswahili. This does not imply that he strictly adheres to standard Swahili usage either. His use of non-standard words such as when he pluralizes words that are not usually in the plural form by adding the prefix "ma" (e.g. "mahuzuni" in "Kifungoni" (14), and "mamama" in "Mimi ni Mimi" (12) etc) illustrates how he is not averse to deviating from conventions of Standard Kiswahili grammar as well.[9]

Nevertheless, there are striking resemblances in the thematic concerns in the two anthologies. In a sense both poets embark on a psychic journey and philosophical journey, which entail articulating a wide range of "voices" as a means of dealing with the reality of incarceration. The multivocality of the multiple "I"-s that inhabit the poetic universe of their collection of poems represent multifarious conceptions and narrations of self and confinement. Both poets capture in the carceral imagination and experience the aporia and uncertainty of the revolutionary struggle (e.g. in Mazrui's "Ni Ipi Njia Yetu?"/ 'Where Do We Go From Here?'(32), and "Hisia"/ 'Feelings' (3) and Abdalla's "Telezi"/ 'Slippery Ground' (24); and "Njia Panda"/ 'Crossroads' (79). Interestingly Mazrui's shorter "Jana Leo na Kesho"/ 'Yesterday Today and Tomorrow' (*Chembe,* 42) is almost a replica of Abdalla's longer "Jana na Leo na Kesho"/ Yesterday and Today and Tomorrow' (*Sauti*,42). Both poems philosophize on the passage of time that inevitably preoccupies the incarcerated self to whom both the "when" or "whether" of release almost always assume unmistakable urgency with them.

It bears stating, however, that having been sentenced to a specific prison term, Abdalla may have kept his focus more on when rather than whether he would be released although there was the remote possibility of early release through a presidential pardon that was never to be. However, for a typical political detainee like Mazrui, as Ngugi wa Thiong'o states in *Detained,* it was presumably both a question of when and whether one would be released. But the passage of time is pivotal whether one is incarcerated in prison or detention. The primacy of time during imprisonment is perhaps what accounts for the Swahili colloquial expression for incarceration "*kula kalenda*" whose literal translation would be "eating up the calendar." In both denotation and connotation *kula kalenda* is closely allied to the English expression "doing time" which significantly is the title for any number of printed or cinematic prison texts e.g. American Morion Sobell's prison memoir *On Doing Time: Life in the Big House* and Japanese Yoichi Sai's film *Doing Time* and his compariot Kazuichi Hanawa's film *Doing Time*. Although Mazrui does not kula kalenda or eat the calendar in the manner of a convicted prisoner who has some idea when he will be released, his preoccupation with time in his prison poetry is symptomatic of the universal centrality of the concept of time in the psyche of the incarcerated.

Like Abdalla, Mazrui also thematizes truth in for instance "Kweli"/ 'Truth' (50) and "Maudhui"/ 'Content' (69). In "Kweli" Mazrui writes;

Kweli wambwa ni uchungu
Hauliki abadani
Ni mwiba wa nungunungu
Ubambuaye lisani
Na kwetu 'si walimwengu
U sumu mwetu moyoni

Lakini nakuuliza
U mchungu kwake nani?
Fukara asojiweza
Wamuumiza nini?
Ana kipi kiliwaza
Asipokukini?

They say truth is bitter
It is not palatable at all
It is the spike of the porcupine
That hurts the tongue
And for us humans
It is poison in our hearts

But let me ask you
To whom is it bitter?
How does it hurt
The poor one who has nothing?
What does he lose
For speaking the truth? (50)

In "Kweli"Mazrui reverts to the motif of truth as bitter, poisonous and unpalatable, and politicizes truth as much as Abdalla in "N'shishiyelo ni Lilo" / 'I am Unshakeable.' The persona in Mazrui's poem contends that the response to the kind of truth propounded here is contingent upon one's class status. One could say it is Marxian or Mazruian truth that defines the rift between the haves or have-mores and have-nots, between peasants and plunderers. Both poets seem to perceive truth as synonymous with exposing the misdeeds of the ruling elite, thereby equating truth with opposition to misrule. This truth is therefore reductive and tendentious and is confined within the political matrix of the struggle between reactionary and revolutionary forces. That is why for instance, the poor person in Mazrui's poem would lose nothing by both thinking about and articulating the truth concerning the connection between his poverty and the greed of the ruling elite. It is the perpetrators of his poverty, who would be incensed by the truth of that connection, hence the selective bitterness that this kind of truth elicits. The subject of political or politicized truth exemplifies the extent to which Mazrui's prison poetry dialogues and generally concurs with Abdalla's.

Nonetheless, the personae in Mazrui's *Chembe cha Moyo* do not seem to be on the same page on matters of religious truth with their counterparts in Abdalla's *Sauti ya Dhiki*. To be sure both anthologies display a passionate revolutionary stance that blurs the line between religion and politics. Their stances also entail envisioning a universal positive change across the continent of Africa as demonstrated by poems such as Abdalla's "Mamaetu Afrika"/ 'Our Mother Africa' (36) and Mazrui's "Kilio cha Afrika"/ 'The Cry of Africa' (30); "Nilivuka"/ 'I Crossed' (10). But it is their articulation and projection of religious fervor that sets them apart. It needs to be reiterated that both Mazrui and Abdalla were brought up against a backdrop of deep Islamic religious tenets. Yet the personae of Abdalla's poetry tend to evince more religious devotion than Mazrui's, believing and trusting in Allah's intervention in human affairs. In Abdalla's "Tuza Moyo"/ 'Take Heart' (6) the persona has a deeply prayerful attitude:

> *Akhi tuliza mtima, uwate kusononeka*
> *Hakuna lisilokoma, siku 'fika 'tatoka*
> *Kusubiri ni lazima, na kumuomba Rabbuka*
> *Wasiya wako 'meshika*
>
> Dear brother take heart, and stop mourning
> There is nothing that has no end, when the day comes I will be free
> It is imperative to be patient, and to pray to God
> I have heeded your advice. (*Sauti* 6)

To the contrary the personae in Mazrui's poetry are typified by misgivings and doubt about Allah's willingness and ability to intervene. In "Risala"/ 'Message' (24) the persona expresses doubt about God's ability to read and respond to a written petition from all struggling and suffering humankind. The persona states:

> *Lakini enyi mafukara wa dunia*
>
> *Hofu yangu kubwa nawambia*
> *Mungu huenda ikatukia*
> *hajui kusoma . . . hili nachelea*
>
> But eeh! Your wretched of the earth
>
> I will reveal to you my biggest worry
> It may well be that God
> I suspect, is illiterate . . . (24)

The persona of Mazrui's poem therefore does not share the same level of profound belief and implicit trust in God as that of Abdalla's poem. The invocation of the image of God as either unwilling or unable to read also implies unwillingness or inability to respond promptly to pressing human needs particularly those pertaining to the poor. On the whole, the personae in Mazrui's poetry at once question and subvert received religious truth as they do any number of time-tested and tried Swahili aphorisms (e.g. the questioning of the proverb 'Hasira Hasara,' 'Wrath is Profitless,' in "Hasira Hasara?"/ Is Wrath Really Profitless?'(23)). It is in this respect that one could read in *Chembe cha Moyo's* personae both traces of nihilism, agnosticism, deisticism or the Nietzchean God-is-dead notion.

It bears clarifying that the poems present us with several invented selves through the various voices or personae that the poets employ. We should, therefore, beware of conflating the poets' personae and the person of the poets as historical individuals. As Sidonie Smith and Julia Watson have stated, the historical person is almost unknowable. Our focus in analysis should hence, be on the self and any number of selves resulting from the poets' art of self-invention or self-creation. Because the poets "create" themselves in several images, it would be missing the point of their poetic endeavor if we were to conclude that the poems are an exact representation or reflection of the poets' personalities. In other words, it would be foolhardy to try to gauge the poets' religious devotion on the basis of the personas they have created in their poems by perhaps suggesting that Abdalla is more devoted than Mazrui as a perfunctory interpretation of their poems would suggest. Moreover, the task of differentiating between a good Muslim and bad Muslim, to borrow, Mahmoud Mamdani's phrase from his book *Good Muslim, Bad Muslim*, is not within the province of this analysis.

In sum the recourse to poetry as refuge hardly loses its saliency as poets narrate themselves and their confinement in multiple voices and "I"-s while they undertake the psychic and philosophical journey that their poetry makes both possible and expedient. Mazrui's thematic concerns are as multi-layered as Abdalla's although for both poets, incarceration is the quintessential pivot around which the poems revolve. Stylistically Mazrui demonstrates how he selectively accepts conventions of Swahili poetic conventions such as meter and rhyme but rejects being their prisoner. His quest for solace from poetry takes priority over rigid adherence to received conventions of writing Swahili poetry.

Mazrui's quest for solace from his prison poetry goes without saying. However, what perhaps goes with saying is whether indeed he attains the intended solace. Yet one could say even the dim prospects of attainability do not at all diminish the poet's quest. The emergence of *Chembe cha Moyo* from within the prison walls is both a consequence and an index of the resilience of this quest for solace. The quest is of and in itself a sustaining endeavour, a desperate attempt by the incarcerated to reclaim personhood and subjectivity, and the right to write and to live, the right to be human. Further, the quest for solace in prison poetry is clearly a form of protest against the detaining authorities that intended for detention to be a silencing mechanism for Mazrui's dissidence and dissent. *Chembe cha Moyo*, therefore, affirms Mazrui's anti-government political engagement that was presumably more radicalized during and after detention. Together with his play *Shadows of the Moon*, *Chembe cha Moyo* stands as Mazrui's monumental attempt to give an account of himself and to challenge what Mechthild Nagel would call "logic of revenge," inherent in the practice and principles of detention without trial so widely espoused by African despots (78).

Conclusion

Human beings participate in history as actors and as narrators.

—Michael Rolph Trouillot, *Sillencing the Past*

[N]o writer on social issues can be non-partisan.

—Mahmoud Mamdani, *Imperialisma and Fascism in Uganda*

The thrust of *Narrating Prison Experience* was to excavate fundamental issues related to human rights, self, and nation from what political prisoners said did happen, to paraphrase Michael Rolph Trouillot. The validity of paying attention to these other voices cannot be overemphasized. This does not mean that we either ignore what actually happened or cast aspersions at all other versions of what happened. But every so often it is the official version of things that enjoys supremacy and obfuscates alternative perspectives, which would otherwise abundantly illuminate the situation or raise red flags over crucial errors of omission and commission, where necessary.

If we should give the official narrative the benefit of the doubt, albeit with its self-evident motives for skewing the "truth" sometimes, the law of natural justice dictates or demands that we accord other versions of events the same benefit of the doubt. But to pay attention to a genre or subgenre such as prison writing, often branded an outlaw is to grant it respect some think it does not deserve. Nevertheless, no acute intelligence is necessary to see the importance of avoiding blind credulity when we encounter the official narrative or restraining a display of icy contempt when we encounter the unofficial narrative. It is imperative, I think, that we read both the official and the unofficial narrative against each other. Ultimately, we become the richer when we read both narratives at once with disbelief and with suspension of disbelief, gleaning something about the human condition from each side, as this book has attempted to do with regard to the prison narratives of political victims of state rage.

But just what do we glean from the constellation of the prison accounts of political prisoners? In *Narrating Prison Experience* I strove to investigate and demonstrate what these narratives reveal about human rights and their abuses, and to examine the extent to which narrating confinement is in and of itself an act of self-exploration, exploring a self that is necessarily implicated in the collective or collectivized. Equally important was seeking to find out the explicit and implicit motivations for narrating confinement; the link between the context of confinement and the text; and the narratological tools that these narratives of confinement employ. Other related questions for which answers were sought included: Is form/genre relevant or irrelevant in narrating and narrativizing confinement? What is the relationship between the narration of confinement and trauma, memory, truth telling, and the I-pronoun?

Most prison narratives seem on the surface to be personal life histories in which incarcerated individuals narrate themselves into existence in a desperate attempt to reclaim their selfhood and sense of humanity. But it seems to me that close reading of these narratives indicates that prison literature is a frame through which we can read a country's history, a tool with which we can feel its national pulse. Also, while pre-colonial oral narratives of incarceration may be appropriated to allegorize the colonial and postcolonial realities of Kenyan peoples, the colonial and postcolonial narratives tend to cannibalize the state. Lastly, these narratives of confinement lend themselves towards rumination on the double function of the state as a "source of security" and as an "agent of destruction and death" as Simon Gikandi put it, albeit in a different context. It would seem more often than not they emphasize the image of the state as the peoples' nemesis "standing literally between subjects and their local and global desires" (Gikandi, 84).

Clearly, that a perpetual *agon* exists between the incarcerated self and the rulers is beyond all doubt. Inevitably, there is no guarantee that either side of the struggle would win over public sympathy and support every time everywhere. At any rate, it would be impractical to expect a uniform and unanimous response to both the authorized and unauthorized national narratives. It would seem quite possible for even an individual to display malleability and variability in responding, reacting differently to the same narrative at different times and places. If the late Oyekan Owomoyela's essay "Dissidence and African Writers: Commitment and Dependency?" (1981), is anything to go by, there are indeed individuals in and outside Kenya for whom it is improbable or impossible for the narrative of the incarcerated self to persuade or convince.

Owomoyela casts aspersions at African rebel writers' claim to humanism and faults the "tendency in Africanist and international circles to claim the struggle between them [writers] and rulers is one between enlightenment and anomie" (85). He finds particularly reprehensible dissidence in African societies that is fashioned after the Western world or is sponsored by it, terming such dissidence "anachronistic and misguided" (84). To Owomoyela these rebel writers are principally motivated by megalomania. Therefore, according to this logic, the so-called antithesis between darkness and light that is often invoked in what we may call an alternative version of things is simply and squarely a power struggle between the rulers in power and the power-hungry writers who are anxious to take over with the support of the Western world. Adopting Owomoyela's viewpoint implies discounting the incarceration narratives and the "truth" the incarcerated selves purport to tell through them. On the other hand, there are those who would stand on the side of the "dissidents" and disbelief the official rhetoric and narrative and who would perhaps regard Owomoyela and like-minded individuals as ostensible paramours of the ruling class and its egregious pattern of endless instances of human rights violations and misrule across Africa. But returning to Owomoyela's suggestion about the African dissident writer in general, one or two questions beg for answers: Is it possible, for instance, that the entire gamut of incarcerated selves analyzed in *Narrating Prison Experience* exhibit unbridled ambition for political power? Are they anachronistic and misguided, always driven by the lack or loss of power? These are questions for which I have no definite answers for the moment.

What appears definite to me, however, is that these narratives of political confinement suggest the existence of what we may call the paradox of patriotism. The incarcerating authorities claim they incarcerated political prisoners or detainees to rid the nation of unpatriotic elements; those who narrate their incarceration claim they are incarcerated because of their patriotism, their love for nation or country. Indeed from colonial to postcolonial times, the thread that runs through the narratives of political confinement is that of vilification of state brutalization of dissenters, but also an explicit message that victims of state terror, particularly the detainees and prisoners, are almost without exception veritable patriots. What we have then is juxtaposition between the official or authorized national narrative and the alternative national narrative that are dialectically opposed to each other. In other words, the incarcerating narratives also tell the national narrative albeit in an odd way that gives it a spin that deviates from the official narrative which posits the state as always already pure, infallible, and just. They instead paint the wheelers and dealers in the state as violators of human rights, greedy, corrupt, despotic, anti-people, anti-freedom, and unjust. In a sense both the authorized national narrative and the alternative national narrative vie for public space, to be heard and believed by a public whose credulity is often stretched to the limit.

In his magisterial *Writers in Prison,* Ioan Davies proposes prisoner narratives often project the innocence of the narrator/protagonist. This study has found a predisposition among prison narrators towards parading or proclaiming their innocence, bearing out Davies's claim. It is as if, as Davies remarks, the writers are posing the question: "What did I do wrong?"(44). This question is bound up with thoughts of and solidarity with other prisoners of conscience or detainees in the same or similar circumstances. It is significant for instance, that those writing in the postcolonial moment, link their "undeserved" suffering with that of those of the colonial period, whose innocence they invoke and identify with. The writers even try to make connections with prisoners and detainees beyond the Kenyan historical reality, traversing temporal, spatial, and geopolitical considerations. This victim solidarity is part of the crucial glue firmly sticking the narrating and narrated "I" to the collective and collectivized "we."

The preoccupation with the interplay between self and society perhaps explains the preponderance of multiple "I"-s in the whole range of prison narratives. The polyvocality of the "I" in each narrative problematizes the simplistic interpretation of the stories as representing the historical "I" whose name appears on the cover of the book. This multiple and fractured mode of self-representation tend to appropriately signify the fragmenting and disorienting attributes of the carceral experience and imagination on the tortured self. Quite often there is also a tendency to embed the collective "we" in the narrating and narrated "I." But it seems to me that the notion of an African self as being peculiarly selfless, unselfish has every so often been blown out of proportion. At the core of every autobiographical act is, at the very best a concern and the very worst, an obsession with self and that rather than the individual's complete dependency on society often emphasized, these prison narratives suggest a level of reciprocity between self and society.

In theorizing on the possible motivation for the writing of the narratives, this study has found that apart from a desire to reclaim selfhood, an attempt to give counter-hegemonic accounts of themselves, incarcerated writers are inspired by the therapeutic attributes of writing. In other words scriptotherapy or writing as therapy is an important consideration in their decisions to narrate their tales of incarceration. This implies that the carceral experience is far from being simply an allegoresis for narration or narrativization.

If it is true as Joana Summers remarks that crisis is seminal for the autobiographical act, the prison context presents a unique crisis for the autobiographical act. The prison writers present or represent themselves as witnesses who claim credibility for their narratives. They therefore posit their stories as nothing but the "truth," including things they never personally witnessed such as Gakaara wa Wanjau's diary which contains entries of events he never witnessed but which he claims are true or J.M. Kariuki's narration of fighting in the forests although he admits he never was there. This study has shown that insistence on veracity and verification in these prison narratives may lead to fallacious and frustrating conclusions. One could perhaps argue that these narratives should rather be taken as the truth of fiction or autobiographical truth, showcasing as Georges Gusdorf pointed out cogently: "Every autobiography is a work of art . . . [I]t does not show us the individual seen from outside in his visible actions but the person in his inner privacy, not as he was, not as he is, but as he believes and wishes himself to be and to have been"(45). In a similar vein Paul John Eakin in *Fictions in Autobiography* has sublimely said of autobiographical truth that it "is not fixed but an evolving content in an intricate process of self-discovery and self-creation, and… the self of that is the center of all autobiographical narrative is necessarily a fictive structure" (3). However, Eakin is attentive to issues of normativity and social accountability that encumber the autobiographer beyond which one ventures only at the risk of shattering the autobiographer-reader relationship. He singles out three rules governing autobiographical truth, namely; 1) misrepresenation of biographical and historical truth; 2) infringement of the right of privacy; and lastly 3) failure to display normative models of personhood.

The question of truth of autobiography continues to animate debate in the 21st century as it did in the last century. The intensity of the debate has been heightened by what some have called blatant lies by perceived autobiographers of which the American James Frey and Guatemalan Rigoberto Menchu are notable instances. Ophrah Winnfrey hosted Frey in her Ophrah Book Club in which he touted his *One Million Pieces* as a true story of redemption from alcoholism. The whole business became scandalous when it became evident that Frey's criminal past was extravagantly exaggerated and police records did not match his claims. Similarly, Menchu suffered the historical assault of historical anthropologist

David Stoll who discounted some of her major claims after meticulously scrutinizing the actual historical facts. Binjiman Wilkonmmirski's Fragments (1995) has also been found to be an autobiographical hoax of the holocaust experience. But if Frey, Menchu and Binjimamin Wilkommisrski may be accused of breaking the first of Eakin's taboos of autobiographical truth, there are also cases of those who transgress against the rights of privacy and failure to display normative models of personhood. Kathryn Harrison's *The Kiss* (1997) is a case in point. As Eakin aptly argues, Harrison's candid account of incestuous affair with her own father renders her "a martyr to autobiography's rule of telling the truth"(39). He is judged harshly, Eakin adds, "for violating privacy—both others' and her own—than for breaking the incest taboo" (42).

Given this seeming disquiet or scepticism associated with autobiography we are bound to dismiss the truth claims of the alternative narratives analyzed and/or excerpted in this book. There could those who would invoke the intimacy between autobiography and fiction, which intimacy necessarily distances these life narratives from historical reality. Others do not see the distinction between autobiography, and fiction on the hand and history on the other as tenable. This seeming incongruity calls to mind Trouillot's question: "Does it mean that the line between history and fiction is useless? (9). I hope not.

I suppose that life narratives in general have not necessarily earned themselves a bad name simply because of few bad apples, if they may be called so. We cannot afford to throw away the baby with the bathwater. The majority of life narratives are substantially truthful in the true sense of truth while all of them are truthful in the autobiographical sense. Regarding accounts of prison experience, my hunch is that we would be missing the point of autobiography if we totally discounted what Paul John Eakin terms, 'the authority of the literature of witness," since in the first place the prison writers experienced or witnessed what they recount (37). One of the things that seem to hold true, is that the thematization of truth in these narratives is a commonplace, suggesting the centrality of truth as a thematic preoccupation in narratives of incarceration. Although the accounts of prison that we encounter are not absolute truth or gospel truth, they tell a kind of truth. Yet it bears adding that it is perhaps what we may call revolutionary truth rather than simply the truth of fiction that drives the narratives of confinement. This revolutionary truth tends to exert a massive magnetic force upon these writers and upon their works, defying verisimilitude and veracity and putting change on the front burner. Put differently, whether the truth the narratives tell is factual, autobiographical, imagined, or fictional, it seems to be a kind of truth that is defined by the ethics and politics of revolutionary change. But more importantly, there is little evidence that these prison narratives transgress upon Eakin's three principles of autobiographical truth, which as he states are normally tacit but become explicit only when transgressed upon.

It is cogent to conclude that prison literature crosses many and varied genres and subgenres. There are certain parallels between oral narratives that narrativize incarceration, some of which seem to be set in the mythical past (e.g. the Sela and Mwambu story from the Bukusu of Western Kenya) and the written colonial and postcolonial narratives of incarceration. These parallels include the use of songs as counter-hegemonic tools and the portrayal of the incarcerated as victims rather than villains. The incarcerated are projected as worthy of audience sympathy, empathy, and identification due to the underlying innocence, the inscription of a highly persuasive self that is often foregrounded in these tales. On the whole the narratives adhere to conventions of their genre or subgenre. To the extent that prison narratives adhere to generic conventions, they can be said to be prisoners of genre. Yet what also emerges in some of these prison narratives is a tendency to transgress conventions, refusing to be prisoners of style and genre. Gakaara wa Wanjau's deviation from the fundamental "tenets" of the Western diary in his *Mau Mau Author in Detention* and Alamin Mazrui's revolt against Swahili prosody in *Chembe cha Moyo* are cases in point.

Where the texts do not directly transgress generic conventions, they are still "transgressive" because they were not officially supposed to be told or written in the first place. Coming from individuals dubbed dissidents, dissenters and dangerous, prison texts are something of an outlaw genre. They are necessarily tendentious, partisan, polemical and unapologetic about the prisoner's ideological and political stance. As Barbara Harlow correctly observes, the reading and writing of these texts itself is transgressive since it constitutes a counterstrategy against the grain of the incarcerating state and its apparatuses (4). In other words even the audience or critic is enmeshed in a quagmire for which it is impossible or improbable to remain completely neutral.

Equally noteworthy in these texts is the description, sometimes really detailed and graphic, of the trauma and torture visited upon the incarcerated self. The narratives, whether they are fictional or non-fictional, in prose form or poetic form, almost always foreground the ferocity and barbarous force employed by state apparatuses to "uncreate" the prisoners and detainees, to dissolve the victims' world. The torture is either physical or psychological or both and begins from the very moment of arrest when the individual loses freedom and agency. Whereas it is possible to say that representing details of individual or collective torture and trauma serve to help heal from the wound, hence the apprehension of telling or writing as therapy, it is also apparent that telling or writing it also constitutes an expose of the government's underhand activities. In other words, as Wahome Mutahi's *Three Days on the Cross* demonstrates, the state masquerades as a civilized and human entity while it secretly and savagely tramples upon human rights of individuals it perceives as enemies, real or imagined. It therefore, behooves the survivors of state torture, terror and trauma, to tell, to expose these atrocities to the unsuspecting public.

Regarding the silences and near-silences of the colonial and postcolonial period, one could say that the paucity of female voices in the colonial and postcolonial narratives of incarceration is a salient feature. The female narrative of incarceration is itself metaphorically incarcerated or classifiable as "missing in action." The women who attempt to narrate their incarceration are few and far between, and when they do so, as Wambui Otieno of Kenya does in *Mau Mau's Daughter*, and Frances Baard of South Africa in *My Spirit is not Banned*, they tend to be swimming against the formidable current of phallocentricism and phallocracy. This paucity of written texts by women is in stark contrast to the practice of telling oral narratives which as any number of scholars have observed is principally regarded as the role of women who serve as both custodians and reservoirs of the oral tradition. One could surmise that the low levels of literacy among women political prisoners in the colonial era account for the paucity of oral texts of incarceration by women. But in Kenya, for instance, the Kenyatta and Moi era saw significant increase in literacy levels across gender. Women political prisoners, who could have written about their prison experience, such as Philemona Chelagat Mutai, did not. And those who did exhibit certain levels of reticence as exemplified by Otieno's muted reference to her rape while in detention.

And yet it is what these narratives tell us about the scope and spread of violations of the human rights of the incarcerated that exposes democracy in Africa in general and in Kenya in particular for the hollow that it really has often been. Most accounts of the prison experience in the colonial and postcolonial period are emphatic in their exposé, and trenchant critique of how the state deals with those it considers guilty of the "crime of opinion." If these narratives expose the underbelly of a state that flaunts its respect for human decency, human rights, and democracy, it is because they are unafraid to tell what the state considers untellable. From Josiah Mwangi Kariuki whose *Mau Mau Detainee* inaugurated the publication of personal prison accounts capturing colonial Kenya, to Ngugi wa Thiong'o's *Detained* in the Kenyatta era and Alamin Mazrui's *Chembe cha Moyo* in the Moi regime, these prison narratives manifestly indicate the path not to take to destination democracy.

The narrators present themselves as voices of dissent that suffered incarceration at the hands of the ruling elite but did not, even then, succumb to state apparatuses, including the prison industrial complex, aimed at muting or silencing them. As Rolph Trouillot states in his *Sillencing the Past*, "Human beings participate in history as actors and as narrators" (xix). Unbreakable and unyielding, the prison writers therefore fashion themselves first as "actors," in Rolph Trouillot's terms, participating in the history of struggle for real freedom in their respective countries, in their capacity as political prisoners and activists; and secondly, as "narrators" of an alternative national narrative. Their stories collectively, could, therefore, be considered as a crystal through which Africa can and should look at itself, to see its dreadful human rights record, complicit silences, sham democracy, individual and national hypocrisy, and bungled promises; and perhaps to count its blessings wherever and whenever they have been experienced.

Appendix: Interview with Ngugi wa Thiong'o

On January 4, 2011 Ngugi wa Thiong'o, who was detained without trial by the Kenyatta regime in Kenya for close to a year from December 1977, graciously accepted my request to interview him on matters related to narrating prison experience. Below is the full text of the interview:

Waliaula: You have mentioned on a number of occasions that you wrote your childhood memoir, *Dreams in a Time of War: A Childhood Memoir*, for your children that they may know what you went through in the turbulent period of your formative years. Why did you write *Detained*?

Ngugi: Although Kenya, since its colonial days, has had many political prisoners, there were very few memoirs of their experience. Harry Thuku was in for seven years; Makhan Singh for a similar number of years; and of course the famous Kapenguria six of Jomo Kenyatta; Bildad Kaggia; Achieng Oneko; Kungu Karumba; Paul Ngei; and Fred Kubai. They never wrote memories of their day-to-day experience. There were writers as well: Gakaara wa Njau; Stanley Kagia, again they had not recorded their experiences. In the post independence era, Oginga Odinga, Bildad Kaggia, Achieng Oneko and others; again no prison memoirs. But memoirs like those of J.M. Kariuki's *Mau Mau Detainee*, did give us glimpses but more as part of their autobiography. I felt that this lack of recorded experience played into the imprisoning authorities in that it made political imprisonment and detention that much more mystical and hence dreaded. My memoir was like a literary act of breaking the silence.

Waliaula: Is there a sense in which you see your individual story as a collective story, your history as the history of a larger entity transcending your singularity as a human subject?

Ngugi: I tried to look at my experience in the context of Kenya colonial and postcolonial history. Perhaps I could have been more detailed in terms of the everyday of prison life.

Waliaula: What does narrating incarceration orally or in the written form do for and to you?

Ngugi: It is therapeutic. It is self-empowering. It is writing freedom. You channel anger and bitterness into something positive.

Waliaula: Do you ever have the sense of telling your experience as re-opening an old wound and leaving it open?
Ngugi: No, silence is what keeps wounds alive. They fester inside a person. It's like giving your opponent continued power over you.

Waliaula: What aspects of your prison experience does *Detained* not mention and why? What would you have presented differently were you to rewrite your prison memoir?
Ngugi: As I said above, I could have been more detailed about the everyday. I could have drawn portraits of fellow prisoners. But I felt I could not adequately represent them, that they should tell their own story.

Waliaula: Do you think issues of style and form matter at all for a political prisoner trying to give an account of their prison experience? Did these issues matter to you when writing *Detained*?

Ngugi: They do matter – every writer chooses the angle and form that would adequately help tell his/her story convincingly. In the case of the Detained, the narrative is literally framed as reflections hours before and after my release. The body is like a flashback. I don't know if many critics have noted this.

Waliaula: In experiencing and writing political incarceration, how do you feel connected to others in similar circumstances across time and space?

Ngugi: Very important. In my case, every story of previous experiences by others under similar circumstances, imprisonment of political and intellectual activists, was a learning experience. So also every story of survival under difficult conditions!

Waliaula: In *Detained* you mention that people would ask you whether you were tortured and you respond that incarceration itself is torture. Could you elaborate more on the nature of torture and trauma—psychological and physical that incarceration engenders?
Ngugi: There's no doubt in my mind that every imprisonment leaves a mark, a scar, on the life of the imprisoned. The scar can be physical, social or psychic. Family life and relationships are often affected. But the most valuable, is the positive appreciation of freedom.

Waliaula: Are you piqued by the curiosity people may have towards what happened to you or what happens to other political prisoners while incarcerated? Are you ever concerned that some are essentially driven by the appeal of the shock value or by voyeuristic tendencies? Do you sometimes or always find questions about your detention bothersome?

Ngugi: I don't feel offended in anyway. People are naturally curious the human spirit of survival. They are drawn to it. They are sometimes wondering how they would have done under similar circumstances.

Waliaula: In your situation you were incarcerated by President Jomo Kenyatta, himself a former political prisoner during the colonial dispensation. Is the pain of incarceration heightened by this transformation of former victims into your victimizers?

Ngugi: One would hope that a former political prisoner would perhaps understand, particularly the conditions. But this does not always happen. It's the same old story of human being not learning from what has gone before. How many times have we seen nations that were victimized themselves becoming victimizers sometime employing even more severely the very measures they used to decry when used against them? We should perhaps look again seriously at the whole question of the psychology of oppression.

Waliaula: What is your conception of how true and abiding justice can and could prevail, given that every so often after each wave of political activism against an unjust system, there is this persistent regression or retrogression? Doesn't it seem like the vicious circle keeps repeating itself as the Kenyan experience since independence tends to suggest. I am thinking, for example, of Kenyatta and the apparent metamorphosis of your fellow former political detainee Koigi wa Wamwere when he became assistant minister for Information and Broadcasting and how he seemed to have exhibited his other side.

Ngugi: I am not in a position to pass judgement on individual cases. What's important is the necessity of continued resistance to repression. The challenge is to every person to take up the weapon of struggle and not to stand on the side and demand the previous bearers of the weapon continue doing so to the satisfaction of those of those still watching on the side.

Waliaula: What place do you think narratives of political incarceration occupy or should occupy in the national memory and psyche in Africa and beyond?
Ngugi: They should occupy a central place because they are also narratives of resistance to oppression and of affirmation of freedom. Look at the slave narratives for instance; they are narratives of freedom. They are eternal variations of the Promethius unbound.

Waliaula: The late Nigerian literary critic Oyekan Owomoyela claimed in his article "Dissidence and the African Writer: Commitment and Dependency?" in African Studies Review 24.1 (1981): 83-98, that African intellectuals and activists opposing governments are motivated by their own greed for power. As a victim and an implacable critic of successive post independence governments in Kenya, what do you say to that?

Ngugi: I have no idea what he means. I don't know much he had studied and was recipient of the motives of those who resist social evil. I presume that many of these writers and intellectuals do not oppose government as such but systems and practices of repression. For me, I believe that progress, freedom, empowerment, development, should be looked at and evaluated not in terms of the needs of those at the top of the mountain but from the needs of those at the bottom of the mountain.

Notes

This book's epigraph is from a personal interview with Ngugi wa Thiong'o on January 4, 2011 whose full text is in the appendix of this book.

Introduction

The epigraph is from Wole Soyinka, *The Burden of Memory, The Muse of Forgiveness*, (New York: Oxford University Press, 1999), viii.
1. There are several texts that specifically tackle human rights in Africa or human rights as they relate to the prison industrial complex in Africa and these include Jeremy Sarkin's magisterial edited volume *Human Rights in African Prisons*, (Athens: Ohio University Press, 2008). These texts make huge contributions to our understanding of the state of human rights on the continent. However, instead of merely rehashing the arguments in these earlier texts, *Human Rights and Narrating Prison Experience in Africa*, makes texts by political prisoners as a window through which we can look at human rights violations in Africa. This is certainly not the only way we should or could look at human rights in Africa, but is for sure another vital way through which we make sense of the institutionalization of the specter of human rights violations.
2. See for example, the interview with Ngugi wa Thiong'o in part II of this book for the therapeutic value of narrating prison experience.

Chapter 1

The first epigraph is from Winnie Madikizela Mandela's *Part of My Soul Went with Him,* edited by Mary Benson, (New York: W.W Norton, 1984), 105.
Abdellatif Laabi's *Rue du Retour,* translated from the French by Jacqueline Kaye (London: Readers International, 1982), 73-74.
1. Over the centuries there has never been a univocal position on the function of mimetic art of which literature is part. Plato is among the earliest known detractors of mimetic art. In his trenchant critique of drama and poetry in the *Republic,* Plato argues that dramatization as a form of writing (in plays, poems, and epics) is a devious device that was a threat to the existing social order. It is therefore not at all surprising that Plato banishes the poet from his ideal republic. Others who have viewed literature as inimical to the stability and morality of society include puritanical Christians of Medieval Rome such as Tertullian and to a lesser degree St. Augustine. Aristotle is one of the most famous defenders of art. In his various treatises, such as *Poetics* and *Rhetoric,* he clearly negates Plato's negation of art. Similarly, in proclaiming, "Poetry is the work of a gifted person," Aristotle recognizes artists as talented people and art as something of positive

value in society. But it is English critic Sydney who places the literary artist above all other professions of knowledge.
2. Gideon Were has proposed that Mundu's sons were in fact three and these are the ones who became the eponymous founders of three distinct but closely related sub-groups namely Muvukusu, the eponymous founder of the Babukusu), Mukishu or Mugishu (the eponymous founder of the Bagishu) and Masaba (the eponymous founder of the Bamasaba. (*A History of the Abaluyia*, 43)
3. See for example the story "Orphans" about Obong'o and his sister Awuor in B. Onyango-Ogutu and A. A. Roscoe's *Keep My Words: Luo Oral Literature*, Nairobi. East African Educational Publishers, (1974): 83-85.
4. See Bethwel A. Ogot's "Politics, Culture and Music in Central Kenya: A Study of Mau Mau Hymns, 1951-1956" (1977) and Maina Kinyatti's *Thunderstorm from the Mountains: Mau Mau Patriotic Songs* (1990)).
5. See Madoshi, "The Meanings of the Word Mswahili" In *Kiswahili* 41, no. 1 (1971), 75-81.
6. See Alamin Mazrui and Ibrahim Noor Shariff, *The Swahili Idiom and Identity of an African People*, (Trenton NJ: Africa World Press, 1994); F.E.M.K Senkoro, *Ushairi: Nadharia na Tahakiki*, (Dar es Salaam: Dar es Salaam University Press, 1988).
7. In the Zanzibar version of the epic Liyongo's son was seized by the people and killed him, so that he did not get the Kingdom that he had been promised as a gift for betraying his father. But in Muhamed Kijumwa's *Utenzi wa Fumo Liyongo*, the son dies of illness, dejected and forlorn after the king's failure to keep the promise (Wamitila, 98-99).

Chapter 2

The first epigraph is from Pierre Janet but quoted in Bessel A. van der Kolk and Onno van der Hart's "The Intrusive past: the Flexibility of Memory and the Engraving of Trauma," in *Trauma: Exploration in Memory*. Edited by Cathy Caruth. (Baltimore: Johns Hopkins University Press, 1995), 175.
The second epigraph is from Vincent B. Leitch's introduction to his edited volume *The Norton Anthology of Theory and Criticism.* (New York: Norton, 2001), 21.
1. Gakaara wa Njau's *Mau Mau Author in Detention* is a diary written in detention and smuggled out of detention during the Colonial epoch, but was not published until 1980s.
2. See London-based correspondent Paul Redfern's report "UK Snubs Compensation Claims by Mau Mau Victims," in *The East African*, January 31, 2010.
3. See Stephen Muiruri's investigative piece "Another Witness goes to the Grave with the secrets of JM Murder" in the *Sunday Nation*, August 13, 2006.
4. See Dominic Odipo's article "JM's true epitaph remains unwritten" in *The East African Standard,* February 2, 2010.

Chapter 3

An earlier version of this chapter appeared as "Reading Ngugi's Detained as a Manifesto," *in Du negre Bambara au Negropolitain: Littérature des mondes contemporains.* (Metsz: University of Metsz Press, 2009), 247-62.

The Epigraph is from Sidonie Smith and Julia Watson's *Women, Autobiography, Theory: A Reader*Madison, (Wisconsin: University of Wisconsin Press, 1998), 369.

1. *Negropolitain* is term referring to African or African-descended migrants from former colonies residing in the metropole. It draws attention to the dislocation their condition as migrants engenders, whereby there are essentially separate from both the African world that they left behind and the cultural space which surrounds them in the metropole. Ngugi's exile in Britain and later the United States situates him within this category of African migrants.

2. In his *Rigoberta Menchú and the Story of All Poor Guatemalas* (1999), anthropologist David Stoll claims the Gautemalan Nobel Peace Prize Laurete stretches the truth too much in her testimonio, *I, Rigoberto Menchu*. He accuses her, for instance, of claiming her own brother was brutally murdered by government forces contrary to Stoll's own field findings in Guatemala.

3. Taylor, Diana. DisappearingActs: Spectacles of Gender and Nationalism in Argentina's "Dirty War." Durham: Duke University Press, 1997.

4. Ngugi's life narrative has been read variously. In "*Detained* as a Modern *Consolatio*" Govind N. Sharma situates Ngugi's prison narrative within the tradition of the *consolatio*, a genre that both Saint Augustine with his *De Civitate Dei* and Cicero with his *Consolatio,* inaugurated in the first century A.D. (521). Simon Gikandi has read *Detained* as a prison memoir; drawing attention to prison as a "site of reflection" and an occasion for establishing affiliation with the tradition of literary resistance"(198). Following Gikandi's emphasis on literary resistance, the late Yvonne Vera reads *Detained* as a "diary of imperialism and insurgency" (135).

Chapter 4

This chapter is a revised version of "Poetry, protest, and polyphony in Abdilatif Abdalla's *Sauti ya Dhiki*," which appeared in *Research in African Literatures* 40, no.3 (2009), 129-48.

The epigraph for this chapter is from Kunle Ajibade's *Jailed for Life: a Reporter's Prison Notes* (Ibadan: Heimann Educational Books Nigeria, 2003), 87.

1. See the *East African Standard* (March 20, 1969).

2. Paradoxically *Sauti ya Dhiki* clinched the 1974 Jomo Kenyatta Prize for Literature with President Jomo Kenyatta personally handing over the prize to Abdalla at the award ceremony.

3. Chacha Nyaigoti Chacha, *Sauti ya Utetezi: Ushairi wa Abdilatif Abdalla*,(Dar es Salaam: University of Dar es Salaam Press, 1992), 19.

4. For more on the fundamentals of motivation in prison narratives see, Joana Summers's *Late Medieval Prison Writing and the Politics of Autobiography*, (Oxford: Oxford UP, 2004), 3,4.

5. Human Rights Watch, Where Silence Rules: The Suppression of Dissent in Malawi, (New York, 1990), 74.

6. A contrasting image of crocodile as a positive image can be seen in Camara Laye's *The Dark Child*, in which the ferocious reptile is projected as the totem of the autobiographer's mother.
7. See Ken Walibora Waliaula, "Poetry, Protest, and Polyphony in Abdilatif Abdalla's Sauti ya Dhiki," *Research in African Literatures* 40, no.3 (2009), 142.

Chapter 5

The epigraph for this chapter is from Mechthild Nagel's "I Write What I Like: African Prison Intellectuals and the Struggle for Freedom," *Journal of Pan African Studies* 2, no. 3 (March 2008),78.
1. Ali Mazrui makes references to the honor bestowed upon him by the Foreign Policy Magazine, Washington, DC, 2005, as well as a host of other honors in an interview with Seifudein Adem in "Witness to History? Interview with Ali Mazrui." HollerAfrica.
<http://www.hollerafrica.com/showArticle.php?catId=1&artId=259
(Accessed December 4, 2008).
2. For a comprehensive, if not exhaustive, list of political prisoners in the Moi era see the appendix in Njuguna Mutahi and Njuguna Theuri's Mutahi, Njuguna and Mugo Theuri. *We Lived to Tell.* (Nairobi: Friedrich Ebert Stiftung, 2003), 70-74.
3. For details on what may have motivated critics see Ken Walibora Waliaula "Poetry, Protest, and Polyphony in Abdilatif Abdalla's Sauti ya Dhiki," *Research in African Literatures* 40, no.3 (2009), 142.
4. Alamin Mazrui in an informal email exchange on March 6, 2007.
5. Mechthild Nagel, "I Write What I Like: African Prison Intellectuals and the Struggle for Freedom," *Journal of Pan African Studies*, 2 no.3 (March 2008), 73.
6. See also Kunle Ajidabe's *Jailed for Life*, (Ibadan: Heinmann Education Books, 2003), 107-09. In his prison memoir Ajibade points to the sustaining power of religious activity and narrates how "We [Nigerian political prisoners] found solace in Christianity and Islam as we waited for [President Sani] Abacha to decide our fate" (107).
7. Ioan Davies, *Writers in Prison,* (Oxford: Basil Blackwell, 1990), 54.
8. Nagel, "I Write What I Like," 78.
9. I am indebted to Mwalimu Abdul Nanji for enlightening me about the occasional use of the word augmentative "mamama" for huge women in Swahili to stress the sense of extraordinary size, awkwardness and ugliness as opposed to the diminutive "vimama" or "vijimama" during an informal conversation at Columbia University on April 9, 2010. It would seem ordinarily that is not a construction that "purists" would expect or condone in "grammatical" Swahili in its written and spoken form.

Conclusion

The first epigraph is from Michael Rolph Trouillot's *Sillencing the Past.* (Boston: Beacon Press, 1995), xix.
The second epigraph is from Mahmoud Mamdani's *Imperialism and Facism in Uganda.* (Nairobi: Heinmann Educational Books, 1983),1.

References

Abdalla, Abdilatif. *Sauti ya Dhiki.* Nairobi: Oxford University Press, 1973.

Abdulaziz, Mohamed H. *Muyaka: 19th Century Swahili Poetry*. Nairobi: Kenya Literature Bureau, 1979.

Achebe, Chinua. *Hopes and Impediments: Selected Essays 1965-1987.* New York: Anchor-Doubleday, 1989.

Afejuku, Tony E. "African Prison Poetry." In *Encyclopedia of Life Writing.* Edited by Margaretta Jolly. London: Fitzroy, 2001.

Alabi, Adetayo. *Telling Our Stories: Continuities and Divergences in Black Autobiographies.* New York; MacMillan, 2005.

Alber, Jan. *Narrating the Prison: Role and Representation in Charles Dickens' Novels and Twentieth Century Film*. Youngstown: Cambria, Press 2007.

Allen, J.W.T. *Al-Inkishafi: Catechism of the Soul*. Nairobi: East African Literature Bureau, 1977.

___."Swahili Prosody." *Swahili* 37, no.2 (September 1967): 171-79.

Amana, Boukheit. *Malenga wa Mvita*. Nairobi: Oxford University Press, 1982.

Amri, Abeid. *Sheria za Kutunga Mashairi na Diwani ya Amri*. Nairobi: East African Publishing House, 1954.

Anderson, Benedict. *Imagined Communities: Reflections on the Origin and Spread of Nationalism*. London: Verso Books, 1983.

Anderson, David. *Histories of the Hanged: The Dirty War in Kenya and the End of Empire*. New York: W.W. Norton and Company, 2005.

Anyidoho, Kofi,ed. *The World Behind Bars and the Paradox of Exile*. Evanson: Northwestern University Press, 1997.

Appiah, Anthony Kwame. *In My Father's House: African Philosophy of Culture*. New York: Oxford University Press, 1992.

Aristotle. *Rhetoric.* Mineola: Dover Publications, 2004.

___.*Poetics.* Edited and Translated by Stephen Halliwell. Cambridge: Havard University Press, 1995.

Austin, J.L. *How to Do Things with Words*. Cambridge: Harvard University Press, 1975.

Baard, Frances. *My Spirit is Not Banned*. Harare: Zimbabwe Publishing House, 1986.

Barthes, Roland. "The Death of the Author." *Image / Music / Text.* Translated by Stephen Heath, 142-147. New York: Hill and Wang, 1977.

Bellamy, Richard and Darrow Schecter. *Gramsci and the Italian State*. New York: Harvard University Press, 1993.

Beverly, John. *Testimonio: On the Politics of Truth.* Minneapolis: University of Minnesota Press, 2004.

Bloom, Harold. *The Western Canon: Books and School of the Ages.* New York: Harcourt Brace, 1994.

Breyentbach, Breyten. *The True Confessions of an Albino Terrorist.* London:Faber and Faber Limited, 1984.

Brutus, Dennis. *Letters to Martha, and Other Poems from a South African Prison*. London: Heinmann, 1968.

Butler, Judith. *Giving an Account of Oneself.* New York: Fordham University Press, 2005.

Carnochan, W. B. "The Literature of Confinement." In *The Oxford History of the*

Prison: The Practice of Punishment in Western Society. Edited by Norval Morris and David J. Rothman, 427-456. New York: Oxford University Press, 1995.

Caruthers, Cathy, ed. *Unclaimed Experience*. Baltimore: John Hopkins University Press, 1996.

___. *Trauma: Explorations in Memory*. Baltimore: John Hopkins University Press, 1995.

Chacha, Nyaigoti Chacha. *Ushairi wa Abdilatif Abdalla: Sauti ya Utetezi*. Dar es Salaam, Dar es Salaam University Press, 1983.

Chakava, Henry. "Introductory Essay." In *Publishing, Books, and Reading in Sub-Saharan Africa: A Critical Bibliography* by Hans M. Zell. Lochcarron: Hans Zell Publishing, 2008.

Chance, Roger. Book Review of "Mau Mau Detainee." *Race Class,* 5, no. 3 (January 1964): 1976-1977.

Chimera, Rocha. *Kiswahili: Past, Present and Future Horizons*. Nairobi: Nairobi UP, 2000.

Chinweizu e al. *Toward the Decolonization of African Literature*. Lagos: Pero, 1987.

Chiraghdin, Shihabdin and Mathias Mnyampala. *Historia ya Kiswahili.* Nairobi: Oxford University Press,1977.

Clough, Marshall S. *Mau Mau Memoirs: History, Memory, and Politics*. Boulder: Rienner, 1998.

Conrad, Joseph. *Heart of Darkness*. London: Penguin, 1995.

Daniels, Anthony. "Mau Mau Revisited." *The New Criterion* 23, no. 10 (June 2005): 21-26.

Davies, Ioan. *Writers in Prison.* Oxford: Basil Blackwell, 1990.

Dostoyevsky, Fyodor. *Notes from Underground and the Gambler*. Translated by Jane Kentish. Oxford: Oxford University Press, 1991.

Dumila, Faraj. *Wasifu wa Kenyatta.* Nairobi: Jomo Kenyatta Foundation, 1971.

Duncan, Martha Grace. *Romantic Outlaws, Beloved Prisons: The Unconscious Meanings of Crime and Punishment*. New York: New York University Press, 1996.

Eagleton, Terry. *Literary Theory: an Introduction.* Minneapolis: University of Minnesota Press, 2003.

Eakin, Paul John. *Living autobiographically: How we Create Identity in Narrative*. Ithaca: Cornell University Press, 2008.

Egan, Susanna. *Mirror Talk: Genres of Crisis in Contemporary Autobiography.* London: University of North Carolina Press, 1999.

Elison, Alexander. "Opening the Circle: Storyteller and Audience in Moroccan Prison Literature." *Middle Eastern Literature* 12, no. 3 (December 2009): 289-303.

Elkins, Caroline. *Imperial Reckoning: The Untold Story of Britain's Gulag in Kenya*. New York: Henry Holt, 2005.

El Sadawi, Nawal. *Memoirs from the Women's Prison.* Berkeley: California University Press, 1983.

____. *Woman at Point Zero*. London: Zed Books, 1983.

Errante, Antoinette. "But Sometimes You're Not Part of the Story: Oral Histories and Ways of Remembering and Telling." *Educational Researcher* 29, no. 2 (March 2000): 12-27.

Fanon, Frantz. *The Wretched of the Earth*. New York: Grove Press, 1963.

Filson, Floyd V. "The Journey Motif in Lucas Acts." *Apostolic History and the Gospel: Biblical and Historical Essays Presented to F.F. Bruce on his 60th Birthday*. Edited by W. Ward Gasque and Ralph P. Martin. Grand Rapids, MI: Eardmans Publishing Company, 1970. 68-77.

Finnigan. Ruth. *Oral Literature in Africa*. Nairobi: Oxford University Press, 1970.

Foley, Barbara. "Generic and Doctrinal Politics in the Proletarian Bildungsroman." *Understanding Narrative* 43-64. Edited by James Phelan and Peter Rabinowitz. Columbus: Ohio State University Press, 1994.

Foucoult, Michel. *Discipline and Punish: The Birth of the Prison* [Surveiller et Punir; Naissance de la prison]. 1975. Trans. Alan Sheridan. New York: Vintage,1979.

Franklin, Bruce, H. *Prison Literature in America: The Victim as Criminal and Artist.* New York: Oxford University Press, 1989.

Frey, Northrop. *Anatomy of Criticism.* New Jersey: Princeton University Press, 1973.

Giddens, Anthony. *The Consequences of Modernity*.Standford: Standford University Press, 1990.

Gikandi, Simon. "Postcolonial Theory and the Specter of Nationalism." *CLIO* 36, no.1 (Autumn 2006): 69-84,151.

___. *Ngugi wa Thiong'o.* New York: Cambridge UP, 2000.

Gilmore, Leigh. "Jurisdictions: *I, Rigoberta Menchu, The Kiss*, and Scandalous Self-Representation in the Age of Memoir and Trauma." *Journal of Women in Culture* 28, no. 2 (2001): 795-718.

Gusdorf, Georges. "Conditions and Limits of Autobiography." *Autobiography: Essays Theoretical and Critical.* Edited by James Olney. New Jersey: Princeton University Press, 1980.

Hale, Dorothy. *The Novel: an Anthology of Criticism and Theory.* Massachussetts: Blackwell, 2006.

Harlow, Barbara. *Barred: Women Writing, and Political Detention.* Hanover: Wesleyan University Press, 1992.

___. *Resistance Literature.* New York: Methuen, 1987.

Human Rights Watch. *Where Silence Rules: The Suppression of Dissent in Malawi*. New York: Human Rights Watch, 1990.

Indede, Florence Ngesa. "Madiliko katika Umbo la Kiswahili na Athari zake katika Ushairi wa Kiswahili." *Swahili Forum* 15(2008): 73-94..

Irele, Abiola. *The African Imagination: Literature and The Black Diaspora.* New York: Oxford University Press, 2001.

___. "In Praise of Alienation." In *The Surreptitious Speech: Présence Africaine and the Politics of Otherness, 1947-1987.* Edited by .V.Y.Mudimbe. London: The University of Chicago Press, 1992. 201-224.

Itote, Waruhiu. *"Mau Mau" General.* Nairobi: East African Publishing House, 1967.

Jameson, Fredric. "Third World Literature in the Era of Multicultural Capitalism." *Social Text,* 15 (1986): 65-88.

Johnson, James Weldon. *The Autobiography of an Ex-Coloured Man.* New York: Vintage Books, 1989.

Johnson, John Williams. *The Epic of Son-jara: A West African Tradition*. Bloomington: Indiana University Press, 1986.

Kanneh, Kadiatu. *African Identitiess. Race, Nation, and Culture in Ethnography. Pan-Africanism and Black Literatures.* London: Routledge, 1998.

Kenyatta, Jomo. *Suffering Without Bitterness: The Founding of the Kenyan Nation*. Nairobi: East African Publishing House, 1968.

Kezilahabi, Euphrase. "Book Review" *Sauti ya Dhiki*." Unpublished paper, 1974.

Kihoro, Wanyiri. *Never Say Die.* Nairobi: East African Education Publishers, 1998.

Kinyatti, Maina wa. *Kenya: a Prison Notebook.* London: Vita Books, 1982

___. *Thunder from the Mountains: Mau Mau Patriotic Songs.* London: Zed Books, 1980.

Kiriamiti, John. *My Life in Crime.* Nairobi: East African Education Publishers, 1984.

Klopp, Charles. *Sentences: Memoirs of Italian Political Prisoners.* Toronto: University of Toronto Press, 1999.

Laabi, Abdellatif. *Rue due Retour*. Translated by Jacqueline Kaye. London: Reader International,1982.

Laye, Camara. *The Dark Child.* New York: Hill and Wang, 1954.

Lazarus, Neil. *Resistance in Postcolonial African Fiction.* New Haven: Yale University Press.1990.

Leitch, Vincent B.,ed. *The Norton Anthology of Theory and Criticism.* New York: Norton, 2001.

Likimani, Muthoni. *Passbook Number. F.47927: Women and the Mau Mau in Kenya*. New York: Praeger, 1985.

Lindfors, Bernth. *The Blind Men and the Elephant*. Adelaide: Centre for Research in New Literatures in English, 1987.

Lovesey, Oliver. "Chained Letters: African Prison Diaries and "NationaAllegory."*Research in African Literatures* 26, no. 4 (1995): 31-35.

Lwanda, John, "Gathering Seaweed: African Prison Writing." *Torture* 14.1 (2004): 60-63.

Lyon, Janet. *Manifestoes: Provocations of the Modern.* Ithaca: Cornell University Press, 1999.

Makilla, F.E. *An Outline History of the Babukusu of Western Kenya*. Nairobi: Kenya Literature Bureau, 1978.

Mamdani, Mahmoud. *Imperialism and Fascism in Uganda*. New Jersey, NJ: Africa World Press, 1984.

Mandela, Winnie Madikizela. *Part of My Soul Went with Him.* Edited by Mary Benson. New York: W.W. Norton, 1984.

Mapanje, Jack. *And The Crocodiles are Hungry at Night: A chronicle of a poet's imprisonment under life president Banda of Malawi*. Banbury: Ayerbia Clerke, 2011.

___.,ed. *Gathering Seaweed: African Prison Writing*. Oxford: Heinmann, 2002.

___. "Of Orality and Memory in Prison and Exile (A Personal Notes on How to Survive the Chaos of Incarceration)". *The Word Behind Bars and the Paradox of Exile*. Ed. Kofi Anyidoho. Evanson: Northwestern University Press, 1997: 1-19.

___. *The Chattering Wagtails of Mikuyu Prison.* Oxford: Heinmann, 1993.

Marx, Karl and Friedrich Engels. *The Communist Manifesto*. Trans. L.M. Findlay.Peterborough: Broadview, 2004.

Matsuda, J. Mari. *Where Is the Body? and Other Essays on Race Gender and Law*. New York: Deacon, 1996.

Matundura, Bitugi. *Shujaa Liyongo*. Nairobi: Phoenix Publishers, 1999.

Maupeu, Herve and Patrick Mutahi. *Wahome Mutahi's World*. Nairobi: Transafrica Press, 2005.

Mazrui, Alamin. *Swahili Beyond the Boundaries: Literature, Language, and Identity*. Athens: Ohio University Press, 2007.

___. *Shadows of the Moon*. Nairobi: East African Education Publishers, 1991.

___.*Chembe cha Moyo*. Nairobi: East African Education Publishers, 1988.

Mbele, Joseph L. "Women in the African Epic." *Research in African Literatures* 37, no. 2 (Summer 2006): 61-67.

Mbembe, Achille. *On the Postcolony*. Berkeley, University of California Press, 2001.

Menchu, Rigoberta. *I, Rigoberta Menchu: An Indian Woman in Guatemala*. New York, Verso Books, 1984.

Miehe, Gudrun, et al. *Kala Shairi: German East Africa in Swahili Poems*. Koln: Arciv Afrikanistischer Manuskripte, 2004.

Miller, Christopher. *Theories of African*. Chicago: University of Chicago Press, 1985.

Millet, Kate. *The Politics of Cruelty: An Essay on the Literature of Political Imprisonment*. New York: W. W. Norton and Company, 1994.

Mills, Charles. *The Racial Contract*. Ithaca: Cornell University Press, 1997.

Morris, Norval, and David J. Rothman, eds. *The Oxford History of the Prison: The Practice of Punishment in Western Society*. New York: Oxford University Press, 1995.

Moukhlis, Salah. "The Forgetten Face of Postcoloniality: Moroccan Prison Narratives, Human Rights, and the Politics of Resistance." *Journal of Arabic Literature* 39, no.3 (2008): 347-376.

Mpasu, Sam. *Political Prisoner 3/75 of Dr. H. Kamuzu Banda of Malawi: A True Story*. African Publishing Group Harare, 1995.

Mudimbe, V.Y. *Invention of Africa: Gnosis, Philosophy and Order of Knowledge*. Bloomington: Indiana University Press. 1988.

Mugo, Micere Githae. *African Orature and Human Rights*. Roma, Lesotho: Institute of Southern African Studies, National University of Lesotho, 1991.

Mulamali, Mohamed. *Ikisiri ya Inkishafi*. Nairobi: Longman, 1980.

Mulokozi, M. M. "The Nanga Bards of Tanzania: Are they Epic Artists?" *Research in African Literatures* 14, no. 3 (Autumn 1983): 283-311.

___. "Protest and Resistance in Swahili Poetry 1600-1885." *Kiswahili* 49 no.1 (March 1982): 25-54.

Mutahi, Njuguna and Mugo Theuri. *We Lived to Tell*. Nairobi: Friedrich Ebert Stiftung, 2003.

Mutahi, Wahome. *The Jail Bugs*. Nairobi: Longhorn, 1992.

___. *Three Days on the Cross*. Nairobi: East African Education Publishers, 1991.

Nagel, Mechthild. "I Write What I Like: African Prison Intellectuals and the Struggle for Freedom." *Journal of Pan African Studies* 2, no. 3 (March 2008): 68-80

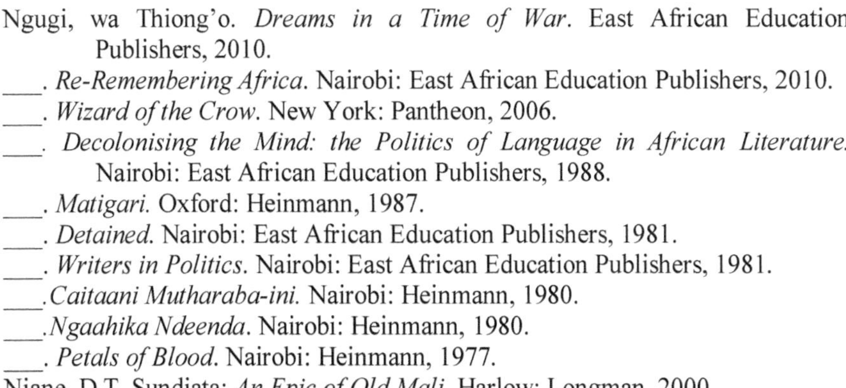

Ngugi, wa Thiong'o. *Dreams in a Time of War*. East African Education Publishers, 2010.

___. *Re-Remembering Africa*. Nairobi: East African Education Publishers, 2010.

___. *Wizard of the Crow*. New York: Pantheon, 2006.

___. *Decolonising the Mind: the Politics of Language in African Literature.* Nairobi: East African Education Publishers, 1988.

___. *Matigari.* Oxford: Heinmann, 1987.

___. *Detained.* Nairobi: East African Education Publishers, 1981.

___. *Writers in Politics*. Nairobi: East African Education Publishers, 1981.

___.*Caitaani Mutharaba-ini.* Nairobi: Heinmann, 1980.

___.*Ngaahika Ndeenda*. Nairobi: Heinmann, 1980.

___. *Petals of Blood.* Nairobi: Heinmann, 1977.

Niane, D.T. Sundiata: *An Epic of Old Mali*. Harlow: Longman, 2000.

Njarama, Karari and Donald L. Barnett. *Mau Mau From Within: Autobiography and Analysis of Kenya's Peasant Revolt*. New York: Modern Reader, 1966.

Njau, Gakaara wa. *Mau Mau Author in Detention.* Translated by Paul Ngigi

Njoroge. Nairobi: East African Educational Publishers, 1988.

Njogu, Kimani. *Reading Poetry as Dialogue.* Nairobi: The Jomo Kenyatta Foundation, 2004.

___. "Gakaara Wanjau: In Memoriam 1921-29 March 2001." *Research in African Literatures* 32, no.4 (2001): 140-142.

Njogu, Kimani & Herve Maupeu (eds). *Songs and Politics in East Africa.* Dar es Salaam: Mkuki na Nyota, 2007.

Njogu, Kimani and Rocha Chimera. *Ufundishaji wa Fasihi: Mbinu na Nadharia.* Nairobi: Jomo Kenyatta Foundation,1999.

Odhiambo, Atieno E.S. "Matunda ya Uhuru, Fruits of Independence: Seven

Theses on Nationalism in Kenya." *Mau Mau and Nationhood: Arms, Authority, and Narrative*.Eds. Odhiambo, Atieno E.S and John Lonsdale. Athens: Ohio University Press, 2003.

Ogot, Bethwel .A. and W.R. Ochieng. *Decolonization and Independence in Kenya: 1940-93*. Nairobi: East African Education Publishers, 1995.

Ohly, Raymond. "A Review of Abdilatif Abdalla's *Sauti ya Dhiki*." *Kiswahili* 44, no. 2 (1974): 82-91.

Olney, James. *Autobiography: Essays Theoretical and Critical.* New Jersey: Princeton University Press, 1980.

___. *Tell Me Africa: An Approach to African Literature.* New Jersey: Princeton University Press, 1973.

Okpewho, Isidore. *African Oral Literature: Backgrounds, Character and Continuity*. Bloomington: Indian University Press, 1992.

___. *The Epic in Africa: Towards a Poetics of Oral Performance*. New York: Columbia University Press, 1979.

Ong, Walter J. *Orality and Literacy: The Technologizing of the Word*. London: Routledge, 1988.

Otieno, Wambui Waiyaki. *Mau Mau's Daughter: A Life History*. Boulder: Lynne Rienner, 1998.

Owomoyela, Oyekan. "Dissidence and the African Writer: Commitment and Dependency?" *African Studies Review* 24, no.1 (1981): 83-98.

Plato. *The Republic*. Mineola: Dover Press, 2000.

Puchner, Martin. *The Poetry of Revolution: Marx, Manifestos, and the Avant-Gardes*. New Jersey: Princeton University Press, 2006.

Rodrigues, Dylan. *Forced Passages: Imprisoned Intellectuals and the US Prison Regime*. Minneapolis: University Press of Minnesota, 2006.

Sarkin, Jeremy, ed. *Human Rights in African Prisons*. Athens: Ohio University Press, 2008.

Scarry, Elaine. *The Body in Pain: The Making and Unmaking of the World.* New York: Oxford University Press, 1985.

Scheffler, Judith, ed. *Wall Tappings: The International Anthology of Women's*

Prison Writings 200 to Present. New York: Feminist Press at the City University of New York, 2002.

___."Women's Prison Writing - An Unexplored Tradition in Literature." *Prison Journal* 64, no.1 (Spring/Summer 1984): 57-67.

Scheub, Harold. *The Uncoiling Snake: South African Storytellers and Resistance*. Athens: Ohio University Press. 2010.

Seitel, Peter. *The Powers of Genre: Interpreting Haya Oral Literature*. New York: Oxford University Press, 1999.

Senkoro, F.E.M.K. *Ushairi: Nadharia na Tahakiki*. Dar es Salaam: Dar es
Salaam University Press, 1988.

Shafi, Adam, Shafi. *Haini.* Nairobi: Longhorn, 2003.

Sharma, Govind N. "Ngugi's *Detained* as a Modern *Consolatio." Research in African Lireratures* 19, no. 4 (Winter 1988): 521-28.

Smith, Sidonie and Julia Watson, eds. *Women, Autobiography, Theory: A Reader.* Madison: University of Wisconsin Press, 1998.

Solzhenistsyn, Alexander. *One Day in the Life of Ivan Denisovich.* Translated by Max Hayward and Ronald Hingley. Chicago: Dramatic, 1963.

Soyinka, Wole. *The Burden of Memory, The Muse of Forgiveness*. New York: Oxford University Press, 1999.

___. *The Man Died: Prison Notes of Wole Soyinka*. New York: Noonday Press, 1988.

Steere, Edward. *Swahili Tales as Told by the Natives of Zanzibar*. Nendeln: Kraus Books, 1970.

Summers, Joanna. *Late Medieval Prison Writing and the Politics of Autobiography*. Oxford: Oxford University Press, 2004.

Taylor, Diana. *Disappearing Acts: Spectacles of Gender and Nationalism in Argentina's "Dirty War*." Durham: Duke University Press, 1997.

Teffeteller, Annette. "Orality and the Politics of Scholarship," 67-86. *Politics of Orality*. Edited by Craig Cooper. Leiden: Brill, 2007.

Tesfagiorgis, Abeba. *A Painful Season & a Stubborn Hope: the Odyssey of an Eritrean Mother*. Trenton, N.j.: Red Sea Press, 1992.

Thuku, Harry. *An Autobiography*. Nairobi: Oxford University Press, 1970.

Vera, Yvonne. *The Prison of Colonial Space: Narratives of Resistance*. Diss. York University,1996.

Wafula, Robert J. *Circumcision among the Bukusu of Western Kenya: an African System of Epistemology and how it Impacts Western Forms of Learning in Bungoma District*. Diss. Ohio University, 2006.

Wali, Obiajunwa. "The Dead End of African Literature." *Transition,* 10 (1963): 13-16.

Waliaula, K.W. "Prison, Poetry, and Polyphony in Abdilatif Abdalla's Sauti ya Dhiki." *Research in African Literatures* 40, no. 3 (Autumn 2009):129-148.

___."Reflections on Knowing as a Problem in Alamin Mazrui's *Shadows of the Moon.*" *Cultural Production and Social Change: Building Bridges,* 217-44. Edited by Kimani Njogu and G.Oluoch-Olunya. Nairobi: Twaweza, 2008.

___."Staging masculinity in an East African Epic" in *Masculinities in African Literary and Cultural Texts,* 13-24. Eds. Helen Nabasuta Mugambi & Tuzyline Jita Allan. Banbury; Ayebia Clarke Literary Agency & Publishing Ltd, (2010): 13-24.

Wamitila, K.W. *Uhakiki wa Fasihi: Misingi na Vipengele Vyake*. Nairobi: Phoenix, 2002.

___. *Archetypal Criticism of Kiswahili Poetry*. Bayreuth: Bayreuth University, 2001.

Wamwere, Koigi wa. *Conscience on Trial*. New Jersey: Africa World, 1988.

Were, Gideon. *History of the Abaluyia of Western Kenya*. Nairobi: East African Publishing House, 1967.

Williams, Raymond. *Marxism and Literature*. Oxford: Oxford University Press, 1977.

Wimsatt, William K. and Monroe C. Beardsley. "The Intentional Fallacy." Sewanee Review, 54 (1946): 468-88.

Wolf, Jan J. de. *Bukusu Stories*. New Brunswick: Transaction, 2005.

___. *Bukusu Tales*: Munster: Lit Verlag, 1995.

Yaeger, Patricia et al. "The End of Postcolonial Theory? A Roundtable with Sunil Agnani, Fernando Coronil, Gaurav Desai, Mamadou Diouf, Simon Gikandi, and Jennifer Wenzel." *PMLA* 122.3(2007): 633-49.

Ylvisaker, Marguerite. ""Mau Mau" Detainee: The Account by an African of His Experiences in Detention Camps, 1953-1960 by Josiah Mwangi Kariuki." *The International Journal of African Historical Studies* 9, no. 4 (1976): 643-49.

www.ingramcontent.com/pod-product-compliance
Lightning Source LLC
Chambersburg PA
CBHW071127100726
47908CB00008B/2511

* 9 7 8 1 6 1 2 2 9 2 1 6 8 *